McPhee Gribble/Penguin Books

GENERATIONS

Grandmothers, Mothers and Daughters

DIANE BELL is professor of Australian Studies at Deakin University. She holds degrees in anthropology from A.N.U. and Monash University. Her publications include *Daughters of the Dreaming*, *Law: the old and the new* (co-authored), *Religion in Aboriginal Australia* (co-edited) and various articles. She is working on a community study of Geelong.

PONCH HAWKES is a Melbourne-based freelance photographer. Her work is held in the collection of the Australian National Gallery. Her photographs have been widely exhibited and published.

Pat,

Hope you enjoy this. We are awaiting a letter telling us that you're journeying to Melbourne. We need you!

Best wishes
Marilyn Woolley.

Thank you for your stories:

Elaine Aikins
Louise Allison
Susan Andrews
Shirley Armstrong
Muriel 'Una' Armstrong
Jessie August
Margaret Bates
Janet Bell
Sue Bellamy
Marian Black
Myriam Bonazzi
Debbie Booker
Barbara Brown
Joy Caddie
Daphne Campbell
Athol Chase
Fran Coghlan
Jo Conway
Madge Cope
Paula Cristoffanini
Joy Damousi
Ruby Davis
Bev Dinn
Megan Dorrough
Jennifer Doust
Elizabeth Durack
Chester Eagle
Mary Fisher
Nina Fletcher
Ros Fraser
Joyce Fuller
Annie Gastin
Ann Giles
Mary Giles
Pat Giles
Myrna Gwyther
Floss Haig
Yvonne Hallett
Cheryl Hannah
Susan Hawthorne
Barbara Bishop Hewitt
Mary Anne Jebb
Allan Johnston
Lena Kay
Val Kear
Michele Kosky
Emmeline Lahey
Margaret Lanigan
Jane Lloyd
Lillian Lloyd
Pam Lyndon
Isabel McBryde
Ann McGrath
Mabel MacKay
Pip McManus
Susan Magarey
Jean Mateer
Louise Moran
Doreen Monro
Patti Monro
Daphne Nash
Topsy Napurrula Nelson
Marguerite Newlove
Penny Peel
Jennifer Rainforth
Nancy Reis
Martha Ricardo
Michaela Richards
Patricia Richards
David Ritchie
Chloe Roe
Margaret Ryan
Shelley Schreiner
Meg Sekavs
Janet Shaw
Susan Sheridan
Isobel Skoczek
Bron Stevens
Gertrude Stotz
John von Sturmer
Una von Sturmer
Peter Sutton
Mimi Taylor
Gertrude Thrower
Belle White
Sally White
Rosemary Wighton
Katie Wilkes
Wendy Wright
Elspeth Young

And to those who chose not to be named.

GENERATIONS

Grandmothers, Mothers and Daughters

Diane Bell
Photographs by Ponch Hawkes

McPhee Gribble/Penguin Books

McPhee Gribble Publishers Pty Ltd
66 Cecil Street
Fitzroy, Victoria, 3065, Australia

Penguin Books Australia Ltd
487 Maroondah Highway, P.O. Box 257
Ringwood, Victoria, 3134, Australia
Penguin Books Ltd
Harmondsworth, Middlesex, England
Penguin Books,
40 West 23rd Street, New York, N.Y. 10010, U.S.A.
Penguin Books Canada Ltd,
2801 John Street, Markham, Ontario, Canada L3R 1B4
Penguin Books (N.Z.) Ltd,
182-190 Wairau Road, Auckland 10, New Zealand

First published by McPhee Gribble Publishers
in association with Penguin Books Australia 1987
Reprinted 1988
Copyright © Diane Bell, 1987
Photographs copyright © Ponch Hawkes, 1987
Designed and typeset by Pam Brewster
Edited by Jane Arms
Typesetting processed in Goudy by Deblaere Typesetting, Sydney
Made and printed in Australia by Griffin Press Limited

All Rights Reserved. Without limiting the rights under copyright reserved above, no part of this publication may be reproduced, stored in or introduced into a retrieval system, or transmitted, in any form or by any means (electronic, mechanical, photocopying, recording or otherwise), without the prior permission of both the copyright owner and McPhee Gribble Publishers Pty Ltd.

National Library of Australia
Cataloguing-in-Publication data

Bell, Diane, 1943
Generations: grandmothers, mothers and daughters.

ISBN 0 14 011094 1.

1. Women - Australia. I. Hawkes, Ponch,
1946-   . II. Title.

305 . 4 ' 0994

The photograph of Josephine Bussel on p. 186 is reproduced, with permission, from *The People of Perth* by C.T. Stannage, Carroll's Publishing, 1979.

This publication has been funded by the
Australian Bicentennial Authority to celebrate Australia's Bicentenary in 1988

For Diane's grandmother Peg,
mother Floss and daughter Genevieve,
Ponch's mother Ida Elizabeth Ponchard
and grandmothers, mothers and daughters everywhere

CONTENTS

CHAPTER ONE
The Order of Things 9

CHAPTER TWO
Waste Not Want Not 30

CHAPTER THREE
Women Have Always Worked 49

CHAPTER FOUR
Tales of Treadles 72

CHAPTER FIVE
The Fabrics of Life 90

CHAPTER SIX
Familiar Things 107

CHAPTER SEVEN
Daryl Got the Farm and Mum Got the Pearls 127

CHAPTER EIGHT
The Telling Things 150

CHAPTER NINE
A Fortunate Life: Mimi Taylor 171

CHAPTER TEN
A Literate Tradition 186

CHAPTER ELEVEN
Everything a Woman Ought to Know 204

CHAPTER TWELVE
Someone's Daughter: Someone's Friend 226

CHAPTER THIRTEEN
Heirlooms and Hand-Me-Downs 243

CHAPTER FOURTEEN
In Search of Australian Women 257

Chapter Notes 269

Acknowledgements 279

CHAPTER ONE

THE ORDER OF THINGS

Monday was wash-day. Tuesday was ironing and kitchen-day. Wednesday was your sort of day when you do the sewing and mending, and Thursday was the bedrooms. Friday you straightened up the kitchen again, went out and did your shopping. Saturday you cooked. Sunday was for family. Well, that was the week taken up.

A familar routine for many women, no doubt. All members of the family knew what was expected of them. 'Mum was a good manager,' the voices of generations of women tell us; she ran that home, and she did it by sticking to the rules. They were rules that provided order and security, but they were also restricting: woman's place was in the home. The routine recalled here is that of Gertrude Thrower, fondly known as Nar by her grand-daughter.

Those rules were pretty rigid, and all my young life that's the only way I remember it. If Mum wanted to clean up, come hail, rain or high water, that cleaning up was done, and you wouldn't walk in if that floor was wet. That's the way Mum ran her life.

I did the same for a good few years, and then suddenly you wake up to yourself - there's more to life than this. You think, I haven't done it today, it can be done tomorrow. But it's a case of old habits dying hard. I suppose life was more orderly then, and if things were done regularly, you perhaps had a bit of time for other things. You knew where you stood.

The experience of Nar, her daughter Gertrude and her grand-daughter Meg spans over a century. Nar, born in England in 1887, educated to the

GERTRUDE JESSIE
1887-
|
GERTRUDE McLAREN
1910-
|
'MEG'
1934-

age of fourteen, began her working life 'in service' to a retired army officer. On arrival in Australia in 1923, she settled with her husband and two children in Perth. Gertrude was apprenticed to a tailor, widowed in the second world war and struggled to raise her four children alone. Both she and her mother still live in Perth. Meg, who completed a degree in 1971, teaches history in a Canberra college. Each generation has worked, going from 'in service' in people's homes, to learning a trade, to a professional career. This is not an uncommon pattern.

Life for Meg is very different from that of her mother on a war widow's pension, or her grandmother, now in a nursing home in Perth. Meg's weekly routine is shaped by the demands of work, family and study. Her grown-up children and those of Egils, her husband, visit, but mid-week rather than Sunday. In a two-wage household, it is possible to employ help in the home and to eat out. Still, as Meg observes, the tyranny of the week's routine remains: 'I have the routine in the back of my mind that certain things should be done by a certain time of the week, and I feel bad if they're not.'

Our lives may be very different from those of our mothers and grandmothers, but their voices and practices still largely shape our routines. We are all someone's daughter. But we are not all someone's wife or mother, nor did we all grow up in nuclear families in the suburbs with our mother as a model. For some the loss of a mother meant housekeepers, orphanages, fostering, or life with another relative. For Katie Wilkes, born in 1913, it meant organizing the house from the age of eleven on.

I didn't have a mother running after me, did I? I didn't have a father. I ran after my father. I had to get up at five o'clock, even though I was going to school, to give him breakfast. I'd go back to bed, and then I'd get up and get my brother off. Then I'd go back to bed, or I'd stay up and get myself off to school.

A woman needed an independent income.

Susan Hawthorne, of an age to be Katie's grand-daughter, draws on a very different heritage. Her grandmother's sisters, the 'maiden aunts', as she calls them, inherited property from their father who had done well in the land booms of late nineteenth-century South Australia. Of the eight children, the two sons did slightly better in the property division while the daughters were given a start that enabled them to develop their independence of spirit.

I always assumed that women alone could not only survive but live fulfilling lives. One of the earliest values I remember my mother imparting to me was that a woman needed an independent income. At the time I knew them, during my childhood years, all my great-aunts as well as my grandmother were independent women. They were all either widowed, unmarried or not yet married. They all had their own means of support. I squeeze domestic chores into my Saturdays. I see those things as necessary but not central to my life.

Topsy Napurrula Nelson, like many Aboriginal children of her age, was separated from her parents and kept locked in a girls' dormitory at night. Her life on the mission at Phillip Creek in the Northern Territory allowed some contact with family. Not all Aboriginal children were so fortunate. Many were forcefully removed and reared by foster parents or in institutions with foreign routines.

During her childhood Topsy, a proficient hunter gatherer, went hungry on land that now supplies sustenance, both physical and spiritual, for her and her family. Her routine in the 1950s:

```
NANGALA
1880s-1942
  |
NAPALJARRI
1900-1960s
  |
TOPSY NAPURRULA
1937-
```

In the morning, we would come and eat little bread, little scones. We would still be hungry. Drink. We would have one little drink. Cordial, like that. We'd stand up, line up. All the Warumungu, Warlpiri and Kaytej - all mixed up. He used to ask us for a song. 'Come on, you kids, what song are we going to sing?' I still remember one. We would kneel down and sing that one. Then we'd eat.

The monotony of the week was broken only by church services on Sunday.

Briefly, in the 1970s, while living on a government reserve, Topsy stayed in a standard three-bedroom house, but because of an administrative bungle, the electricity was not connected. The house was difficult to manage. Today she is back on her own land, where she cooks on an open fire, washes in a bucket, carts water in a drum. 'Now,' she says, 'I'm rich in country.'

Topsy's mother remembered the police parties that swept through the desert regions of Central Australia in the late 1920s. She lost her first husband in one reprisal. Topsy's grandmother saw the intrusion of cattlemen and missionaries on her country. Her routine was a response to the rhythms of the land, her life shaped by the seasons, kin and country. Nar, Katie, the maiden aunts, Topsy: very different Australias.

The hardships of the depression and the need to make do in the country were common memories for many of the daughters and grand-daughters of this generation. Mabel MacKay, born at the turn of the century, recalled her household tasks. At that time, Mrs Mac was looking after her father and three brothers, the youngest of whom was only six years old.

I did everything, cleaning, cooking. Washing meant heating water in the copper, scrubbing the clothes on a glass washboard, boiling them, hauling them out on a pot-stick into a tub of cold water, rinsing them and then into a tub of blue water, put through the wringer and then on the line, held up with a clothes prop. Then they had to be ironed with a flat iron or a box iron. There was never any problem of scorching. We starched a lot of things. When Mum was sick, I had her washed and tidied up, the bedroom done, and I was waiting for our doctor when he called. I had a little white apron on with a bib, starched, of course. All that by ten o'clock in the morning. I was still not yet fifteen.

There is no longer any need to use white-wash and red ochre on the fireplace. The boards are no longer scrubbed, the stove no longer blackened. At the flick of a switch, a machine is called into action. We do not find the same number of women going into service or staying at home to help mother, they manage their own homes, and many also work, sometimes cleaning for others or minding children. Help must now be paid for.

Before the second world war, wood stoves and coppers required constant care and special handling; resources were limited, and the storage of food a problem. Today, pre-set timers on ovens, deep freezers, automatic washing machines, driers and similar gadgets give freedom. Woman's time may be used elsewhere. As women learnt to drive after the war, they became mobile. They could visit and shop at their convenience. But many found that they were spending hours driving children to school, sport, child care and other activities far from home.

With smaller families and more devices, the households that women run

now are much different from those of the women before them who ran a wood stove, an ice-block, a flat iron, and provided home remedies for every ill. In those days, it was a matter of pride not to call the doctor but to know how to dose yourself.

Washing machines with automatic cycles mask the time spent on the household wash. This routine task, which had occupied the better part of a Monday, has gone from the family chores. And it is no longer Dad's job to cut and pile the wood by the outhouse, a neat, full stack a sign that he was doing his job; a clean shirt comes without a heated copper. But now the woman is left to load and unload, hang out, to bring in and fold, as if the existence of the machine removed the need for any help. Overall, little time is saved.

The Order of Things

Monday was washing day.

Mum was boss of the copper, the Reckitt's Blue rinse, the Velvet soap shavings, the starch mix; she organized wash-day and had troops to call on. Wash-day was not changed lightly. In families where mothers supervised correspondence school work, Saturday might become wash-day and time found to iron on Sunday, but most of us grew up knowing that Monday was washing-day.

We hated coming home from school on Mondays because we knew Mum had spent the whole day washing and hanging out the clothes. With the leftover soapy water, she washed the floor, did the back steps with Lysol, which was straight caustic soda. No rubber gloves then. We didn't expect much humour from Mum on Mondays, and we usually ate leftovers. I suppose I did the same early in my marriage, but we moved into a new place in the 1951, and that was the end of the wash-house.

At school we practised the skills of our mothers as we sang, 'This is the way we wash our clothes' and rubbed the stained garments up and down on the corrugated board. Work-clothes got an extra vigorous action. My dolls' house from the 1940s had a miniature glass scrubbing board. It's a piece of prehistory as far as my daughter is concerned, but the song is still taught. On holidays we helped to slosh the blue bag up and down, and we marvelled how it made the clothes white not blue. We watched the starch mix as it turned from stringy white to blancmange and as the tablecloths, pillowcases, and tea-towels were dunked. With each new item the solution weakened until, last of all, the hankies would go through.

Preparations for the Monday wash began on Sunday. In the country, new wives learnt to put the moleskins in drums to soak overnight; Aboriginal women rubbed and soaped the heavily soiled work-clothes. On Monday, the wash could then be supervised by the missus. In town, the clothes went into the copper or trough with soap shaved from the bar of Velvet. Stubborn stains were worked on by rubbing the bar of soap on the fabric flat against the trough.

And that's how we kept the clothes clean.

Sometimes if you left the clothes damped down for ironing too long in warm weather, mildew would grow. Then we'd cut a lemon and put the juice on the sheet, or whatever, on the lawn in the sun. They all came out so white. Of course, they were all cotton - sun, salt, lemon, ammonia for spot cleaning, yellow

> ETHEL
> 1887-1976
> |
> *FLOSS HAIG*
> 1918-
> |
> DIANE
> 1943-
> |
> GENEVIEVE
> 1967-

soap, boiling water - that's how we kept the clothes clean. It was only Mum and us girls, so right through the late twenties and thirties we did the work of getting the copper ready. Then, when I was married, it was war time, and I was still preparing the wash alone, but now I had nappies. It was hard to adjust the routine when the boys came home.

Floss Haig has seen many wash-days, hard work, which she considers was made lighter when laundries adjoined the house and you could listen to the cheery patter on the radio.

I listened to Nicky and Tupper on 3UZ, and Nicky would say, 'Now, Mum, turn around when I'm talking to you. I don't want a face full of steam.'

Copper, concrete troughs, garden tools and home-made beer shared the wash-house, which was often some distance from the house. There, if someone in the family had a heavy cold, the handkerchiefs soaked in a bucket of salted water. And out of sight, under the trough or the pine lid covering the trough, was a cold-water bucket with the menstrual cloths. Floss Haig recalls the rituals in the 1930s.

We must have had a month's supply because the rags stayed in the bucket until the next Monday wash. We'd clunk them down with the copper stick, then tip out the water and run clean through. That went on until the water ran clear. They were rubbed against the trough side or on the scrubbing board, like the collars, and kept aside for a separate boil. They came out white and fluffy. Shirts, the ones with detachable collars, lasted several days. People with a little extra money sent them out to a 'Shirt John' (from the Chinese laundry). Labour was so cheap then.

Even after a woman got an electric washing machine, the old copper was preferred for the sheets. It held more, was more hygienic and the sheets came out cleaner, but the weight of water-logged clothes made the work dangerous.

Mum scalded herself from the copper, and she lost four stone. She treated the burn with radium and a salt-water mixture. We had to get help from the people in the Victoria Market, where she sold confectionery. I was too small to take her place at that time.

The copper survived until recently. Some are now garden tubs, at least one serves as an ice bucket for grand parties, and another is used to boil the Christmas ham. The copper stick, a nicely turned piece of wood, eventually became too soggy at one end, and it was pensioned off as a tomato stake.

Had Mimi Taylor's daughters not bought her a washing machine when she was in hospital, she may have still been sitting on the verandah washing in her old tub. It was one she regarded with great affection. She remembered it, as a child, in 1910, stacked with everything her parents, brothers and sisters owned. It was slung on a boat as the family moved from Rockhampton to Mackay and was slightly crooked from the way it had been strapped. But it was a good old tub and never leaked.

No matter how hard we'd wring out the clothes, they still dripped: the grass under the line was green.

The amount of washing and the difficulty of wringing by hand could be seen by the greenness of the grass under the clothes-line. Mangles, the hand-turned and powered models, were a boon, but buttons got smashed, fingers were jammed and creases were firmed up.

The Whizz-Dri, a nifty piece of washing-day technology of the forties, was one solution. Made of two cylinders, a metal outside and baked enamel inside, it clamped to the trough and through the hose attached to the tap; the rushing water set it spinning. It was vicious and vibrated many a cement trough off its base.

My neighbour asked that I let her know when I would be using it. Her wash-house backed onto mine, and the Whizz-Dri had shattered all her jars, and the shelves had collapsed. During times of water restrictions, we couldn't use it, but it certainly did the trick with the nappies. We left it in that house when we moved to one with an inside laundry. Mum brought me a mangle then. She said a timber floor and frame wouldn't stand the Whizz-Dri. The house would lift off its foundations.

Jo Conway recalls the 1920s in rural New South Wales: *The washing-line was unbelievable during the depression when we had our family, twelve children, Mum and Dad, and the cousins who came and lived with us because they needed a roof over their heads.*

MARY JANE
|
VIOLET
1885-1958
|
'JO' CONWAY
1920-

There were miles of work-clothes, and lengths of line between whatever, trees and clothes props. The rotary hadn't been invented then. The line went for miles around the paddocks, and Mum was so particular about pegging clothes on the line in a proper way - all the towels in a row.

We continued to hang out the washing, the way Mum did, in a proper way; more to please her than anything. The socks were kept in pairs; that way, you knew if you'd lost one, and it made storing easier. We pegged shirts by the tails, undies at the waist and pinnies from the bib. The tablecloths and napkins were hung so that they could be damped down for ironing with no extra creases from crooked hanging or twisting. To the inside, away from the gaze of outsiders, especially men, even those in the family, went the 'unmentionables' - the underwear.

Row upon row of sheets, towels, hankies, dishrags, clothes of all descriptions hung out as early as possible, competing with the neighbours, waiting for a breeze. The towelling nappies that replaced the old winceyette ones in the sixties needed more hours of sunshine than you got on a winter's day, at least in southern Australia. But when health centre sisters insisted that the nappies be hung outside, and that an efficient mother could manage with three dozen, every day was wash-day. Disposable nappies were expensive and frowned upon, as were plastic pants. 'Just wash, rinse, lots of sun, and there'll be no rashes,' was standard advice.

I always had a little line somewhere.

As the wife of a member of the fire brigade, Katie Wilkes rarely lived in self-contained quarters. Early in her married life, establishing rights to the wash-house was not always easy.

When I went to Carlton, I had to share the wash-house with three women. One of them said, 'If you do as you're told and do the right thing, we won't have any trouble.' I said, 'Well I've never had any trouble before, and I'm not likely to now.' I didn't know what to say. And she said, 'I'm having Monday now.' There was all this nastiness going on, but I always had a little line somewhere; I put it up on the balcony.

Several years later, while living in apartments with a communal washing area on the roof, Katie was able to offer sage advice to a new arrival.

There was this very nice young lady, she came here as a bride. She was crying one day up in the wash-house. She'd walked over the top of the roof where her husband was sound asleep, and I said, 'Look, you're just new to this place, dear. You do what you want to do. If you want your washing hung out, you've got to walk on that roof. You'll find out that they have parties there until three o'clock in the morning, and they're not going to worry about anyone else sleeping. So dry your tears.'

If a woman remained with or near her parents or in-laws, she was taught the traditional family ways. *Ma lived one block to the left of her daughter-in-law and, on Monday, when she was hanging out the washing, there'd be this tap,*

tap on the window to lower the line so she that didn't have to stretch. Ma considered it very bad to stretch when you were pregnant. Mum was terrified of washing-day. She thought that her mother-in-law would be watching.

When the Hill's hoist came on the market after the war, backyards across Australia were dominated by it. Every new home had one. The risk of a broken prop in a high wind dumping clothes on the ground had gone, but the hoists had their own quirks. After a while the mechanism jammed, or the outside line suffered from its use as a merry-go-round. Some were locked into place by a bolt to avoid take-off in a high wind. The Hill's was impossible to disguise, although some sported colourful canvas covers in summer. Replacing the rotary with a hideaway line restored the back garden but involved digging out the substantial concrete moorings. The Hill's had been installed to withstand most onslaughts.

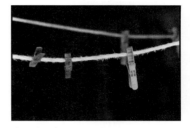

Tuesday was ironing-day. I've always liked that smell of ironed linen, but Mum said, 'Only brides iron their sheets.'

Women used a range of irons in the early days of this century. Floss Haig remembers the gas iron that was used in the 1920s in inner Melbourne.

There was a tap on our gas stove just before the jets, which you connected with a piece of tube to the iron. Then you would light the tap, like a griller, and wait for it to get hot, then disconnect the iron. It was exceedingly dangerous, but then, of course, so was the first electric we had. It plugged into the socket in the overhead light and swung as you ironed.

The flat iron sat on the one fire stove and got black and dirty. We used bar soap to clean around the edges. We'd run it over brown paper and onto a sheet. Ironing was skilled then. We had a separate sleeve board for doing those big leg of mutton sleeves and the cuffs at the small end. You always had to be careful with the black up the sides of the iron.

Meg Sekavs, despite her moves, has kept her grandmother's iron stand. Her father made it for her. *It has a clover leaf stamp on it, very faint. It's practically worn off. It's a brass iron stand. The whole set, the tongs, the clinkers, the iron, they were stored under the house when she went electric. I have the iron stand because it was given to me, and I've seen the clinkers. You lifted up the back of the iron, and they fitted in.*

Meg's mother, Gertrude, has the newer model, the 'Mother Potts', with the removable handle. *I've still got two, which I've covered. They became so worn in the middle that they were dangerous to use. We bent a piece of conduit and fitted it underneath them because it was too dangerous with the handle. You'd pick it up, and the thing would drop off; it wouldn't grip it properly. Then Doug took them to work, and that handle's a fixture now. I've covered them, and they stand by the doors, as door stops. I won't part with those.*

Drip-dry clothes and synthetics reorganized wardrobes and lightened the burden of ironing. *Mum doesn't iron. She's always worked, and it was quite novel for me when I began work in 1985 to decide to buy clothes that weren't drip-dry. It was a sort of luxury. I didn't read the 'care instructions' at first, but it wasn't long before I changed. I think twice now before I wear things that need ironing.*

From Jessie August at Nutwood Downs station in the Northern Territory I heard of the coal iron, a particularly treacherous instrument. It was filled with coals and, as you ironed, it spat sparks, scorched the material and scarred the operator.

I was still working when I was having kids, washing clothes for the missus, Mrs Wood, ironing shirts, dresses. Hagar [her sister-in-law] was the 'laying-the-table girl' and I was the 'laundry girl'. Iron sheets and pillowcases, too. Lovely, put them back along cupboard, fold the towels, put them along cupboard. With a coal iron and a little bit of water in front of it. Level it up, shirts: you know, you do the sleeve first, then the yoke. Curtains, too; we used to wash dirty ones. No machine, only finger work. Soap we made too, boil it down, with fat.

Jessie had little use for an ironed dress shirt; nor did her husband, Sandy. But like many Aboriginal women, she had worked in the house of the station manager or owner and was familiar with a technology that was only a dim memory to an urban dweller. She lived in a tin shelter in the camp about 300 metres from the station homestead. Jessie has not saved the iron. She has, however, retained her grinding stones, the ones used by her mother and what she calls 'the first generation', those who remember the old people, in the closing decades of the nineteenth century, when the land was 'opened up' and people 'settled down'.

All the older gardens had a lemon tree. People didn't move around so much then.

In settling down, in the making of a home, establishing a routine ordered time and space, spelt out certain expectations, offered a sort of security.

The Order of Things

In Mimi Taylor's kitchen, Sunnybank Hills, Queensland, the cannisters that her daughter Ruby bought with her first pay

Mary Giles, Leederville, Western Australia

The Order of Things

Jodie Mitchell and her mother Virginia Mayo, Alice Springs, Northern Territory

Bernadine Harrington, her daughter Gillian Gerard and her grand-daughter Pia Gerard, Leabrook, South Australia

Inside, women managed household affairs; outside they wrought order in gardens, created areas of shade, colour, utility and significance. Establishing a garden is one of those acts of faith: we will be there long enough to enjoy it. With gardens comes a sense of stability and a commitment to maintaining more than just the house.

When family and friends visited, the minimum courtesy was a cup of tea and a walk around the garden to discuss the aspect and the soil; the balance of colour and scent; then a pause to admire a particularly fine bloom, a vigorous vine; examine the pieces potted since the last visit; advise on ailing shrubs; hear their histories. You were told the stories of plants: the fuchsia called, 'My Mother', planted by a daughter; the white rose, a symbol of purity, planted when Kay entered the convent and always known by her name.

In very powerful ways, plants evoke people and places, their continued growth a link with the past and hope for the future. We can move and re-make our homes around familiar things such as teapots and favourite chairs, routines can be adapted to different situations, but our gardens are our roots in a real sense.

Where gardens are alive with meaning, moving house is wrenching. In the garden of my childhood, we buried our pet terrier under the plum tree, and we hoped that the new people would respect that space. It was where she sat in the sun. I said goodbye to the trees I'd kept alive with the kitchen slops and upturned bottles during the years of drought and water restrictions, and I transplanted some of my favourite plants to a neighbour's garden so that I could take a cutting at a later time. The garden, where my children had played as toddlers, had eased my frustrations as a house-bound mother. Creating a garden was one possible outlet for my energy; I could work in fits and starts. Any other more sustained creativity depended on both children having their naps at the same time. At least in the garden there was something to show for my time, and it didn't get unmade everyday like the beds. I've driven past that garden, but I haven't trusted myself to venture in, to ask, did the almond trees I rescued from sure death with excessive pruning still produce fruit, and did the crimson rosellas still eat the best fruit just before the harvest weekend?

Gardens carry their own histories, but these may easily be lost. I was distressed when, on leaving my Canberra garden, one I'd worked quite hard to establish, the new owner did not want to look at it with me, did not want to know what would be coming up in a month's time. It was a garden that reflected my interests, full of Australian plants put in to attract the honeyeaters. The children, by then in secondary school, did not need to be protected from spiky bushes. And there was no need to set aside a sunny spot for the sand pit, or an expanse for the Hill's hoist. It went, and the backyard became a garden.

I planted a tree for each of the children; that one there when my son was born.

To the eye accustomed to lush gardens in eastern Australia, or the tropical growth in the north, a large jacaranda in a Perth garden is not extraordinary, except to the woman who put it there. In dry sandy areas, sustaining a garden requires dedication.

I planted that big tree when my son was born, my first son. It's as old as he is. He was born in 1960, and I planted it for him then. I planted a tree for each of the children. The big one, that's a jacaranda, and we've got lots of jacarandas in this area, that's for him. I've cut it back just recently, for the first time; it's lovely in the summer. It's so hot here, and we've got that shade. The rhus tree was my daughter's and the willow my son's. It's a lovely tree, in bud now. I've replaced the rhus tree with a peach and hopefully that'll grow and take off.

Throughout her married life, one marred by long periods in hospital and a great deal of unhappiness, the garden was a refuge. *When I was first married, I used to survive in the garden.*

My husband and father-in-law drank and gambled all weekend and then started to look after themselves on Sunday to go to work on Monday. I survived by gardening and looking after my children. That was my relaxation. And I can see it now, you know. I'm in the garden all day Sunday. On Sunday night my husband would come and say, 'What's for tea?' I was stupid enough to go and get it. But then, of course, there were the kids that had to be fed.

Now that she is living at home, the garden is her joy.

When we moved in here, it was a desert and, now, when it's mowed, it looks lovely. The kids play cricket and bowl down there and love it. My husband always used to have straight lines. He was a bricklayer, and everything had to be straight and level. I like nice curved ones, and I'm gradually breaking them down. I've got fruit trees because I'm on the pension, and I can't always afford to buy fruit. Most of the fruit trees were birthday presents. The kids bought them for me. I've got a few vegies and strawberries and rhubarb in my garden. And

I've got the ever-faithful greenery that stayed there over the years when nothing else grew.

Plants can even come to represent people. In one family, the standing joke was that the personalities of each of the three daughters could be attributed to where they were found: the first was said to have been prickly because she was found under a rose bush; the second was found under a bougainvillea, and the last under an oleander. 'Draw your own conclusions,' said the eldest.

In Penny Peel's family, her mother managed to grow a rose where her grandmother's attempts had failed.

Gran would send away for roses from a nursery that's still near Bundaberg, Langbeckers. They'd send a catalogue, she'd order, and it would be sent by train. Every year she ordered a yellow rose, and we'd plant it in the same place, but it'd never survive. One day she saw Dad mowing it down. When Gran died, Mother insisted on a yellow climber for Gran. It's in my house now.

Whenever I visit her, she gives me cuttings. All of mine are from familiar places.

Rather than a garden recording just one time in your life, it often brings together a lot of your past. Mary Fisher has lived in many parts of Australia.

I love gardening, and my cuttings are from familiar places. My friends from Broken Hill have given me manure. In fact, I demanded some as a wedding present from them. That's the red dust in my garden in Sydney. I have cuttings from the old rosemary bush in the Senate gardens from when I worked there in Canberra. The bush is no longer there. Some of the plants are from my parents, some from the gully at home in Adelaide. It's a peaceful place, full of trees, old beeches, oaks, elms. I haven't had any success with Lily of the Valley. It grows in the Adelaide Hills but cannot survive the humidity of Sydney.

Looking at many of the pieces struck from cuttings, the bulbs shared out when they were last lifted, the plants nurtured from seeds, I'm struck that it is not the exotic plants but the ordinary ones that are sought. Geraniums, daisies, sweet william, lavender bushes are moved from garden to garden around Australia. In one Melbourne garden, a Western Australian climbing geranium flourishes. A mother, now living in the country, visits her daughter in the city and takes cuttings from plants in her garden, some of which were in the original family home. 'I'll bring a trailer next time I come down,' she declares. In the meantime, the cuttings sit in a bucket in the boot of the car.

It takes time and care to find the variety that will blend or contrast with your own garden's lay-out. Geraniums come in such a range of colours, such a variety of leaves; they climb, they survive a savage pruning. I remember my mother taking pieces from various botanical gardens around Australia. Then we all took cuttings from hers. She'd bring them back in her luggage and regale us with stories of how she 'pruned' the creeper in the Hobart Gardens. She had a magnificent range of geraniums. She didn't bring soil, so she reasoned that she wasn't violating quarantine regulations.

Always on the look-out for the plants that will keep the balance of the garden, the preference is to have something in bloom most of the year. By the back door, near the gully trap, over the outhouses, you planted something sweet-smelling like lavender. Plants with the overpowering and heavy scents were kept at a distance from the house, at least one child being allergic to the spring pollens. The precious pieces were put where the dogs didn't dig and the fragile growth was protected from the ravages of the mower and the car backing down the driveway.

Taking cuttings from a home garden was mostly by invitation. Only those on very close terms would presume to do so without being asked. Even with my mother, who is forever potting out pieces, I feel strange asking for cuttings unless she offers. It's more that I admire a plant, she'll pot it out and then, on a special occasion, the new plant will be presented to me. Those are small gestures that give pleasure to the giver and receiver - but the anxiety when it doesn't flourish! - it is almost an omen.

Colour in the gardens reminds me of colour chalks.

Not all women grew up with gardens, but the need to create one is strong. Nancy Reis lived with her parents and three brothers in a hotel until she was twenty-one, when she left to marry. Later in her married life she was to return to hotels in partnership with her husband. She now lives in Brighton, Melbourne. To Nancy, a garden means home.

Living in hotels, you're different from other people. It wasn't a hostile atmosphere, but I was the little girl who lived in a hotel. I didn't have a yard to play in; I had no garden to walk in. We were opposite Melbourne University in Parkville, and we'd walk in the gardens and feed the ducks. My first taste of living in a house was when the hotel was being renovated in 1924-6. To be able to have a door you could leave open and to have a door bell, to hear it ring and to go to the door, I'd never thought about those things before.

The years I was a boarder at Genezzano in Kew were among the happiest in my life because I had the companionship I'd yearned for and also there was a garden. Every morning, before school, we would have a walk around the garden a couple of times to get some fresh air. Colour in the gardens reminds me of the colour chalks Miss Howe would use on the board - always something decorative to start the day's work. That was when I was at Parkville Grammar, and we used to push Miss Howe around the school because she was in a wheelchair.

Nancy now has a grown-up family, five girls and four boys and sixteen grandchildren. From her daughter's garden in Perth she has some mother-in-law tongue, but it's not doing as well as the geraniums. Her son is the one with the 'green fingers'. As a young mother she created a garden in an unusual setting.

We didn't have much of a garden at the hotel. I don't think I've got much left from there. Up on the roof, the flat roof, when Anthony was only about six or seven, we had a little bit of a garden there. We put in lobelia, and it was beautiful. We had a couple of camellias in tubs, and it began in him a love of the garden, really. I've always got a pot of whatever I want to grow, and I pot the piece. He doesn't. He can put it straight into the ground, and it comes up.

Many gardens were divided into domains, each with its purpose and own gardener. Nancy Reis's husband would sometimes help. *When I was re-doing my gardenia from here, I had to get my husband to help move the pot down under the tree. I didn't think to start to try to do it. I've got a weak back, and I just don't want to do those things. I could be male and feel exactly the same.*

The lawns, by and large, were for the men to mow. Indeed, it was a liberating moment for many women to get the hang of the pull start and operate the motor mower. The vegetable garden may also be a male domain, although the herbs, for cooking and medicinal purposes, tend to be looked after by the women.
   Penny Peel's Gran tried her hand at roses and was also an avid gardener.

She grew and developed strains from seed. It was very difficult, and she did fruit trees as well. There was only one tree we were allowed to climb. It was the mulberry, and she used to make mulberry pie. We were encouraged to pick the best from the top.

We relax in our gardens, work in them, read our past from them. We only leave those we trust in charge of our plants when we go on holidays. We may even ask for photographs of a particular piece in bloom, or a leaf if we are absent for long. As a newcomer to Australia, as one who grew up in Europe, Gertrude Stotz was intrigued by the traffic in plants, the moving, the potting, the creation of gardens. In each house in which she lived in inner Sydney suburbs, she planted a gum tree - quite an investment in the locale and the future.

They are so graphically beautiful, and I'm trying to accommodate myself to a new environment. It's the opposite of the greener lush of my home in Austria, and planting a gum tree is quite the opposite of what many Australians do.

I need that space and time to be away from the clutter of city structures.

Gardens reveal personal histories and social change. The gardens of immigrants who came here after the second world war, for example, were not filled with roses, and the vegetables growing in their front gardens shocked people accustomed to a neat path and spring bulbs. Only recently have Australian gardeners shown confidence in using local plants. In the last few decades 'native gardens' have come into fashion; 'the bush' has invaded the suburbs.

Each generation has planted its own garden. And now it's as if our gardens have moved back in sympathy with the landscape. Chloe Roe, whose family is part of the pastoral history of Queensland and New South Wales, was born during a drought that didn't break until the mid-1940s

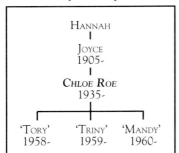

I feel a mystical relationship to the landscape around western Queensland. I was born in the drought, and it didn't rain until I was ten years old. Dryness was a constant preoccupation, especially when there were starving stock to consider. I saw the coastal regions as a more luxuriant landscape, not as hostile to people as the interior. It was as if people were irrelevant. As a child I had a powerful feeling that all man-made structures were ephemeral and at night the earth breathes and in the morning everything would be as it was. The dry country was the origin of my aesthetic sense - the landscape elements - the broad horizon and the bowl of the blue sky. They've influenced my appreciation of art and architecture.

After an absence of some years, Chloe re-visited the area. *I was in fear and trepidation that perhaps the bush would be boring, but it was just as I remembered. I need that space and time to be away from the clutter of city structures. It stems from the enforced isolation of my childhood.*

We've only got one history, here.

Topsy Napurrula Nelson speaks of her mother's country, that of her father, of her mother's mother, that of her birth. Each rock, tree, sand ridge, creek is a visible marker; each tells the history of her ancestors, of a time past when the land was given shape and meaning. She would no more be at home on the coast than Chloe. But Topsy's relationship to the land is underwritten by the law of the dreamtime.

You can move to another place. You've got plane, Toyota. We pass away here. We die in one place in our country; in our land, people don't move. We've only got one history, here.

Settled and ordered but no need to make a garden.

CHAPTER TWO

WASTE NOT WANT NOT

Now, it's easy to get romantic about the wood stove, a warm hearth around which the happy, well-fed family members cluster after eating their fill of the perfect baked dinner. The very shape of the house and its rhythms seem to flow from the rituals of the stove.

The skills and timing are all part of the day's routine. There is a sense of satisfaction that the kettle is boiling on the back, the bread rising, the yoghurt turning, the boots drying - you open the door and see the sparks glow. On the back of the stove sits the hand-cream mixture: melted sheep's fat and sulphur, and rosewater to give the scent. From the cavernous ovens comes a dry, wholesome smell, a reassuring crackle, a sense of order, of mother at the helm.

The smell of yeast still reminds me of reading.

The kitchen was the hub of women's activity, the wood stove a magnet. On the large, homely table of Australian wood, the family meals were eaten; in between, snacks of bread, butter and home-made jam were laid out, peas were shucked, the mincer clamped and turned. While bread was kneaded at one end, children puzzled over their homework at the other. For Janet Shaw, who studied by correspondence in the forties, 'The smell of yeast still reminds me of reading.' In the pantry, rows of Fowlers Vacola paid tribute to bottling skills. The ice-box or Coolgardie safe held food that would perish. In the galvanized basin in the porcelain sink, a soap-saver, and beside the sink the shavings and remains of the ends of the bar soap. The wooden sideboard was scrubbed down with sandsoap, and where there was no sink a basin stood alone. When you had to cut the wood to boil all your water, you economized on the size of the container.

It was not much fun splitting the kindling, cleaning the ashtrays, washing down the soot lodged on the walls and laundering the greying curtains. It may have been comfortingly warm in winter, but where hot water depended on the stove being lit, a hot summer was less than pleasant. The routine was relentless: by mid-afternoon, at the latest, you had to re-kindle the fire so that the oven heated, the water boiled and the cup of tea was ready for Dad when he came home from work. Woe betide the new wife who failed to get the temperature right, the daughter who served the meat raw in the middle. Dinner was on the table by six.

After the war, the electric fridge, hot-water service, fan-forced oven and dishwasher streamlined the kitchens. With the saving of space came the possibility of replacing the large table with a breakfast bench or smaller table, and with it the loss of somewhere for the family to meet and talk. Women were isolated in the kitchen with no sure call on the labour of other household members. No longer the need for a cunning ruse by which to prevent unpleasant smells, a crust under the lid of boiling cauliflower, clove sticks and herb bags. Instead all odours are whisked away by the extractor fan.

New technologies, new skills: the ability to fine tune a wood stove is no longer in great demand for women in the city. It is more a cherished memory or an item of nostalgia in a weekend cottage. Even on the station homesteads in the remotest areas of the Northern Territory, on the fringes of the Simpson Desert, one finds a microwave oven being used to bring a frozen slice of bread to life. And with the technology comes a change in the flavour of hospitality. The kettle and favourite teapot bear little resemblance to a teabag in a cup that is zapped into life in the microwave in a matter of minutes.

With the wood stove came the tools for opening, closing and cleaning, the little blackening brush, the enormous baking trays. Few of these tools of trade have been handed down. The passing of the wood stove was the death knell for a number of objects: the heavy iron-based kettle now full of nasturtiums finds a place in the garden. Women no longer need to scour the bottom of the kettle. The Robur teapot need no longer be instantly filled for visitors, or left to draw in its hand-knitted cosy. The baking trays are too large for the modern oven; now they hold the children's Lego blocks or odd nails in the garden shed.

So what connects our kitchens of the 1980s to those of our mothers and grandmothers? In a few the wood stove survives or, at least the space, perhaps filled by a gas or electric range. Old pieces of pottery, teapots and the more formal dinner services sketch the style of these homes. Recipe books make the link.

Recipe books included not just ingredients but also the tricks of the trade.

Recipes were not shared randomly: they were only given to women who were close, trusted and worthy. Care in the selection of those who might be allowed to try a hand at your culinary ingenuity reflected the relationship of women to their kitchen produce. Recipe books included not just a list of ingredients but also the tricks of the trade: how to read the signs of a quirky wood oven; hints for dealing with less than fresh eggs; what to do with milk on the turn (cottage cheese hung to drip in a linen hankerchief); how to set brawn (always have a broken window sash); how to allow for humidity; cold fingers in kneading pastry (work in the early morning); how to mix fruit cakes (drop three times to remove the air bubbles). Knowing how to crisp up the Yorkshire pud or the potatoes was a secret only shared with those who were close. (One manual advised the cook to add a small amount of snow to the batter - not an option for many Australian women.)

The worn book which, to an outsider, appeared like a collection of scrap paper held together with the remains of long-gone feasts included recipes, remedies and household tips. People who were not liked were not recorded; only good friends would give the right quantity.

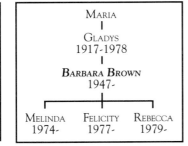

In Mum's brown book of recipes, there was a section on handy hints, including how to remove stains from concrete, make soup, truss chicken and many recipes from Martha Gardener's radio programme. Beside each recipe were details of the date, person and source of the recipe. Mostly they came from friends, neighbours and relatives. There was one for tomato sauce, pickles, pudding and a twelve-egg butter cake. Of course, there was Mother's recipe for punch. I'd given it to her originally and making it at Christmas had become a tradition. That's the recipe that made me notice that the book was no longer there. I came down with my family for

Christmas, but I didn't bring my copy of the recipe because I thought it was in Mother's book.

After Barbara Brown's mother died, her brother, his fiancée and father cleaned up the house and moved some of her belongings to the old family home.

They did it as a kindness. Their attitude was, 'Keep what is useful and new.' When I discovered the book was not there, and my brother was not sure of its fate, I panicked. My sister, who was still grieving for our mother, was distraught. My brother knew from the tone of her voice that something was amiss. We found the book had been taken up to the old house and retrieved it. It's now with my sister down at Warrnambool. I suppose our family is sentimental, but it's because of those links. It's more than just hoarding, it's part of ourselves.

By the time Mrs Beeton's *Book of Household Management* was first published in 1861, Australian women had already begun making their own recipe books, a blend of old traditions from the home country and new wisdom acquired in the colonies. From Queensland came the story of how to store citrus. 'Cut the lemons from the tree with stalks still on, and coat with vaseline, bury in the sand with stalk peeking out.' This is remarkably similar to the way in which Aboriginal women in Central Australia stored native oranges for thousands of years. They picked the fruits in season and stored them for lean times.

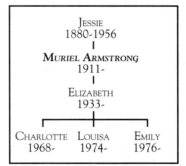

When the *Women's Weekly* appeared in the late 1920s, it was another source of recipes. Remember the 1938 Christmas cake recipe from the *Women's Weekly*? Muriel Armstrong received it from her mother and passed it on to her daughter. It is now with her grand-daughter and is made for the family and for competitions. The radio was also a source of recipes and hints of what to do with foods that were in season, cheap in the markets or plentiful in the home gardens. Preserving by bottling, drying, smoking and salting was recorded and, alongside the recipe, the name and the occasion; an acknowledgement of the creator, a form of copyright.

Cookbooks put out by community groups, especially churches, filled an important gap. Reliance on works such as the *Presbyterian Women's Mothers' Union Cookbook* and *The Treasury of Good Recipes* was strong. It was where you could find a section on tuna mornay and 'luxuries with leftovers'. It was where you found the formula for 'minute per pound' roasting of various meats, charts of weights and measures, advice on the dietary merits of a range of foods, a list of welfare services.

Home-made recipe books, featuring local produce, and household manuals included improvisations; some borrowed from the Aborigines and some from Chinese market gardeners. These recipe books became family treasures. They reflected the dedication to excellence in the kitchen of the generation who had compiled them and gave later generations access to that knowledge. Selected friends and relatives were able to use them or sometimes to copy the recipes.

What of the farmers' wives who cooked the sheep from one end to the other? Who boiled the flaps until the bones popped out and then smothered the dish in a white sauce with tomatoes, onions and bacon? What of the famous fruit cakes? Aunt Mildred's was probably in a dozen recipe books. But it was hers we used. We would have felt guilty, otherwise. What about the daisy cake, the pastry that never flopped, the pavlova that was always sticky inside? What of the cook who could gauge the temperature of a stove with a sheet of tissue paper? Much of that expertise is lost.

The good cooks, the plain cooks, the bosses of the wood stove, like Lena Kay's mother, produced slabs of cakes for the shearers.

Well, she used to make a cake that we all loved. It was a fruit cake, and she put vinegar in it. I've never been able to get that recipe for that vinegar cake. Well, perhaps she just made it up, I don't know. She used to make it in very big slabs for the men, working, for their morning and afternoon tea.

Several younger women noted that rather than recipes being handed down they were passing recipes up the generations. With travel and the variety of cookbooks about, daughters no longer need to rely on their mothers for all their culinary skills.

Life is so full for my daughters. They're not standing around in the kitchen cooking. My older daughter is a good cook. She finds her own modern recipes in the Women's Weekly. *My cooking is not quite up to it. I've watched and learnt from her. She makes her own butter, and I still make my own bread. We all borrowed mother's old hand-written recipe book and copied out recipes when we were married.*

Of course, learning continues, and we each develop our own kitchen rituals. We draw on the traditions of other families, our friends, respond to new ideas, different ways of doing things. Patricia Richards adopted a practice from a friend.

It's ways of doing things more than actual recipes, because when I left home I couldn't actually cook. I taught myself, but I guess a lot of it is observing customs.

Like I have a friend who spreads out a piece of butcher paper over the tops of her cupboards when she's going to do the vegetables and then just rolls it up and puts it in the garbage. I saw her doing it one day and said, 'That's marvellous.' She said, 'Well, my mother always did it, and so I always do it too.'

Mothers may have been memorable cooks, but they were not always good teachers. Often they were too busy to fool around with the experiments of children, and it was grandma or an aunt who had time to supervise the first attempts. Sometimes it was a sense of the kitchen, of certain traditions rather than skills, that was passed to the next generation.

With Mum, it wasn't just the time she spent cooking but all the preparation. You were either pickling or baking or salting and curing food, or pickling cucumbers in their pots in the laundry, and she'd even be making her own noodles. I didn't learn to cook from her. I just got a sort of appreciation because we always had such nice food. Then, when I was eighteen and left home to go nursing, I had to live with other women in little boxes, no heat and horrible food. It was my first experience of non-Polish cooking.

Isobel Skoczek's response to Australian food, especially institutional food, is not unique. Other migrants who spent their early days in Australia in hostels were similarly dismayed by the food. An arrival in 1947 said of it:

Australians in those days would not eat garlic: they wouldn't eat a lot of things. I know, because when I first came here, I worked as a cook at the hostel at Bathurst. My training was as a nurse, but my English was not good enough. I hadn't done much cooking at home in Yugoslavia, so I had to learn as I went along. The cooks in the hostel kitchens were all Europeans, but the Australian staff wanted their cabbage boiled in water. Pigs would not eat it that way. We like it this way: cook first garlic in butter, add some tomato, then the cabbage until it's cooked - beautiful.

Spice racks, additions to the kitchens of the sixties, tell us something of the degree of daring. Many of the neatly labelled jars were unused. To milk drinks, pies and cakes perhaps mixed spice, nutmeg or cinnamon was added. Herbs from the garden - parsley, rosemary, mint and chives - were in demand, but garlic was not used until much later.

  Not all women regarded the kitchen as a creative place, and several were clear that cooking was not part of their life.

I don't cook much, but I have some recipes from women I've shared houses with. When I make them, I think of those women. I think I probably rebelled against my Jewish mother. But I'm not at home, and the woman I live with has always had help in the home, so she doesn't cook much either. We eat out a lot.

For many families, food for the week was grilled meat and boiled vegetables, with the possibility of a casserole made from the leftovers. On Sunday, vegetables were baked with the roast. For some mothers, the daily production of 'chop and two veg' was a form of rebellion, the obsessive bottling of the older generation spurned. Trapped in the kitchen, they were damned if they were going to provide gourmet meals every day. They turned out their standard good plain cooking, day in, day out.

When the number to be fed dropped, as children left home, or perhaps a partner died, the change could be difficult.

After Dad died, Mum just didn't eat properly. She'd had a lot of trouble re-adjusting to cooking for just them after we all left home but, by herself, she always cooked too much or couldn't be bothered. I went looking for a 'Cooking for One' recipe book so she could see it was still worth preparing a decent meal.

The smell when you came in from church, the assurance that friends and relatives would be there to share the occasion, the roast evokes the home; it is a symbol of family. Once in the oven it required little attention; it was just basted and the cover removed when everyone was home. The leftovers provided another meal or sandwich fillings for the week.

There was a recipe for Yorkshire pudding, but to learn how to roast a leg of lamb, to crisp the potatoes, you had to be in the kitchen. It was a matter of acting when it looked right. In Penny Peel's home, this was the time for her Gran, Cecile, to air her views.

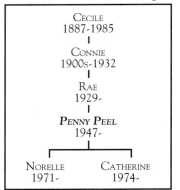

We learnt how to cook the leg without being told. We were taught to raise pork crackling in the same way. We'd sit around the big kitchen table, and Gran would be talking about what the stupid miners were doing while she was rubbing salt into the pork. Politics - we learnt politics in the kitchen. She had strong opinions and could back them up. One thing, she never got used to the idea that her one-time playmate had gone on to be prime minister. When she saw the Canberra suburb Fadden named after him, she said, 'Oh well, I suppose he must have grown up, but he'll always be "Arty" to me.'

The meat was often over-cooked, but meat that fell from the bone was admired. In the Anglo-Saxon view of baking, only foreigners, the French, ate their meat red. Some roasts were carved at the table, an elaborate ritual, where the head of the table had charge of the meat and could favour one or the other with special servings: the sweet knuckle bone or the crispy end. Others were dished up on the kitchen bench and brought to the table, gravy and vegetables already served, with any possibility of a second serve or the pickings out of sight. Now we hear complaints about confusions with serving dishes, of the silver of the dining room and the pyrex of the kitchen being interchanged, now that there are no longer servants to separate the kitchenware from the dining silver. 'A generation in decline,' say the few who remember the gracious old days.

While no one, it seems, has a written recipe for roast lamb, the dessert that followed was recorded carefully and copied by one generation after another. There are plenty of recipes for sweets, desserts, suet puddings and Anzac biscuits. And somehow or other Sunday wasn't properly observed unless there was a variety of cakes on the table.

If I have visitors and I'm preparing ahead, I don't think I've done the whole bit unless I've got the meal and sweets and a cake. It was a special treat, because you didn't have it through the week. You just had your meat and vegetables.

The traditions of high tea were brought from the United Kingdom. *I used to make a cake every Sunday, but now I do it for visitors only. It was part of growing up in Scotland and part of achieving status as a woman. I still do it, but I don't want to get fat.*

A greater health consciousness now limits the production of certain treats. *I wouldn't dream of using a lot of the recipes. They're too full of sugar, and who would use a dozen eggs in one dessert?*

There were few wordly topics on which Mother spoke with ease, and food was one of the ways she gained his attention.

Although it is no longer her routine, the memories are vivid for this daughter of one of Australia's pioneering families.

The gong went at 4 a.m. to rise, dress and do the chores. Breakfast between 6 and 6.30 in summer (an hour later in winter), smoko was at ten, lunch at noon, afternoon tea at four and then drinks between 6 and 6.30 followed by dinner. Breakfast was always cooked, and we served ourselves from the hot plate, except on Mondays and Tuesdays, which were washing and ironing-days. Then the housemaid cleared away. On those days, we helped Mum. Lunch, like breakfast, was on the seersucker cloth, and there were cold cuts on a silver dish. For those working away from the homestead, mutton and chutney sandwiches and billy tea. Morning tea was scones or pikelets, while the afternoon break was little cakes. Tea was served with all food.

Everyone changed for dinner. After soup, which mother served, the courses were brought in response to the bell she would ring. There were rules about eating, which knife to use: cut toast, break bread. Father was head of the table in every way. His monologues were tolerated by the governess, the jackaroo, the family. Mother, at the other end of the table, was very much overpowered by him. They did not communicate during meals. Their only conversation went like this. Mother: "Don't give me so much." Father: "You'll die if you don't eat." There were few worldly topics on which she spoke with any ease, and food was one of the ways she gained his attention.

There was always a pot on the stove, and we'd boil up the scraps for soup.

Memories of a mother living in the Gulf country, Queensland, in the 1930s stress self-sufficiency and making do.

She was a plain cook and measured by the fistful not a cup. Cooks would come and go, but she had to be able to manage in between. It was necessary to keep remedies for all ills, and castor oil was a great favourite. A matter of necessity to know how to treat the sick.

It was a big day when the fresh food arrived. The flour would be weevilly, and we would have to sift it. Sometimes we would kill a goat, but mostly we had beef. We had a vegetable garden at Lawn Hill, and vegies went to the stock camp, too. Not all stations did that. I'd go out with my husband and stay overnight and sometimes take the children to the stock camp. We had drip safes and got our first fridge by World War II. In the winter we had cow's milk, when there was a bit of green feed. Up north the Aboriginal women did the milking; I never learned. Tinned butter came by ship, and we buried it in the sand under the store to keep it cool. It was hard to keep it firm in the summertime.

The frugality of our grandmothers is now the stuff of stories for grandchildren rather than the basis for survival. Emmeline Lahey's memories of life in rural Queensland reach back into the mid-nineteenth century when her grandmother's generation was born.

I hate waste. Everything is precious in the bush, and you have to look after it. We were brought up with, 'Not even a Mintie paper should be thrown out,' and our children have followed our example on that. But now it's a throwaway society. We made do with everything. We ate everything. There was always a pot on the stove, and we'd boil up the scraps for soup. Soup for lunch in winter and summer. In the old days, we went out and cut the corn and harvested the corn and spent most of the day at it. We made it into flour or porridge or whatever. Most of our time was spent just acquiring and processing the food we were going to eat. It's nothing like that now. We've lost our ability to fend for ourselves. We've become very dependent.

Rose Chalmers and her daughter Heather Goldsworthy, McDonald Downs Station, Northern Territory.

Joy Caddie and her daughter Jill Taylor, Browns Plains, Queensland

Goldie Blyth, her grand-daughter Jamey Blyth and daughter Mary Blyth, Kakadu National Park, Northern Territory

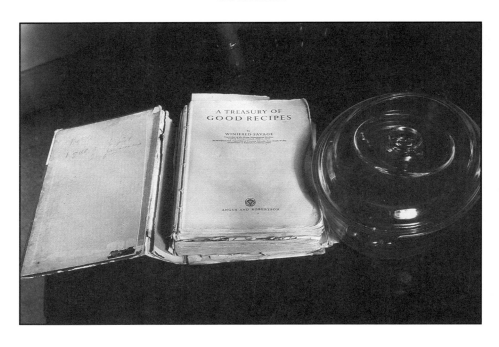

Patti Monro's precious objects: a recipe book from her mother and a dish from her grandmother

Most families have a bunch of recipes for dealing with a glut of fruits. In Queensland, mango chutney is the celebrated answer. Penny Peel:

When you grow up in North Queensland, where everybody has trees, and when they're ripe, you can't eat them all, so everyone does something with their mangoes. Gran's recipe has chilli, the little red ones, in it. I never used it while I was living in the southern states but now I'm back here in Queensland, I do. She never wrote it down for herself. I made it with her and learned that way. I asked for the recipe when she was living with her daughter, my aunt. She dictated it, and I wrote it down. She was giving amounts, and her daughter disputed them. I wrote hers down. I suspect, nonetheless, she had her own bit of magic. She had one recipe with cannabis in it. People grew it then. My father said it was the best chutney he'd ever had. When we realized what it was, it went.

The leftovers re-worked through the mincer provided another hot meal. *Dad was very skilled at breaking the bones, and I have a very clear memory of the meat cleaver being used to actually break the long bone of the roast into several sections to get at the inside of the bone and the stuff from the knuckles. Absolutely anything edible from the Sunday roast they'd put through the mincer. It was made into meat loaves and rissoles, which were eaten with gravy and Mum's tomato relish, the one made with green tomatoes.*

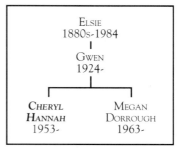

Growing up in the fifties in New South Wales, Cheryl Hannah remembers sitting on a small stool on the table to balance that mincer. By the time her sister Megan was old enough to help, it was no longer in use. Leftovers were a thing of the past.

Mum's still got the mincer, but I'm sure it hasn't been used for ten years or more. It took quite a lot of physical strength to grind up the bits and pieces. There was raw pumpkin with the skin still on, and sometimes raw meat. If he was going to put onions through, I'd be quite happy for one of the boys to sit on the stool.

One of the most savoury additions to a good plain Australian meal was chutney. Served with the cold meat from the Sunday roast or added to sandwiches, it was a favourite. Almost any fruit, the glut crops bartered with neighbours, those picked wild, could be turned into jam, pickles, chutney. Jo Conway:

We had an orchard but not a fantastic one. Our neighbours had more cherries than they could cope with, and you'd go out picking blackberries by the ton; melons grew in our own paddocks; other neighbours had plum trees, apple trees. In the country, everyone worked together in that respect. So Mother was always making jam of some description, or preserving. She loved her preserves.

This was not necessarily the experience of the next generation, as a daughter of the fifties explains. *Grandma made everything. She had a Vacola bottling set. Mum refused. It was her act of rebellion. She wasn't going to stand around anyone's hot kitchen making preserves. She quite liked making pickles and relishes. I remember green tomato and paw-paw. We would only have been able to make that in my Grandma's place in northern New South Wales. So if Mum made it, she must have gone up there and brought it back to Sydney. Grandma made everything, and she won prizes at the local show for her stuff. She was an absolute perfectionist. Her bottles were beautiful works of art, and the things were delicious to eat.*

She continued to make marmalade until the second-last year of her life. A very strong tradition.

In the southern states, it was marmalade that showed the calibre of the cook. Elspeth Young has brought her Scottish marmalade recipes to Australia and adapted them to the conditions of places where she has lived: Canberra and Darwin.

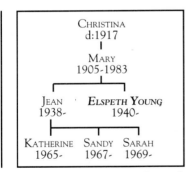

Scottish housewives go out Saville orange-spotting in the shops late January. When I've bought them in Canberra, which is usually in August, or so, I've had to have a long discussion with the storeholders at the market, most of whom assume, I think, that they're sweet oranges. I've used the same recipe with other fruits too, because in Australia you've got more access to other kinds of citrus. I've made it with limes. I think that's probably the best, especially the ones nicked from the N.A.R.U. [Northern Australian Research Unit] garden in Darwin. The very best substitute is cumquats.

I suspect that every Scottish housewife probably had a recipe that she believed in and thought was better than anybody else's. My mother's was one that she used to apologise about sometimes because it was 'a bit easy'. She belongs in the generation where unless it was awfully hard work you didn't justify yourself. Hers was a bit easy because it involved putting the orange peel through the mincing machine. One time she'd eaten marmalade at someone else's house, which she thought was really good - it was extremely coarse-cut marmalade - she decided to make this. We all got pulled into it 'cos this was 'very hard work'. She only made one lot of it, and that was brought out on special occasions. Everybody liked it very much, but she thought it was 'just a bit too much hard work'.

The work involved having the daughters on hand to polish pans, to cut, mince and soak the peel, to stir the pot and sterilize the jars; work spanning several days.

The part which nobody else could do was to make sure it was setting. No thermometers or anything like that, just a cold plate and a little bit of marmalade on it and then turn the plate up and down. There was always a little bit that didn't fit or, if it fitted exactly, she made sure that there was some left over so you could start eating it straight away. She'd fill up a whole shelf in the cupboard and put all the jars there on display.

She continued to make marmalade when she'd given up making a lot of other things. She made it for my sister. She would say, 'Oh, Jean's too busy to make marmalade, but I have to make marmalade every time these oranges come into the shops, every February.' So she probably made it up till about the last, second-last year of her life, even though she hardly ate any of it. A very strong tradition, I think.

Not all the bottling and pickling frenzy was for presentations, display or to be eaten at home. Women like Mimi Taylor, widowed, ineligible for a pension, but unable to work because of her health, made jams for her daughter to sell.

Bland baking dominated Australian kitchens in the era of the wood stove. The recipes that were recorded and those tastes that are remembered tend to be for the fancy desserts, the wholesome cakes and biscuits, what to do with glut fruits and that mayonnaise dressing made from a tin of condensed milk and lemon juice. The 'chop and two-veg' generation had little use for the hints on handling exotic foods. Certainly, other traditions were being pursued. When the Chinese from the goldfields became market gardeners, new foods were available in other parts of Australia. Chinese cooks in the north continued their customs and even influenced station diets. One person complained of her mother who had grown up in the far north: 'Bits of green pepper turned up in a quite random fashion in the salads and casseroles.'

Aborigines continued to cook their food according to their customs. The endurance of bland food in the Australian diet, however, is recorded by the women who lived in the migrant hostels in the forties and fifties. Among some war veterans, there was a strong resistance to eating rice with 'grown-up' food as part of the main course. Garlic was used to keep away evil spirits. The salads, when dressed, came with a glop of mayonnaise. Now we are offered the basics of the delights of another culture in a series of easy steps. Recipe books entice us with the colours and style of the pictures. They are a new fantasy literature, the erotica of the kitchen. Rarely, however, do we realize the promise. Not so with the recipe books of grandma; hers were the tried and proven, if bland, recipes.

I always felt good when I could smell Nar's kitchen in my kitchen.

Recipes provide visible evidence of grandmother's presence. For Meg, the association is more diffuse.

I can remember the way Nar's kitchen smelt. Every now and again I'll go somewhere, and the smell is there. Sometimes in the old house down in Arabana Street, in Canberra, I could smell that in my own kitchen. I always felt good when I could smell Nar's kitchen in my kitchen.

Routines and rhythms of life, memories of the stability of old ways; scepticism towards the new. A tinge of nostalgia? Perhaps. Certainly older women were more comfortable with the distant than the near past. They spoke of happy times, simple pleasures, respect for authority and the security of an ordered existence. 'Hard work and happy times,' rang like an incantation through the stories of the lives of older women. Gertrude:

Well, she got to the stage, when she was close on ninety, when she couldn't do outside as she would like it to be done. I used to go up and clean through for her, now and again, and do jobs I thought she shouldn't be doing, like climbing up on the copper to wash walls in the laundry. If you got there early enough to get to it, you could do it for her. She was quite tough, but she'd led a very sheltered life, and maybe that gave you the idea she was sort of fragile, shall I say. She'd never gone out to work, she'd never been a person who had mixed a lot with other people, but she was quite content and happy in her own home and living in sort of her own little square. But she was tough. She must have been to carry on as she did.

The life of Nar was a subject on which Meg had reflected, but she questioned Gertrude's equation of an ordered life with happiness.

Life was very orderly. You knew that when you came home from school or work what had been done during the day, and you knew because it was something which happened on that day. If I think of what I feel when I look at the sewing machine, I think it's that sense of order. It was not so much happy as belonging. There is an emotional attachment. Smells attached as clean, wholesome and nourishing, and the attachment is part of identity; it's warmth not really happiness. I wonder about Nar. I suppose she was content.

The memories of individual women born around the turn of the century, of their mothers and grandmothers, take us well into the the last century.

In our interviews with women born before or during the first world war, we found a remarkably coherent world, one bound by weekly domestic rituals.

Although our interview group of older women had met each other fairly recently through social activites such as cards and tennis, their pasts were intertwined. The number of shared experiences gave rise to a measure of surprise. The interviewer, herself born, married and retired in the same district, found that her group had similar biographies. The intermeshing of their lives was so fine that they all had associations, as student, teacher, secretary, or P. & C., with one local school. Their reconstruction of their youthful worlds was like that of a stable village community. I began to wonder whether we had done such a poor job of selecting our subjects that we'd missed a major slice of Australian society. When we look at the size and mobility of the population for that time, however, the notion of Australia as made up of village-like communities is not so far-fetched. It was not unusual to live your life within a small radius. Attachment to a locality, knowledge of its geography, its people and problems was part of coming from that place. It was your stamping ground.

On cross-checking with women of a similar age living elsewhere in Australia, there was a similar pattern. Mary Giles, as a young girl, settled in 1914 in Leederville, a Perth suburb, and has been there ever since. Mary, whose household included her five siblings, said: 'Until the thirties there wasn't a house without a granny in our street. Mine died in 1933 at age eighty-three.'

Mary is still in close contact with school friends, and her daughter and grand-daughter live near by: frequent visiting and sharing is possible. The generation born after the second world war is much less likely to have this experience.

The older women recalled their girlhoods in detail most readily and, although the memories were of hard times, the events were far enough away to be safe to talk about, their parts in the events not being open to close scrutiny. The reminiscences did not dwell on alcoholism, although on probing there was plenty of grief. They were clear that their opportunities to work in their later years (whether for interest or necessity) were limited because they had been under-educated or had spent too many years out of the workforce. They were quite explicit about why women stayed in violent marriages or lived at home with parents, but there was also acceptance: 'That's how life was; we made the best of it.' Although the central players in many of these dramas had been dead for years, they would not allow any cruel assessments to be published - dutiful wives and daughters to the end.

It is the daughters of these women, the baby boomers of the late forties, and the new arrivals under Australia's immigration policies who carry on the story; who speak critically of their relationship to their mothers and daughters, of their struggle to order their lives; who reflect upon the image of woman; and who have the possibility of finding a number of answers not available to their mothers or grandmothers.

CHAPTER THREE

WOMEN HAVE ALWAYS WORKED

From my earliest memories, in the early forties, Mum had a series of jars - some families used the teapot - for all the different household expenses: rent, electricity, the insurance man who called at the house, the milkman and the rates. There were endless lists for the greengrocer, butcher, grocer. And somehow or other there were always bits left over for special treats. Dad got an allowance for grog and the S.P. After Mum died, he continued that system of budgeting by lists. We found ones he'd made, just like hers, when we cleaned out the house after he died.

Although women have only recently moved into the paid workforce in large numbers, they have run the house for decades, and they have done so without the need for cheque accounts and overdrafts. Their strategies varied widely but, at the core, was the aim of providing enough for those they cared for. Their skills in managing money ensured that the family was fed, clothed, educated, healthy, happy and housed. Where there was little to get by on, and fresh memories of banks crashing, budgeting was down to earth.

Good managers set standards that were followed by more affluent generations. Home-making skills, modelled on our mothers', persist. Meg Sekavs:

When things were tough, and I was just living with the

boys, I worked out how much money I needed for the whole year, for all my bills, just the way my mother did. I worked out how much I would have to have in the bank out of each pay. So I didn't have jars that I could borrow and pay back; I had an account with the Building Society. But I think I was following the same procedure. That's the way Nar managed her money, too. If you didn't have the amount of money, then you couldn't pay the bill when it came in unless you'd saved for it. If you borrowed from one of those jars, you had to put it back again. You got perhaps two lots to put back out of one week's wages, and that made it harder. It's different now with two incomes.

Doing well with little was the hallmark of a good manager. Lena Kay's parents were farmers; they were not particularly well off, but her mother made sure there was variety for her daughters. Lena, born in 1924, recalls:

When we lived in Balranald, we were self-sufficient in terms of food, and would send to Melbourne for clothes on approval. Mum believed that in a small town like Balranald, where there was only one drapery shop, everyone would have the same thing. She made sure that her daughters would wear different clothes by purchasing clothes in Swan Hill or sending to Melbourne. You would send down an order for so many dresses, and they would send them up, and you would pick out what you wanted, and then Mum would send the cheque down and the rest back; what we didn't like would go back. Oh, that used to be a lovely way of getting dresses. Then our shoes, we used to send to Sydney and get our shoes from there.

---

*It was money that ran the house, that kept us fed,
so that was my mother's role.*

Jane Lloyd's mother had a background in book-keeping and kept a record of where the money went. But the notion that mothers were responsible for seeing the family fed shaped financial arrangements in her parents' household.

> LYDIA
> 1896-1983
> |
> LILLIAN
> 1922-
> |
> JANE LLOYD
> 1958-

Well, in our house, money matters were controlled, worked and operated by my mother. She'd lived at home until her late twenties and used to give her pay packet to her mother. As far as I can remember, my father gave his fortnightly pay packet to Mum. Somehow I just don't think my father wanted to deal with it himself. It was money that ran the house, that kept us fed, so that was my mother's role. She did all the banking; she did all the budgeting; she paid the bills, she used to account for the money. I remember her saying every so often that he would say, 'Where has all the money gone?' I think he queried her, and I think the story goes that in the early days of their marriage she sat down and accounted for every cent that she'd spent and showed him just where it went.

My mother describes him as doing Holmes a'Court takeover tactics.

A generous parent, from the perspective of a child, may have been a spendthrift for the budgeter, and recollections of how our parents organized their financial affairs may be anything but correct. Jane Lloyd's recounting of her family's finances was confirmed, however, by her mother Lillian. It was a regime in which Jane had participated as a child.

I don't remember there being any fights or arguments about money, not that there was much. I think most decisions were made between both of them. When my brother and I became older, we were consulted and brought into this decision-making, too. Probably not so much on financial things but on whether we were going to move, and things like holidays. A couple of times when Mum was in hospital, I was about ten, Dad handed me the pay packet for me to do the shopping.

Now, he's been retired for about a year, and my mother describes him as doing Holmes a'Court takeover tactics. He wants to take charge of everything. He goes for the shopping errands and buys all these flash cheeses and has a sort of mental block at the cash register as he realizes how much it all costs, little things like that. He's lost his work domain, and he's no longer in charge of any staff. He's no longer the boss of the workshop. So he's trying to create another area for himself. My mother is resisting.

When a daughter becomes independent, it may be difficult for parents to reconcile her choices with their experience.

Now I get contradictory messages regarding how they see me running my house. They support me in being independent and owning a house myself but suggest indirectly that my boyfriend might buy into the house. These messages do not come directly from them. It seems to me they are trying to reconcile the ideas and beliefs of their times and generation with new attitudes that have developed in their lifetime. I think my father still sees the man as being the provider.

> *Although it wasn't much, Mum knew how much*
> *he got and, if the packet was open,*
> *there was hell to pay.*

Attitudes to money and ways of handling it are remarkably conservative. Penny Peel was reared by her great-grandmother. In their household, her father handed over his pay packet. It is a tradition that reaches back over a century.

It was all right for the wives who grew up in that sort of household, but a bit hard on the others who did not know how to manage. My husband was away a lot in the services. And he was quite content to let me run the house. Now he's at home, he's interested to see how I manage, but he doesn't want to take it over.

The unopened pay packet was one way of ensuring that housekeeping money was available. *Mum took his pay packet and, if it was open, there was hell to pay. He had to hand it over to her. We would have starved otherwise. It would have all gone on booze with his mates and with the bookies. There were always fights over money. When he was out of work, it was awful. Mum did cleaning and stuff to keep us afloat. It was only when we were at school that Mum went back to work. Then, she didn't have to rely on him.*

If a husband worked irregularly, women still had to manage. *When he worked, Mum would only get ten pounds for the shopping, and that had to do her. If there were any bills to pay, ten pounds, that's all she had. Oh, he'd think about himself; he'd buy two shillings worth of lollies. That was a lot of lollies, really.*

> *My father, fairly typical of his time, wanted*
> *his daughters dependent on him.*

Staying at home to help mother and relying on father until you married was not always accepted passively.

When I left school in 1936, my father, fairly typical of his time, wanted his daughters dependent on him. He was quite comfortably off. He took the attitude, if you want a job, get it. I did, but I had to give it up because my mother developed rheumatoid arthritis. So I was needed at home. I look back now, and I'm full of admiration for the girls who got their matriculation.

In one-income families, where money was scarce, it was a matter of pride for the wage earner to be seen to be a good provider, and a wife who was a good manager helped to make this possible. Although there was little to play with, she at least knew the limits and could get some satisfaction from knowing that the bills were paid. In families in more comfortable circumstances, mothers were often cared for but uninformed about money.

Mum had never signed a cheque until after Dad died. Money was not scarce, Mum just had no idea of the financial affairs; her allowance appeared magically each month. She made decisions about how money was spent, all right. But, because Dad was the breadwinner, it was his pride at stake. He handled the cheque book. It was his name on the piece of paper which the outsider saw.

Over the last decade, the widespread use of credit cards has revolutionized the paying of bills. Arrangements are as diverse as plastic money permits. Women's incomes, however, remain central. Their jobs are often more vulnerable, part time, and they earn less than men. Women's ability to be joint partners is limited. If housekeeping bills are paid from a wife's wage, more choices are open to her: the possibility of splurging, indulging in luxury foods, saving for something special. But if she lost pay, was put off, or had to leave, she was back depending on housekeeping from the male wage, an allowance often begrudgingly allocated until she went back to work.

The need to be well organized, to make ends meet, is clearly attested. For many women, there was little opportunity to cheat on the housekeeping or to salt it away. The only way of making that little bit extra was through labour that was independent of the 'breadwinner'. Keeping fowls was seen as 'inside work'. It was part of the domain that included the kitchen, wash-house, vegie garden and the run for the hens. The egg money was women's money.

If married women took on paid work, it was often for a specific goal: the second mortgage, a holiday, some stylish furniture, even a front fence.

I had a very narrow upbringing, and I'd never been away from my mother until I was married, and I was twenty-six then. Eight months after we were married, we had to move to Canberra, and I said goodbye to my mother and burst into tears. I thought that the most dreadful thing was happening. I went straight into a job and was there six years before I became pregnant with the first one. We just saved money. I didn't think of it as a career, just getting together the necessary money.

She nearly died when Dad retired because he was in her hair all the time.

As long as dinner was on the table at 5.30 when Dad walked in the door, he didn't really care what Mum had been doing. She nearly died when Dad *retired because he was in her hair all the time. She couldn't go anywhere without him, and she hated it. It took her a long time to adjust. She had to adjust, he didn't. If she wanted to go shopping, he'd follow her, everywhere. He'd talk to her about what she was choosing and tell her it was wrong. She'd had all these years while he was working where she could at least be herself for six or seven hours.*

Much part-time work was set up so that it wouldn't interfere with the children's schooling or the preparation of the evening meal. Although such work rarely provided the basis for a career, it did allow women to make choices.

As we got older, my mother got employment, and she always kept a separate bank account. She kept that money to one side. Occasionally, he'd get a bit sort of funny about it, and she often used that for specific purposes for us - not things he wouldn't have agreed to - but she didn't have to explain or reason with him this way. She invested in my career, and that was her pleasure.

The aspirations of mothers, aunts and grandmothers for the females in the family were more important than the actual achievements of mothers or fathers. Mothers used their skills to eke out housekeeping money to help fulfil these ambitions. As one daughter said: 'What Mum gave me was a sense I had to be trained for something and not rely on marriage.'

When the mother was the manager, as she was in many working-class families, there was not much money to go around. But she would try to use it to allow for a decent holiday, for seeing the carpet down that year, or for allowing the children to finish school.

I look back now, and she went without food to give us an education. We didn't aspire to anything like piano lessons. Mum went out to work a lot because Dad refused to work. He was violent, particularly with her, and she took the easy way out all the time to stop him belting us. He's been dead fifteen years now, and I've stopped dreaming of getting him back, but I still want to vent my anger.

In her family, there were three boys and three girls, and the girls were supposed to stay at home. Her mother owned a guest-house. Mum had four kids under five and was also doing the housework for other people. She was a fantastic manager but, if I wanted to stay on at school, I needed some assistance. I just drifted into teaching. It was a respectable thing to do and a fantastic scheme as far as my parents were concerned. It was a pittance, but it covered my travel and books. It was when

I set up an art room, I was twenty-five, and I was finally approaching something I liked. Now my daughter, she's at an all girls' school. I know she'll make mistakes, but she'll know she's made them and learn quicker.

She wanted to be a teacher: someone got her a job as a stocking mender.

Many women who lived through the depression were determined that their daughters would have more options than they had had, and they considered education to be crucial.

Mum was born in 1906, one of nine surviving children. She was the third youngest, so her Mum goes back a long way. She died when Mum was seven, and her life was sort of lopped off. She went to live with her father's aunt. She went from the wild, free, uncontrolled life of Aberfeldy, a place in the hills outside Walhalla, to this great-aunt who kept a shop in a country town and was very popular. It had its effect in that Mum really valued her independence.

DIANA
d:1914
|
'PEG'
1906-1981
|
BRON STEVENS
1946-

When her aunt died, she was twenty-one and not trained for anything. She'd wanted to be a teacher. Someone got her a job as a stocking mender. It was a bit of a blessing; it paid well and kept on during the depression. She married late, at thirty-one, and kept on working, on a piece-work basis, horrible, close work. She did it on the back verandah. Then, when I was eight, she developed Parkinson's disease, and that was the kiss of death for work.

The depression, whether viewed from the perspective of a daughter or mother, a worker or the unemployed, a dependant or breadwinner, had been survived. World War II had interrupted education, separated loved ones and left young mothers alone to rear children. But for what sort of a future? It had put women into the paid workforce where, assured they were empire builders, they worked until the boys came home, and life was supposed to return to normal. For some that was widowhood, for others a return to domestic labour. Some continued to work.

In factories, at lower wages than men, their nimble fingers did process and piece-work. Women, until the late sixties, had to resign their position in the public service, so they stayed single or worked elsewhere. In the professions, women undertook nurturing tasks as teachers and nurses - rarely as doctors or professors.

Mum was a primary schoolteacher, and she taught for five years to pay off the first mortgage. Then she resigned to start a family. The year she resigned, she was due for her teaching mark, and it meant foregoing promotion. She came back in at the bottom of the scale.

If your husband left you, you didn't get anything. That's why everyone put up with what they had.

Leaving a husband was a hard choice. Families did not always welcome a defiant daughter and instead gave advice on how to manage in marriage.

You had to depend on your husband. There was no child endowment then. If he didn't provide it, you missed out. I got a husband just like my father, and I went along with it. I lived on my own. I reared those kids. He was only there a couple of nights. I had a friend, and her mother went to work, and they kept it quiet because it was not the done thing. The war years, that was the start of women going to work, but I was rearing my children. If your husband left you, you didn't get anything. You had to take him to court. That's why everyone put up with what they had. Once you had kids, you were stuck. You'd made your bed, and you could lie in it. Dad used to say, 'Never let a man hit you. Take the poker to him. Take it once, and you've lost!' And I used to say to my husband, 'If you ever hit me or those kids, I'll hang for you.'

The contrast between how men and women managed when widowed was stark. Men, when left with a motherless family, kept the eldest daughter at home, employed a housekeeper, or re-married. Widows, on the other hand, were forced to return to live with their family, farm their kids out or, more recently, subsist on welfare programmes and social security payments.

After mother died, we had a series of housekeepers. He used to growl about the money and say I was spending it wrong. You couldn't spend it wrong, there wasn't that much to spend! And I remember saying one night to my father, 'If you're not satisfied,' you see I was young, but I said, 'You think I'm not spending the money right, you do it.' So the next time he gave me the money, which was every week, I said to him, 'If you think I'm spending wrongly, you go for the groceries.' He changed his mind.

Working a double day left many women exhausted. Their labour was poorly rewarded in the workplace, and at home it was just part of being mother. A number of daughters were critical of their mothers for doing all the work at home when they also went out to work.

My mother would leave the house about seven o'clock and come at five. She basically killed herself. We were what sociologists call 'latch-key kids'. We virtually lived independent of my parents. She was working in factories, then she'd cook and do all domestic stuff every day when she got home. On the weekend, she would wash tons of clothes by hand. She refused a machine, how about that? She still does everything, by hand, because that's the way they would do it in Greece. She refused to listen. Dad bought her a machine, and we told her how to operate it, but she hated it.

Martha Ricardo recognized the force of tradition in her mother's attitudes to work. Martha, born in Turin, Italy, in 1939, was told by her mother: 'You have got to be a really good girl. You've got to do the right thing at the right time and be capable of doing all the housework.'

My mother had to shop, to knit, to embroider, to go out and nobody would say a word behind her because they knew that she was a good woman. She had to be able to do all those things because no one else would do it for her. She had no money. Mum had to go out to work because, during the retreat of the Germans, the soldiers set fire to the place as a reprisal. Our house was lost, and we lost everything. I was told this; I only remember the flames. To me they were fun, you know. I can remember being carried to a little street with houses on both sides. Walking and a line of soldiers in green walking this way, and they were going to set fire to the houses.

My father died when he was thirty-four, and she was only in her thirties. She could have re-married because she was a widow, but she didn't. So she brought up three children on her own. It wasn't fair on her really, but Mum had to work. She was working in a factory, and the three of us had to contribute something, like lighting the fire and learning to cook. We lived in a house with different apartments, and this lady, we called her Nana, she was really old then, she looked after us. So when my mother went to work, and we were going to school, we came back to her.

She thought it was wrong for a woman to go out at night by herself.

Martha found that the expectations of what was proper for a wife, which had constrained her mother's life in Italy, were also present in Australia. *When we got here we were living in someone else's house, and my privacy wasn't there anymore. We had to share the kitchen and the bathroom. The woman was a widow, and she was from the south of Italy. And she had no idea about the freedom that women from the north are allowed. She thought it was wrong for a woman to go out at night by herself. She called me dreadful names. She thought a woman should stay at home. We're talking about 1969. So, in her eyes, I became a bad person. Mind you, I was trying to integrate, and*

I loved the idea of learning English. If you wanted education, you had to be prepared to go out in the night to get it. No one was going to keep me down, if I wanted to do it.

The patterns are hard to break. Under stress we speak to our children in the voice our mother used; we turn to the same strategies to ensure the smooth running of the house. Like her mother, Mary Anne Jebb works and organizes a house.

Well, Mother was running two jobs. She did the dishes because she wanted us to be professionals as well, and she didn't want us to have that burden. I remember now, looking back and thinking, She came home from work, cooked the dinner, did the dishes, so that we were set down to our studies. So the girls were not expected to help in the house. Mum took on the whole operation. And with my daughter, she's a bit young yet, but yes, I think I'd probably do everything and let them get on with their own lives. I think I'm setting the same pattern. It's quicker, you know, it's more efficient if I do it on my own. They really should do something. Although, I must say, she is far more receptive to housework and into household organization entirely. So that now and again you notice that she's picked something up, and her brother wouldn't have a clue.

Even though there hasn't been a conscious decision of mine to teach her that, like how you put a pillow into a pillowcase - I think that might be a classic - I remember my mother telling me how to put the pillow in a pillowcase. So, even though she wasn't there all the time, there were quite a lot of lessons in housework that I remember as a little girl. I couldn't date it.

We always had housekeepers, and Mum often said to me, whenever she got money, she got a baby-sitter or a housekeeper. Bridge-playing took up a lot of both of my parents' time, but the housekeeper stopped at five, and she came on every night, on the night shift. We both have the tendency to balance the book we're reading in the kitchen so we can read and cook.

> AILSA
> 1927-
> |
> MARY ANNE JEBB
> 1955-
> |
> SARAH
> 1977-

He said that if he wanted to hire a housekeeper, he was sure it would be much cheaper than marrying me.

In Bron Stevens's home, her mother did the work but for very different reasons.

Mum's life had been very hard so she went to the other extreme and totally spoilt her children. When my brother and I ended up in the same house together, having left home at the same time, we couldn't cook and clean. My father would help

Madge Cope, Guildford, Western Australia

Annie Gastin and her daughter, Lily Coates, wearing a dress made for her by Annie's grandmother

Thelma Bock with her daughters Helen Bock and Christine Hemmerling, Glenelg, South Australia

GENERATIONS

Rae Bastin (front) with her daughters Connie Larsen and Penny Peel and her grand-daughters Catherine Peel and Norelle Peel, Eden's Landing, Queensland

with the dishes, but the children weren't expected to. My parents wanted their children to get on with their homework so that they could get on with their education and their lives. Mum didn't like to be looked after. She preferred to look after other people. I like being looked after, and I'm perfectly capable of sitting back and letting other people do things for me. There were always newspapers lying around the house, and Mum had better things to do with her time than pick them up. I think this trait has been passed on to me. I'm grateful that I never feel the urge to get up and clean the house.

My husband had quite a different experience. His mother was a nurse and had two boys and then two girls after a four-year gap. He was quite used to having to wash and clean, and he's much more inclined to clean up than I am. When he proposed to me, I said I had no intention of getting married and being a housewife and washing someone else's dirty socks. He said that if he wanted to hire a housekeeper he was sure it would be much cheaper than marrying me. If Mum hadn't said things like that I would never have thought about it. I was married relatively young, at twenty-two. If I hadn't have said that, we might have gone through the same sorts of traumas and hassles that other friends did.

Annie Gastin, now living in Alice Springs, was quite clear about the conditions under which she began to organize the chores.

Before we had Lily, I wouldn't have bothered doing the dishes before I went to work. We would leave them for several days, come rocking home from work and go out to dinner. No one was spending a lot of time at home. Then you have a kid, and you have to keep up with it. There's this real rut, a domestic internal clock. If you let go, you've had it. You become an efficient organizer.

In Nancy Reis's unusual household, she had responsibilities from an early age. *I was about six or seven, and I had to set the table, and my brothers would fight with me, and we'd race around the table, and then my father would say, 'You kids...' It was the busiest time of the day for my parents because they were running a hotel. I had to cook while they tended to customers and guests. I cooked Huttons frankfurters. I didn't regret that responsibility.*

NANCY REIS
1918-
|
MICHELE
1946-
|
ANNA
1977

I reared those kids in a house on my own... I never expected anyone to do anything for me.

Mabel Mackay had run the house when her mother was ill and had left an apprenticeship with a tailor to care for her father and brothers. It was a tale told by other women of her age, and the pattern of women caring for males persisted into the next generation. Katie Wilkes:

Really, I was allowed to do anything in that house. That house was mine. I would come home to that house, open the door, and then there'd be tea ready for Dad, and I was allowed to cook what I liked. My brother used to help me doing the washing. But I can't remember him doing much else. We had to weed the garden and those sorts of things.

Then my husband, he never wanted a house. He would never let me make it a home, really. I reared those kids in a house on my own. I did everything. They'd come in from school, and I did everything on my own in that house, just like for Dad. I didn't have a mother coming to me and giving me cups of tea. My father didn't come and give me a cup of tea; my husband didn't come to give me a cup of tea. I never expected anyone to do anything for me. The lady across the road said that I ran a restaurant. My daughter would come home from university. She'd walk across, and I'd have dinner at half past four for her, and then she'd go back to her lectures. Then my son would come in at half past five, and I'd have his little bit of stuff if he was going to night class. Then I'd have dinner for the old man at six when he came in.

Not all children were exposed to serious responsibilities. *I had a ridiculously over-privileged childhood in many ways. It seemed quite normal at the time. We were never told to pick up our own clothes or toys. We weren't taught anything about housework. We weren't even allowed into the kitchen. In some ways we had less attention than children today. My parents went out a great deal and, like many of my contemporaries, we spent a lot of time with the servants. Although we had a car, we walked or took trams to school and anywhere else we wanted to go. Nowadays, parents seem to spend half their time driving their children about, especially the mother who has to manage the children. But in our time, we were expected to make our own fun and, if we ever complained of boredom, we were told it was foolish to be bored. Why, there was a household of books to choose from. We were encouraged to read, and we've all remained great readers. Mum went to boarding school during the depression and complained about the horrid conditions.*

Lena Kay remembers that her mother not only had the family to manage but also the workers for whom she cooked. *My eldest son was fourteen when his father died. I continued to do everything for him. Cooked his dinner, ironed his clothes, all through high school and even when he went to university.*

Mum made us clean the doorknobs and silver every week. It had to be done. Everything that was silver had to be polished so that you could see your face in it. Even out on the farm, if we weren't having visitors, it still had to be done. I suppose that's where I get my feeling that I want things to be perfect. When my mother and father got married and had just shifted into the house, her father came to visit. And he said, 'Well, everything is very nice, Gladys, but you want to polish the doorknobs better. They're not shiny.' She said he was really serious.

And when I was working, before the children came, my husband would even polish the tops of the tables because he knew if I came home and found it was not polished... and he had flowers on the dressing table. And I used to have a bath mat. It was lemon with two feet, and I wouldn't have him stand on the yellow part. He had to put his feet where the black bits were.

You had your housework to do, so there was no sitting amid all the mess.

So much hard work, double days, a feeling that inactivity was a luxury that could not be indulged.

If I'm not busy, I feel guilty. I suppose I get that from Nar. It's not a habit that we've picked up from our fathers. Dadda was always busy. But that strong feeling of black and white and right and wrong, and it was wrong to be sitting, and that you should be busy, that there were certain things that were right for the day and others for the night, if you didn't swap them around. So that you could sit and do fancy work in the evenings or in the afternoons, but if I sit for too long, and not so much now perhaps, but it's still there. You had your housework to do, so there was no sitting amid all the mess.

'Nar'
1887-
|
Gertrude
1910-
|
'Meg' Sekavs
1934-

Remember Mum, you'd say to us two girls, 'It's bedroom day today; get that rubbish out of the way. If anything is left lying around, it will go up the vacuum cleaner.' All we used to do was scoop up all this rubbish and put it on our beds and then get it back to the floor. That's what you used to do, and I think Lesley used to throw all hers in the wardrobe, including the sandwiches from lunch, orange peels and apple cores, and then you'd read the riot act - Get that wardrobe cleaned out. So, now it's a case of clean-up because Jan, my cleaning lady, is coming, and she must be obeyed.

Gertrude: I am glad somebody has got you bluffed. I never could.

Meg: I think most people are bluffed by their cleaning lady. And it's funny that Nar in a sense started out as a cleaning lady.

But we've worked so hard and maybe did a job that other people said they wouldn't do.

It was not only new foods that two immigrants brought in the last forty years, but also different experiences of growing up female. Martha

Ricardo's widowed mother had few choices. In coming to Australia, Martha sought a new life, but the hard work continued, and she faced problems finding accommodation, learning the language and coping with prejudice.

When I came out to Australia, I cried my eyes out when I left my city. I cried because I left my mother, I left my sister and my brother. I was married by then, and we'd seen an advertisement in the Sunday paper. I said, 'Hey, this is a good idea.' It invited people with certain trades and qualifications to come. John was working, and we had to pay the rent. I thought, Well, if we don't do it, we'll never see anything. We'll never have the money to go anywhere. We are so stupid living like grubs in the same hole all the time. So, we started writing to places, to the Australian Embassy. We wrote to somebody in Melbourne, and he wrote back. We were really impressed. The Embassy sent us pamphlets, photos and things telling us more or less how it is. Immigration interviewed us to make sure we had no criminal record, or anything. This was in 1968. And I had a little boy. So we came by boat, and we had a holiday. It was lovely. I love languages, and I said I'd learn English if nothing else. We only had to stay two years.

When someone comes here from another country, there are some Australian people who say, 'Look at them, they're new Australians.' I've heard it many times. They'll want to know how we can afford things. But we've worked so hard and maybe did a job that other people said they wouldn't do. To me, money is important. But when I get to the point of having enough, I have a choice, and then money will not be so important. I know that once you've got that choice it's no longer important. If I want to go to night school, lovely, I've got the choice. If I wanted to leave work tomorrow, John would say, 'Well, leave.' He wouldn't stop me. Well, I don't feel it's fair, because that's why I work all the time. I couldn't just dump on him that I'm your wife and here's your family, so provide. I can't dump that on him. Responsibility and reliability, that was pounded into me, that's what makes a good family background when you're little. Of course, some softness would have done me a lot of good, but it wasn't to be.

There's always a good meal on the table for them, but I've begun to put work first.

For other women, the need to separate home from work was critical. To succeed in the workplace, they could not afford to be seen as wives, mothers or housekeepers. To survive, they had to keep their homes running smoothly. Staying sane was quite a feat. Going out to work offered an outlet, a sense of worth and, in time, the chores came into perspective.

I can't imagine anything worse than not working. I'm very determined about getting work finished, but I'd say my pride in my housework has slowly diminished. There's always a good meal on the table for them, but I've begun to put work first. I don't see it just as something to supplement the family income any more. I see it as my career.

The experience of paid work and housework is difficult to separate, for many women; one flows into the other. The routine of Joyce Caddie is a familiar one for many farming daughters.

We had to milk the cows, fifty of them, before we went to school. There were nine of us children. One day, an inspector was visiting the school and demanded to know why we were late. We didn't know, because we were always late. We were sent outside to sit on the verandah until we thought of a reason. My brother and I decided to tell him our mother was sick. He accepted that.

The life histories of older women in town and country show that women have always worked, but often their labour and contribution to the economy were invisible: they were 'in service', day domestics, sewing at home, maintaining the family, working for the farm. Their jobs were essential to the survival of families, but they were not valued beyond the home, and brought little or no financial recognition.

We moved out of the migrant hostel when we were offered a small house on a few acres in return for work on the property of the farmer. My husband continued to work as a butcher, and I worked on the farm. It was not possible for him to stop work at the migrant centre and work for these people. He was a butcher by trade, and that's what he would do. He won't just do anything - he's got pride. Some people might, but not my husband. We're not beggars. We wanted to work. Sure, we had nothing, but no fault of our own.

She ran the house and worked outside, but her labour was unpaid. In her view, there were important advantages to living in the country.

It was very peaceful on the farm. I can walk through the paddocks and it's so nice and quiet. I can do exactly what I think is best and easiest. There are no neighbours to criticize or interfere. This country is a blessed country. If you work very hard, you can lead a way of life that is good. I love it here on the farm. I wouldn't change places with anyone.

Not all women living in the country agreed that such freedoms were compensation for the isolation. For new arrivals, the move to the country was a rupture with family, a relocation within a community dominated by the husband's family, a limiting of opportunity to pursue a career. A number of trained nurses and teachers had spent decades raising children and running farms. But managing the farm restricted the social ambit. Some women resented their husbands' engagement in co-operative work, which gave them access to networks and friendships denied to the women at home.

Australians and migrants kept very separate in those days. There were no other Yugoslavs in the area and, basically, we had no friends. Even now, thirty-eight years after our arrival, we have no friends for socializing; only friends if we need someone. My husband was able to get to know local farmers and business men, and they came to trust him. I went to town to shop and then came home. I was invited to join the C.W.A. but didn't. I didn't want to waste time sitting around having cups of tea and cake when there was so much work to be done. I was separated and isolated because I was not Australian, I had no leisure time, and I had a child to raise.

For a number of women living on the land, finding time to be interviewed was a problem. One was conducted in the hour between cleaning up after the midday meal and preparing the afternoon tea for the shearers. Another was half an hour late for her session after moving the sheep from one paddock to another took longer than expected.

I had to fend for myself while my brothers were set up with properties.

Farming women claiming proudly that no area of work was denied to them, that they were able to participate in outside work, found that by helping their husbands, there was more time that could be spent as a family. Their labour was a contribution to building the property for their children.

I have no desire to work. I'm happy at home, and nursing was purely for financial reasons. I wouldn't care if I didn't go off the place for a year. Farm work is hard but mostly enjoyable. I know not everyone is adaptable to the rural life. A number of women resented that their contribution to family prosperity had a different set of rewards.

It occurred to me at some stage I'd worked equally hard as my brother, was the eldest, but I had to fend for myself while my brothers were set up with properties.

The daughters of the gentry did not always remain captive. *Dad took over management of the property and his eight sisters, my aunts. He was the sixth child of eleven, but he was the oldest son. Five of his sisters went into successful careers: one as an actress, another as a singer and two in the dressmaking business. That was not unusual in the twenties or thirties. The only surviving sister, the youngest, was a champion bottler, won all the prizes at the Sydney Royal Easter Show, and until recently was a judge.*

They all had bonnets and veils and wouldn't go outside in case they got sunburnt.

On established properties, social life, appearances and the institution of afternoon tea were important.

My three older sisters were married before I left school so I helped outside. We all did. My mother wouldn't have done that, and my grandmother certainly wouldn't have done that. They all had bonnets and veils and wouldn't go outside in case they got sunburnt. They were working, but they weren't doing outside jobs.

I really prefer life at that slower pace and enjoy bird-watching, botany, not racing around town. I don't get exhausted, but I am always busy. I know how to pace myself. I am out in the bush doing things younger women say they want to do all the time, but they're too busy. My father was born in 1890 and, for that generation, women were not important people. I feel that, whereas my daughters don't. We were more domestics. I was brought up to make things run smoothly for men. That's what my mother, grandmother and great-grandmother did. We made everything. We were self-sufficient.

Women from farming families compared their lives to graziers, who were assumed to have amassed wealth over a number of generations or to have brought wealth to their properties.

I'm excluded from many things because I'm single... people make too much of the family.

To live an independent single life locked a woman out of some social activities. Breaking the order had serious effects.

There are more opportunities for country girls now. Mum's generation just got on with living, making a home, just being there. I had to board at a school 1,000 miles away and did my tertiary education as an adult. Now I work as an occupational therapist. I don't think the nature of the profession is well understood by medicos. 'You might be able to teach them to crochet,' is the attitude I get. I find going home quite 'hard work'. I have to take the lead all the time. I don't have much in common with many of the women here. Some I quite like, and some are bird-brains. I'm excluded from many things because I'm single, and everything is for pairs - dances, parties. I get quite crabby when I find I'm not invited to dinner because I don't have a partner. People make too much of 'the family'.

My place is with my husband to make home.

Yes, women have suffered discrimination. They have had to seek security in marriage, to accept less than men in return for hard work. Some have tried to provide different choices for their daughters; some have clung to the traditions of their mothers; others have adapted old ways to new demands. From a position of privilege, some women argued that it was family that was important, and that their role as homemaker was their career. Reared in families where father provided and mother was cared for, the thought of pursuing an independent life was threatening. One whose husband's career requires spending time in overseas postings recognized the tensions this created but did not seek changes.

The moves have been hard on the children, and there have been difficult decisions to make about whether to leave them in school or take them with us to another country when my husband was posted. I know some of the younger wives work, but they are making a rod for their back. My place is with my husband to make home.

This position was not one the daughter, now in her thirties, wished to endorse. *I was given every opportunity, but it was to be a certain sort of person, like, 'Learn science so you can talk to your father's guests.' My mother and her friends are all cultured, well travelled, but not particularly well educated, and they've led sheltered lives. In some ways, they see my desire to pursue a career and not see marriage as my future as a rejection of their care. It's not that at all: a good education has made it possible for me to be independent. I suppose, though, I do shield them from some of the things I do, especially my politics.*

I might as well have the game as the name.

Madge Cope, born in 1904, looking back on a century of decisions over work, marriage and home, said:

Women are not as romantic over marriage as they used to be. I went into it thinking you gave up everything for love and didn't expect any concessions; you sacrificed everything for love. You felt tied for life.

So we're better off now because they can work and have equal pay. But the categories are manipulated, and that's where I see capitalism and politics tying up. I asked Katharine Susannah Prichard if she thought I should join the Communist Party. At the time, it was illegal. She said she would never push anyone to join. I told her my husband didn't want me to join. She said I'd have to choose according to my principles. I said I couldn't give up my principles so I joined the party. I thought, If it's good enough for her... That was the first time I joined. I left after twelve months because my husband made such a fuss about me neglecting him. I stayed at home, and we argued just as much so I rejoined. I said, 'I might as well have the game as the name.'

The women we interviewed had worked to support themselves, to supplement family income, for an outside interest, to establish careers, to maintain homes and families. In most families, there was a component of unpaid, selfless labour. They had been advised 'to be trained for something and not rely on marriage' and to 'learn science so you can talk to your father's guests'.

Women have always worked, but the nature and purpose of the work is changing. Some look back to their female forebears and see continuity between the generations; others a disjointed pattern. One daughter recognizes the strength of the women in her line, another rejects all that tradition; others weigh the lives of previous generations and find curious parallels with their own.

CHAPTER FOUR

TALES OF TREADLES

Do you know why Mum gave me that machine? It was because if you ever go bankrupt the two things that they cannot take are your bed and your sewing machine. That's what she said. There are only two things that they can't take from you: one's your bed and the other's the sewing machine. It was because you need your bed to sleep on and you can earn your living on the machine. I gave you a machine when you were married, but I didn't really think about the why of it until you asked.

Neither Patricia Richards nor her daughter had thought about the conditions under which they had received machines from their mothers. But this conversation reminded Michaela of research she had done on charitable organizations of the last century.

ELVA
1905-1964
|
PATRICIA
1930-
|
MICHAELA RICHARDS
1961-

They used to give out sewing machines in the old days as one way to give relief. The Queen's Jubilee Fund was one of several organizations which assisted the 'able' and 'genteel' poor, the widows, single women, deserted wives, wives of incapacitated husbands. It was not for women with relatives who could support them or those who should end their days in an asylum on charity.

Giving me a sewing machine... saved them a fortune.

In 1908 the fund arranged for fifty-three sewing machines, thirty mangles, and one cooking stove to be distributed. In this way, women were encouraged to earn their own living and keep their homes; they were given the means to achieve independence, and the means were protected at law. Since the mid-nineteenth century, a man's tools of trade could not be taken to pay a rent debt. Then, in 1898, the law was extended to include the mangle, typewriter and sewing machine. It seems that families have continued this practice. Daughters are still given machines in the hope that they will begin to support themselves.

When I left school, she gave me a graduation present of a sewing machine and a week's course with Singer. That was very sensible because it saved them a fortune during university when I was able to live on my allowance. It was an electric with a foot pedal bought brand new in December 1963, January 1964.

When Mimi Taylor bought her machine in 1919, it cost sixteen pounds. It was a treadle with a long bobbin, the model that required special skill to thread. It did not come with lessons. Mimi taught herself to sew. Her youngest daughter, Margaret, has her eye on this machine which, with the addition of a motor, has continued to turn out the essentials and little treats for the family. When her older daughters, Ruby and Doris, were teenagers in the 1930s, they would go to town on Saturday morning, buy a piece of material at three pence a yard and ask Mimi to make it up for them for that evening.

Mimi: *I taught myself to sew and was a pretty good sewer at school. We made samplers, and they were only destroyed when we moved from Rockhampton to Brisbane. They'd take mine out to show to the class. I had a button sewn on one and an eyelet and hemming. I could do all that but to start to make a frock… one of my mates said, 'Would you make me a dress?' I had my new machine, I said, 'Yes,' and I was all right till I came to putting in the sleeve, and then I can remember calling Flo, my mate, and I said, 'Hey, Flo, come on in a minute,' and I had to get her to show me how to set a sleeve in, but from then on - you improve with time - I made wedding dresses, Margaret's wedding dress also.*

My grandmother would have sympathized. Throughout the depression she sewed to support herself and her two daughters. Her work was fine, imaginative and meticulous. She'd chalk, pin, tack, gather and ease but would declare, 'There's no such thing as the perfect sleeve.' It was not an excuse, it was exasperation.

The machine was a sacred object in the home.

Penny Peel's mother, born in Queensland in 1929, had one of the early Singer treadles.

She had been given it when she was young. She sewed anything from silk to denim on it. On her birthday, when I was eleven, my father gave her an electric one. She used it once and said it was useless and went back to the treadle. She said she had no control over the electric machine. She would say, 'You can't hem a handkerchief on it.'

The machine was a sacred object in the home, and even the repair man worked under supervision. It gave her financial independence. She could earn with it, and it was her money. When I was pregnant with Aaron, and discovered how expensive clothes were for babies, I started to learn to make clothes. She said, 'When I go, it's yours.' It went to her daughter when she lived there, and it's still there in my Aunt's hall, with an embroidered cloth. I couldn't take it from Phil now, and I couldn't move it while I was in the army. When she goes, I'll take it on unless she gives it to me before.

Ah, Singer sewing machines, the old treadles. Everyone seems to have had one. They have very predictable histories, which can be read like the fly-leaves in family bibles. As women's property, rarely out of sight, frequently locked, they pass from one woman to another. They trace ties of blood and affection, they mark out significant relationships between women. Although the treadle may have been bought first of all by a husband or father, its care was a woman's responsibility; it was under her control, and any money earned, like the egg money, was hers. No need to give account.

Women were quite able to service their machines. The instruction manuals gave clear explanations on the way it worked and how to keep it in working order. My 1915 manual explains: 'To ensure easy and quiet working of the machine it is necessary that all moving parts in contact with each other be covered with a film of oil, and not allowed to become dry.' It was simple. You just followed the chart; nothing mysterious. The list of possible malfunctions, and remedies, was comprehensive. Women like my grandmother never had to call a serviceman, although she would have denied that she was mechanical. In tracing and piecing together stories about the old treadle, I have come to think of it as a shrine, at which generations of Australian women have worshipped, a centrepiece in women's lives.

At home it was used to sew simple things: flannel and drill shirts, children's clothes, smocked dresses with matching bloomers, rompers, pyjamas; it mended, patched work-clothes, turned collars; it reclaimed and transformed, making dressing gowns from unpicked and turned coats, slippers from old felt hats, quilts from scraps; it furnished, with curtains, cushions and pillowcases. Comfortable with canvas or muslin, set to the task of turning sheets or fashioning a wedding dress, sewing work-clothes and Sunday best. Hand models gave way to treadles which, with the addition of a motor, entered the age of the computer and fared badly. There were numerous variations possible once the old treadle was superseded. An electric motor could be added - it only took one screw - and in the words of the manual: 'That little Singerlight, by showing the stitching more clearly, prevents eyestrain and saves time and annoyance when threading the needle. Any Singer shop or Singer salesman will tell you all about them.' Some had a foot pedal and some a handle coming out from the base of the machine, which was operated by applying pressure with your knee.

Despite the advent of computerized machines and the availability of cheap, off-the-rack clothes, disposable garments and polyester white goods, the Singer treadle endures. It takes up its position in the hall or family room, as an occasional table or bench where it is adorned with a pot plant, basket or lamp, the wrought-iron blackened and the wood polished. Some stored in the garage, but always carefully protected, await restoration of the bubbled wood. Those that became encumbrances and went to the tip are mourned, and younger generations scour Op-shops for a treadle to replace the lost one.

Sewing machines found their way into homes across Australia but fulfilled very different needs. Mary Anne now has her grandmother's machine.

Ginger was always first with everything. She had the first electric refrigerator in Perth, and I thought someone had come along and sold her this wonderful sewing machine, but Mum says it belonged to Ginger's mother, Bessie, who had been the matron of the Royal Adelaide Hospital. I don't think Ginger ever used the machine. When Ginger died, I was travelling, and her things were handed out when I was away.

'GINGER'
1891-1969
|
MALCOLM = AILSA 1927-
|
MARY ANNE JEBB
1955-

On Sunday visits, grandchildren waited for a turn - even the boys. There was a trick to the foot-hand co-ordination and, until the rhythm was right, the thread snapped with each backward lurch. The tension was disrupted, or we found our fingers were webbed or nailed to the fabric. So, with the head down or strap disconnected, we practised. Sometimes, with a helper turning the wheel, we'd concentrate on guiding the material through. When at last our feet reached the pedals, we left behind those jerky stitches. Smooth, even stitching was a matter of pride, a real accomplishment. These were the initiation rites.

Often we learned from our grandmothers, or aunts, the older generation who had more patience, who could wait till we conquered the moves, and who would delight in our mistakes and revel in our successes. These were the women who had time to supervise our sewing. It was in their homes that we spent holidays and the odd weekend. Sometimes we learned from our mothers and friends. Skills were refined at school in a quiet afternoon with the needle and thread, in domestic science colleges, such as Emily MacPherson, or working as apprentices and out-workers for back-breaking hours.

If you didn't have a machine when you married, you soon acquired one with the arrival of the first child, whether the machine was mother's, grandmother's or a new one. The hand-me-down was cherished. The tradition of not leaving home and setting up house independently without a machine persisted into the 1950s. When the World War II babies reached an age where they might have begun to sew their own clothes, they bought their clothes off the rack. Home-made clothes no longer competed with bought clothing on quality or price. As the cost of material soared and patterns proliferated, we chose between elementary Butterick and Simplicity patterns and the more ambitious Vogue ones. No more home-drafting with Enid Gilchrist.

Many models competed for the money, and it was possible to buy rather than wait to inherit. And with less regular contact with grandparents, there were fewer opportunities to learn. Much of the process became less personal. Machines came with ten lessons from 'the expert'. Only for the daughters of the 1960s and 1970s is there a generation with no experience of the treadle, who regard the machine as a focus of the past of their female relatives, and listen to stories about it. The treadle has passed into folklore.

We were never idle.

*D*ad *was on the night shift, and Mum would sew in the evenings. We'd be in bed, she'd settle into sewing, and there'd be a roar as the needle went through her finger.*

The motif of constant work, of women's productivity, runs through the stories of a number of women born early this century. Each daughter, looking back on her mother's life, remarks on the business and purpose of the activities.

Emmeline Lahey, who grew up in the New South Wales-Queensland border country recalls:

We were never idle, and my female forebears never just sat. They were always sewing, knitting, crocheting or making something for the family. They made for themselves and were so self-sufficient. They made their own clothes, tea-towels, curtains, hemmed up the sheets, pot holders, tea-cosies. Not now: you just run down to the shop and buy it. My older sister embroidered afternoon tea-cloths for mother, and I still have them. My unmarried aunts, on my father's side, passed on home-embroidered doilies to me. I don't use them because they are too much trouble, and I am too busy to use them, but I am interested to have them because they remind me of the self-sufficiency of those women. My mother made most of my clothes, and I still have the dresses she made for my trousseau twenty-five years ago.

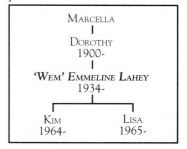

My second sister spins wool and makes jumpers for all her family. Her daughters sew and are good sewers. My daughters both can sew and make their own clothes, but they have more interesting things to do. My third sister makes clothes for the family. I don't sew much because I am not much good at it, and I'm flat out doing the mending. I work outside instead.

Doreen Monro was educated at home because her parents considered the state system to be too rough. It is a choice she has regretted. The pace at home was leisurely. A pleasant afternoon with friends and family included needlework.

My mother taught me to sew when I was very young. I made dresses for her, my children and others. I didn't charge very much. We did a lot of sewing and knitting. We'd sit around talking - gossip, I suppose you'd call it. I'd invite friends over for afternoon tea. It was how women could entertain then, without the men. It involved a lot of cooking, but there were always other women at home to help. There were the sisters who'd finished at boarding school and not yet married, a visiting cousin, an unmarried aunt.

My treadle was bought for me by my mother when I left school in the 1920s. When we went up to the Gulf country in the 1930s, I took it with me. I sold it to the person who came after me at Lawn Hill, and I bought another one when we got back here. I always loved sewing. We always had a machine, a good one, a Singer, and during World War II Mum made Dad's shirts to save coupons.

With no thought of a career, Doreen stayed at home to help her mother; there was always plenty to do. When she was widowed in her fifties, she taught herself to type and worked as a typist.

To Nina Fletcher the afternoons with the needle were very enjoyable. Her machine, bought before she was married, went to the Salvos in her later years. At that time, Doreen's daughter-in-law, Patti, was searching for a treadle to teach her daughter to sew. *I was sick of humping it around Brisbane. I was taught by my mother and passed these skills on to my daughters. We made camisole tops and pants by hand - I was very young then - and the pants buttoned on the bodice. It took me one and a half years to make that set. Then I learned dressmaking in Warwick at boarding school.*

Both Patti and her mother taught their daughters to sew but have always been willing to help in the final steps. *I think if the skill is forced upon them, or you stop them doing it because it's not good enough, then they give up. I made it a game to use the machine. My mother always finished off my sewing for me. It was such a relief, and I've always done that for my daughter. I'll put on the skirt hook and eye, or put in the zipper. The process of doing it is important. You get close to finishing it and then not want to finish it off. My daughter never finishes the dishes either. Still, it doesn't matter. In twenty-five years' time, she'll only remember the raging if I nag.*

Marguerite Newlove, born in 1952, recalls that during the war, her mother used her machine to sew army uniforms and, after the war, beautiful ball gowns. It rarely sewed for her.

Mum and I, we're too close in temperament for me to stand for a fitting with Mum, so my clothes were made by the lady across the road. Mum used a treadle machine but, because of her polio foot, she couldn't handle the foot pedal on the new machines. Mum didn't work for the Australian government during the war. She worked for the Americans, and she made uniforms, munitions, and she worked in their post office. I don't know what happened to her treadle machine, but I think it might have gone to one of my older cousins.

  Mum did try to teach me to sew on the treadle, but it didn't work because she couldn't co-ordinate everything. Then Dad bought a little electric machine and taught me to sew on that. He could co-ordinate on the electric but not on the treadle. I'm not a good sewer, but I manage. I made the kids' clothes when they were little, and sometimes I make clothes now. I use the machine to do all the mending.

The wife of the headmaster frequently taught sewing at school. Una von Sturmer had the task of making a pair of pants for herself.

They were to be all hand-sewn, a tedious task. My mother cut them out, and then I took it to school to make it up. The mistress wanted to sew the waist to the crutch in a way which would have made the pants an impossible undergarment. When I was married, I sewed everything on my machine: the boys' trousers, shirts and pyjamas; I made all Pam's clothes and my own. Shops didn't cater for children, and ordinary people made their children's clothing. The machine was used for mending and turning sheets; when they were worn in the middle, cut them up and stitched the sides up the middle with a French seam.

A page from Nina Fletcher's sewing machine manual

Mary Anne Jebb's Singer; it came from her grandmother, Ginger

Doreen Monro, Goondiwindi, Queensland

Patti Monro, Sherwood, Queensland

For some women, the amount of time spent with the machine by their mothers or aunts was a positive turn off. *I don't like sewing, and Mum's machine will go to my daughter when she wants or needs it. Mum was widowed at the age of thirty-two and found herself alone and having to provide for her five children. Her only work experience before marriage had been in a country store where her husband had been the garage proprietor, but she was willing to work at anything to earn a living for herself and children. She found her greatest asset to be her treadle sewing machine. She made all the children's clothes, including their school uniforms, and sewed for money; not much, just locally. In her later years, she hated sewing because she had been compelled to do so much.*

You might get paid eventually when you could produce something.

Martha Ricardo brought a different attitude to sewing when she arrived in Australia in the late forties.

In Italy we learnt sewing, cooking, and things like that. I was taught by the local dressmaker. You wouldn't get paid, but they'd teach you the trade, more or less. You stayed for as long as you liked, depending if the dressmaker was someone with real business sense. You might just stay on and get paid eventually when you could produce something. At that time, it was done so we would learn something for ourselves and be kept away from the street. Also, it was part of becoming a woman. So when I was very young, there was a textile industry, and that's what I was directed to, not because I wanted, but because that was there. So you just do what was there.

Early in the century, in the home and in the workplace, apprenticed as vest-hands, shirt-hands and coat-hands, Australian women relied on their machines to earn a living. In workshops, in appalling conditions, they toiled from first light till dark. During the war, they made uniforms and after the war, widows, piece-workers and out-workers again, relied on their machines to support themselves.

The treadle machine had its own movements and sounds.

The sewing machine was in Nar's kitchen with the benches and chairs. It was part of a continuity, of belonging, of visiting on Sundays. It's part of my interest in history, of wanting to get to the beginning of things. I am sure at one stage the machine stood under the window in what became the dining room. I remember it being used to do the household sewing, some clothes, some underwear, some household goods. I certainly remember it in Nar's kitchen, just where you went from the kitchen into the hallway. It was next to the dresser, the one with the little bits of leadlights in the window. And, if you just touched those little doors, they slid on the ball bearings, and they rolled easily. The had their own sort of distinctive sound, but the treadle machine had its own movements and

sounds, and the doors on the dresser, with their movement and sound, they were all fitted together in the kitchen.

The machine had all those little drawers, six little drawers, three down each side, plus a little sort of secret area in the front with a drop door. In one of the drawers there was a box with all the screwdrivers and shuttles and things. When we went there on Sundays, there were always those interesting things: beads, buttons, pins, chalk. You knew just where to go to get anything you wanted to use. But be careful. Don't use the dressmaking scissors to cut paper or you'll blunt them. Don't lose the little screwdrivers.

In 1914, shortly after the birth of her second child, Nar was given a machine bought by her mother at the Co-op stores in Beccles, England. It must have been a welcome gift for the young family. As a little girl, Gertrude sat on the table to wind it for her mother. In 1929, Nar's mother bought a treadle from her daughter's employer, and the hand machine passed to Nar's daughter. When Gertrude bought a treadle of her own in 1942, the hand machine passed to her sister-in-law. Later, it was converted to electric and put into a frame so that it became a portable that could be worked on a table. Gertrude still has this machine. Meg has the treadle from Nar. Meg has no daughters, only nieces and a daughter-in-law, so there is no one in her own line who might rightfully receive the treadle. The tale of the treadle terminates with Meg.

Nar's story: 'The machine was how I earned my living.'

Gertrude and Meg reflected on Nar's use of the machine. They agreed that it was easy to spoil the material or the fit. Although Nar would make her own working clothes, she would not attempt 'a good dress'.

If she wanted a costume, she'd probably go to the dressmaker. She wouldn't know how to go about doing that sort of thing. Dressmaker's wages were not like they are today. She was the wife of a carpenter but was a good manager and able to afford a costume when she needed it.

Dadda [Nar's husband] wore a flannel undershirt, a practice he had brought from England. The idea with the flannel was that it absorbed perspiration, and it wasn't cold to the body so, if the wind blew, you didn't feel the cold. He rode a bike to work in those days. He always used to wear just his flannel shirt; it was a working man's uniform.

One of Meg's memories of her grandfather is of him in the garden wearing that flannel shirt. Gertrude remembered the change in men's work-clothes.

Then he graduated from flannel ones to the white ones for summer. Mum used to complain about the jarrah dust in them; she couldn't get it out. But Bill [his son] never wore them. He wore a singlet, and then they brought in the navy blue ones for them at work. They used to make them with a gusset under the arms. That's how they did them in those days. They'd make them with a maygar sleeve, but Mum used to sit and put a gusset in them. Dad wore flannel under his khaki working shirts. Mum used to make a lot of those shirts because it was cheaper to make them than to buy them. You often bought a stronger material, a twill, a khaki twill, I think she used to buy. He used to wear them to work and, when it got a bit hot, he could take the khaki shirt off and still have on that flannel shirt. He wore them in the summer and winter-time.

Meg: *Today we buy them as fashion garments.*
Gertrude: *Oh, my goodness, grey flannel shirts!*
Meg: *Yes, women wear them over their jeans and things, but you can get red ones or oatmeal coloured ones and grey ones. They have a round neck, two or three buttons down the front and short sleeves.*

Pillowcases, Gertrude recalled, also had these buttons. *Well, people didn't buy pillowcases, then, off the rack. Mum made them, and they had tapes on them. They didn't have that bit flapped in because that took extra material, you see. When you gradually got a little bit more money, well, you were able to buy them, and you bought flapped-in pillowcases. But they were not something that's always been there. Even the bought pillowcases had tapes, or sometimes those ones with the buttons.*

Sometimes, she bought what they called forfah, a sort of linen, and you'd cut it through and hem it to make your tea-towels; just the ends not the sides. Mum used to make little bloomers for me, you know, and she made them for you, too, Meg. Purple ones. They'd call you 'Mary purple pants'. When you look back, they were made out of some sort of ripply cloth, a bit harder than seersucker. It must have been rough on your poor old bot. I think sometimes you wore little white ones underneath them, didn't you? Yes, and you always had little pants to match your dresses, which I made.

> Gertrude Jessie
> 1887-
> |
> Gertrude McLaren
> 1910-
> |
> 'Meg'
> 1934-

Mum made her own curtains too, but not like they are today. They were mainly lace curtains at the window with a holland blind. Then, later on, they had the sides, but they were not backed. You didn't back your curtains. They were only put on a rod, with a pocket or with curtain rings. You'd sew the rings on, and you had a valance, but it was nailed to the board of your window. And that hung flat or else you pleated it to give a little bit of fullness.

Gertrude's story: 'The machine did all the household sewing.'

After leaving Perth Girls' School in 1926, Gertrude was apprenticed as a tailor until 1930. She married Gavin McLaren, was widowed during the war and raised her four children in Western Australia.

Well, I'd always liked sewing, and Dad heard about this opportunity of doing an apprenticeship as a tailoress, and that was really I suppose why I went there. I used to go by tram from Victoria Park to Perth. It was in the old Economic Stores. We worked in a room up on the top. There were other tailors up there plus different people. There was a solicitor up there, and that sort of thing. I got to know other girls who went backwards and forwards to work with me, but the other girl there was much older than I was. I was the apprentice, and the other girl there was a full-hand. She did the coats and helped with other things. I was a vest-hand, and the trousers were made outside. Someone else had to do that. And if we were really pushed, the boss, Mr Jervis, used to come and help. His wife taught me. She was there too.

It was a three-year apprenticeship for a vest-hand. It was five years for a coat-hand, and I don't know about the trousers. So, after working for three years, I was a fully fledged vest-hand. I was about eighteen or nineteen then. I stayed on making vests, and sometimes I would help out with coats; not make them, just hand-stitch the edges, that fine stitching that you see around the edge of a coat. You had to do it around the edge of a vest so that you were quite capable of doing it around the edge of a coat. We made them in greys, blues, browns and stripes with a little strap across the satin back. Some had five, some had six buttons if they were a big person and hand-done button-holes.

So we did the lot.
Meg: *But you didn't fit the jacket?*
Gertrude: *Oh, no, hardly.*
Meg: *It's a wonder you didn't get R.S.I.*
Gertrude: *Well, if you did, you didn't know.*

Gertrude, like other women of her generation, began married life with a second-hand machine. *I worked on the small machine that you've got now,*

Meg. When I first got married and needed a sewing machine, I got Mum's little hand sewing machine. She'd progressed to a treadle model, and I got the hand-machine to start me off. I went from that machine, the hand-machine, to a treadle with an electric motor on it. I had 'Grandad London's' big tailor's machine, and he said he wouldn't do work on it any more. It was a big machine, and I can't remember where we were living, but he left it with me and said, 'Look, you can have this. I won't be using it any more'. I never sewed on it; I traded it in. I went down to Egham Road and traded it in. It was the end of the war, when we were allowed twenty-five pounds to sort of help replace things that had been worn out during the war, and I traded it. The government gave it to war widows to help. It was too heavy for me to use, and I traded it in on the one you probably remember. The one in the little polished cabinet. And I bought some mats as well for the bedroom. That was when we were in Egham Road. So I traded in the big machine for the one that Peter made a stand for, and that's the one you learned to sew on, Meg.

You wouldn't dream of throwing out something if you hadn't taken the zip out and the buttons off, and even the press-studs. Anything re-usable you took off, and the place where you stored those bits and pieces was in the sewing machine. Or in a big tin. I used to keep mine in a tin. I had a button jar, which was all right. I've still got that button tin. I went through it before I moved and threw out a lot of buttons that I should have never kept. The old cloth buttons that were worn out, and there was just the brass ring. Do you remember the three little buttons about the size of a ten-cent piece? and they were black velvet, and they had a little painting on the surface of it done with oil paint, a little rose, a spray of roses, or something like that. I haven't got any now, I don't think. You sewed them on to the dress, and they were re-usable. Yes, anything that's worthwhile but, see, zips aren't used much now; your clothes don't have zips in them. Elastic around the waist, and that's it.

Meg's story: 'The machine is now with me in Canberra.'

Those zips are now used for decoration. I think the fact that you were creative when you used the sewing machine, it was like you were setting things to rights, repairing the holes in things and making something useful out of something that might not previously have been of use. Like making the boys trousers out of cut-off men's trousers. You always did that. You didn't throw out a garment because part of it was worn out. You reused it, and you never used new cloth on aprons. They were made from the back of a frock or a skirt or

'NAR'
1887-
|
GERTRUDE
1910-
|
'MEG' SEKAVS
1934-

parts of dresses. There were a number of other things that you wouldn't dream of buying new cloth for. It was always re-used. So that what was thrown away was well and truly worn out.

When Nar went into the home, we had to sort out her things. Others in the family wanted the plates or the Victorian working-class Sunday best furniture. Gertrude took the things which were not keepsakes, like cups and saucers, things to use. She did not take her old bedspreads, but she took newer things which were better value in her view than the old. I wanted the sewing machine.

I used to go home every two years. After my first marriage broke up, I went over to Perth in the Kombi van with the boys. On the second trip, we brought the machine back. Uncle Bill dismantled it and put the iron part on the roof and wooden part wrapped up in the Kombi. We kept it in the old house and had it restored - the wood was bubbling. It stayed in the old house and, then, after three months came to the new house in the back bedroom. Then, when we stripped the new house to renovate it, we used it as a hall table. Then it went into the garage to be stored, and now it is back in the house in my step-daughter's bedroom.

The skills of the mothers and grandmothers are regarded with affection, respect and awe by the next generation, the daughters of the fifties and sixties, for whom life was easier. The machine came as a birthday present, or new as a wedding present, or was bought out of your own savings. Jane Lloyd's sewing machine arrived on her ninth birthday.

I can vividly remember waking up that morning and going to my parents' bedroom with the joy and expectation of presents and getting a yellow swimsuit, which I thought was pretty good. I stayed in their bed for a while, and then I was told to get up, put on my dressing gown and come in for breakfast. I had to go to my bedroom and, 'Voilà!' there was the Singer sewing machine, which I was delighted with. So that's how I got the Singer sewing machine. They bought it at an old warehouse. It wasn't handed down from anybody. Now, as well, I have my mother's old Husqvarna machine, which she bought around the time my brother was born, but it's electric.

I learnt to sew on the old treadle. I used to sit up in my room and sew, but I was also interested in playing bat and ball and going to the football with my father. I brought the treadle up here to Alice Springs at the same time I brought up my books. But now it's not set up as a sewing machine. It has pot plants and fruits and things on it. But I see it as being really important. It was one thing that I wanted to bring up with me. I quite like it as a bit of furniture, too, and there's a lot of sentimentality attached to it. It will be something that I can keep, and probably something that I will hand on to someone else. Whether it's my own daughter or a friend's daughter, or whatever, I don't know. I suppose it was an important mark in my life to receive it.

Cheryl Hannah spent some time with her grandmother and, in that time, learned to sew. And I sewed my fingers under the treadle, and all the drama and the pain of having to dismantle the machine to get the needle out, to get my fingers out. Grandma told me this was something everybody did. It was part of learning to sew and part of being over-anxious and unskilled, and all that sort of stuff. My cousin, Jane, has that machine and still uses it. She's my mother's brother's eldest daughter, who's the same age as me. She stayed up on the north coast and is married to a banana farmer at Grafton and has four children. I suppose she got it because she was close, and I don't have any children. But in fact it wasn't a big deal for me because one of the things I did with my income was go and buy myself a really good electric machine. I bought top of the range Elna. That was in 1972, the first holidays that I earned a good salary. I spent the whole of my vacation salary on that sewing machine.

I had to sew. I really loved to sew my own clothes, and I didn't have access to Mum's sewing machine any more because I'd left home. Mum had a Singer. She had one of the knee-control Singers, which Dad bought her as a wedding present, and she did all her sewing for her own trousseau and everything for us kids on that machine. It literally wore out and ceased to be repairable. When I was in late high school, Dad bought her a new Singer sewing machine, which was never as good. She loathed, cursed and despaired at it because it was made out of plastic. It didn't work as well, and it didn't hold the tension as well. So I wouldn't have wanted Mum's Singer anyway, and as soon as I knew that I could afford to do it, I was going to buy my own machine. I spent months working out what machine I was going to buy, and my Elna cost three hundred and sixty-five dollars in 1972, which was three months' pay.

No need for a charitable fund.

Chapter Five

THE FABRICS OF LIFE

I've just opened the trunk, and what I'm faced with is the fabrics of my life. This array of different pieces is what I've collected or been given over the years. It links me to my mother and her professional area: weaving. There are bits of fabric like raw silk that Mum gave me, and batiks I bought in Indonesia. There is embroidery done by Vietnamese women in the camps in Thailand and Malaysia and a woven piece from a friend in Sumatra. There's some batik from the Aboriginal women at Utopia cattle station and a silk kite I started to make.

The wooden box, made by Jane Lloyd's father when she left home to go to university, is where she keeps these treasures, which tell of her travels, friendships and family.

```
LYDIA
1896-1983
    |
LILLIAN
1922-
    |
JANE LLOYD
1958-
```

There is a shawl made for me by Jan Chaloupka, another woman who has influenced my life. I used to spend a lot of time talking to her during my high school years in Darwin. They lived near us. She is a very creative woman, not just in the ceramic work she does, but also in ideas and thinking. She made that shawl for me just before I went to university. It's a sort of aqua blue, mohair shawl. The other one was made for me by Mum while I was at university. It's made out of berber wool in various shades, and it's a nice warm one.

Mary Anne Jebb had two dresses of her grandmother's. My mother kept them for me. They are the most exquisite hand-sewn dresses that were made by some poor woman, not by my grandmother, in Perth. They are very dear to me. I had been living in New Zealand, the Kimberley and the south-west since I was *eighteen. I'd travelled around Asia and Europe in my seventeenth year. When I came back, it was almost a coming back to the family gift. I arrived back home, and Mum pulled Ginger's dresses out. So perhaps this was Mum's inadvertent symbol of her welcoming home again to me. The two dresses and shawl are still in my cupboard.*

I wore one particular dress for four Christmases. It's a beautiful thing, suits my colouring, and I am the same shape as Ginger, as well. A friend of Ginger's, Aunty Sally, saw me wearing it and stopped in her tracks, visibly distressed: 'Gosh, I thought it was Ginger. You look just like her standing there.' I haven't worn that dress since.

Clothes may make us re-think our images of our mother. *Everything went when she died. Then, in the back of the wardrobe I found a dressing gown which obviously had never been worn. It was old, and only later did I find some honeymoon photographs, and there she was sitting on the balcony of a hotel at the Sea of Galilee in that lovely brocade gown.*

In another story, a nightgown reveals a mother's naive expectations of marriage, love and sex. *It's an embroidered nightgown from her trousseau, but it was never worn. I found it folded in the original tissue paper, out of sight, under a number of heavier clothes in the bottom drawer. She was angry about me rummaging through her things, but I was quite innocent at the time. Now I realize marriage for Mum was not very romantic. It was about scarcity, violence and neglect. If the silverfish don't get it first, I would love to have that nightgown. It was her labour, and she was happy once.*

The fabrics no longer in use are easily lost. Gone are the collections of handkerchiefs in the hand-worked sachet, the fine muslin lavender bags in the linen press and underwear drawers. That soft scent was like the mild evenings when, just at dusk, mother would come to kiss you goodnight. She also had that light lavender scent. Furs, no longer fashionable, the ones with the little clipped fox heads at the neck, went from being dress-ups into the bag for the second-hand shop. The daughter with the task of clearing out the house, thankful that at last she no longer has to divide her time between duties at home and taking care of her mother, feels she is well rid of it. She sees it as part of another world, macabre but exotic. It was too late to retrieve the fur the next time she visited grandma. They shared the loss, but neither mentioned it to the mother.

Fabrics bought to be worn may be put to another use. *I've never forgotten, I'd saved up my pocket money and bought my mother a nightgown for her birthday. I can remember this pink nightgown. I thought it was marvellous. So what does my mother do but have my grandmother buried in it. She didn't have anything else decent to put on her. I was so terribly upset. I wanted my mother to have it. I can understand why she did it. Life must have been awful for her. At one stage, she had my father's mother and his sister and her mother all under the same roof. She was a very patient person. I nursed Mum and was with her when she died. I have a few prizes she won, a few old photographs and her reading glasses. I can't bear to throw them away. I didn't want to cut her off completely when she died.*

A going-away dress has been retained and is claimed by the youngest. Megan was thin enough to wear grandma's dress of the 1920s when she got married. Grandma never minded her going through her drawers She probably thought Megan understood the significance of those things better than the others did. The youngest grandchild is often favoured by the grandparents.

Another woman tells of a wedding dress torn in two after a bitter separation. In yet another house, the gown was burned by the mother-in-law. Those that survive are sometimes worn again, or the lace re-worked for the next generation. Whatever, the emotional investment in the fabric of marriage is extremely powerful.

Some of the clothes, those that survived purges, the moths and dress-up sessions, are still worn.

There's this wonderful blouse of grandmother's I used to wear. I gave it back to Mum because I didn't trust myself with it, and I thought at some future date my daughter might like to do something with it. It was an ordinary day-time blouse, a sort of bluey-green with a raised white polka dot and saddle stitching.

Patricia Richards: *I'm often reminded of my mother because I feel she's been dead twenty-three years, and I'm still using some of her handkerchiefs. I see them and remember her. I've still got her underwear, spencers, and things like that, which I don't wear much. She wore the long woolly knickers. I wouldn't but, I mean, they're there if I want them.*

> *I wouldn't let those things not be looked after. Caring for them is our duty. They're our ceremonial objects.*

One woman has a christening gown made by her mother's mother's mother.

It's minute, made for when babies were christened when very young. It was worn by generations of the women of my line. But now I have only grandsons, to whom should it go? My brothers and sisters had daughters, so this worry is just for my part of the family.

It's yellow now with age, and so beautiful. It's unthinkable to destroy it, so I've kept it in a box in the cupboard with the wedding veil. I wouldn't let those things not be looked after. Caring for them is a duty. They're our ceremonial objects.

The fringed shawl in which the baby is displayed and first photographs taken is kept for special occasions. Pieces of fine work, such as the gown and shawl, pass from woman to woman. Traditionally, these objects are made by a mother for her daughter's child but not actually given to the daughter. Instead the gown is held in trust by the daughter for her daughter's children. Those that survive several generations become highly prized heirlooms, kept carefully folded in tissue paper.  The heavy-duty shawls, the ones in everyday use, are made of sturdier stuff. When they are worn out, they are cut down to become knee rugs or used in patchwork. Daphne Nash has a tartan wool 'working shawl' for her child that is the same as the one she had when she was a baby. The shawl, re-made in the old style, maintains some continuity from one generation of women to the next.

Patti Monro's grandmother knitted each of her grandchildren a huge blanket in box stitch. They are still on their beds. Nancy Reis converted old quilts from the hotel she'd owned in Melbourne into doonas for her grandchildren in Perth. In the 1930s, Joyce Caddie made blankets by stitching together corn bags, filling them with corn husks and covering them with material. 'They were warm, like a modern doona. I don't tell this often because of the reaction it gets.' Her experience was shared in the 1950s by Topsy Nelson at Phillip Creek in the Northern Territory.

We didn't have any decent blankets, just rubbish ones, bags cut open to make blankets. They had wheat in them before. That was in the dormitories. They kept us locked in at night. I ran away once to be with my family. The old people used paper bark for keeping little ones warm, you know.

A hand-embroidered cloth, rarely used, neatly folded in the bottom drawer, the setting for sixteen, with little chance of being used in a home with a small table and breakfast bench, these are women's heritage, fabrics of which women say, 'I wouldn't part with them,' and express a strong belief in using them even though it may involve extra work. *It is linen, not cotton, mind you, my grandmother made it, such patience. I think of her whenever I iron it; she gave it to me when she gave up ironing.*

In some families, production of such things as supper cloths, for daughters, daughters-in-law and grand-daughters was a conscious creation of ceremonial objects which, like christening gowns, are passed from one generation to the next, exhibited at shows, the fine stitching a hallmark of women's skills.

I think of it as as part of my inheritance, all that embroidered work... It's stuff I would never part with.

As Cheryl Hannah observed: *It makes me sad to see all that old work, all the fine work of the 1920s and 1930s, sold for twenty cents at school fetes. It's a loss of family history. It's stuff I would never part with. I think of it as part of my inheritance, all that embroidered work. I don't intend having children, but I'd give it to my sister if she had any daughters, or to my god-daughter. I've already given her some embroidered baby clothes.*

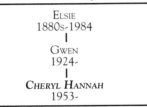

ELSIE
1880s-1984
|
GWEN
1924-
|
CHERYL HANNAH
1953-

Collections of women's fine work were amassed for the glory box. It was here that everything necessary for the establishment of an independent home by the daughter was kept: sheets, towels, table linen, fine lingerie, china, pots and pans. Up until the fifties, the practice of putting together a trousseau was well entrenched. Lena Kay, born in 1924, saw her generation as the last to put together a glory box.

I had one, but my daughter did not. I never bought any linen for eleven years after we were married. I had the glory box, the real glory box, in Swan Hill. My sister Rose sold it for me and sent the money down. I packed everything before I left, tea sets and all. I'd had it from about the time I was eighteen, and I'd see something and buy it and put it in there.

Fine work exhibited at shows was taken by many to be the mark of the accomplished woman. Those who had had an education, however, put less value on these skills. *My mother's mother was portrayed as not being clever in the way that women should be clever, to be able to read, write and be scholarly, to win an argument. She'd always put doilies in the show. She stayed up every night until two or three in the morning, knitting and sewing for the show. I have very little from my mother's mother, and my mother didn't speak of her much. I remember her, but my view is probably very tainted, I'd say, by my mother's impression. She always talked far more about her mother than Nanna.*

My mother has these doilies, and she will pass them on to me. There are also doilies made by female family members dating back to the 1830s. Mum knows who made them and has told me at one time. I expect I'll be told again when they're handed over to the children. We did spend a lot of time with her when I think about it but never with her. There were about nine cousins, first cousins all staying together on the farm. Everyone who was older than you was an aunt or uncle.

Some time in the mid to late fifties, women stopped receiving, buying and making these items for the box. No doubt, this reflects increased affluence, a greater variety of goods from which young married women could choose and the number of women remaining unmarried but living independently. Thus, the duchess set and the lovingly embroidered linens are no longer produced. Indeed, the routines of younger women and the furniture in their homes make constant use of these items inappropriate.

The salesman would call to sell you a trousseau.

Grandma made pillowcases for her daughter's trousseau. The pillowcases have the initials of Mum and Dad intertwined. I admire the patience it required and enjoy embroidery, but Mum was always impatient with fine work.

Within the glory box was the trousseau, sewn with love and hope. The contents of the box were known and reviewed by other women, especially by a potential mother-in-law. One woman commented that a contemporary of her mother had encouraged her daughter, who was 'exceedingly plain', to put a good deal of work into the embroidery in her trousseau.

Table-cloths and napkins coloured and made especially to match the china were bought on lay-by. The salesman would call to sell you a trousseau set once your engagement was announced in the paper.

In lean times, we simply made do, and hand-me-downs were essential. What was passed to the next generation had to be weighed up and what was chosen said something about the relationship between them. Would your old saucepans, which had done yeoman service, but no longer worked on the electric hot plates, be appreciated? Often it was the older generation who saved to buy the new gadget and the younger who inherited the old. We began our married lives with our mother's iron, blankets, tables and what we had put together in the glory box. What was a wedding gift to Grandma, a tea set, cloth or brooch, may become an heirloom in several generations.

Although the formal gathering of a glory box has passed, the notion that mothers will help their daughters set up home has persisted.

She didn't do any fancy work, or anything like that; she was too much of a modern woman. She didn't do anything for a box; it just kind of went out. I helped to get together towels and linen, and those sorts of things, some china. She still hasn't much in the way of china, but she'll certainly get a fair load of mine. I've often thought I must give her some now and give her the pleasure of it because I've got more than I can use. Once she's settled, and they've got space for it in the house, I'll give it to her. Because, you see, firstly, she was at university for all that time, then she went into a flat where there wasn't much space, and then she was in England.

When we had visitors, my mother used to say, 'Well, this is Lilly. She's good with her hands, you know.' I think that should be put on my tombstone when I die.

Lillian Lloyd left school when she was thirteen, and it was not until she took art classes in her late teens that her talents were recognized. Until then, she had always felt in the shadow of her older sister. But with breaks for the raising of her two children, she has developed her talents and, through teaching, passed them on to others.

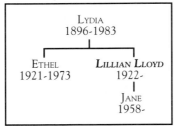

Someone asked me once where I learnt to weave, and I still maintain it was mending socks because I used to get a halfpenny a pair. My mother hated sewing and mending, and she was absolutely hopeless at it. A beautiful knitter, she could do crochet work, but she hated sewing or making things. I remember sitting up and actually trying to make a hole a bit bigger so I could get another halfpenny. You had to mend so many before you could get sixpence to go to the Saturday afternoon matinee.

It was much later that Lillian discovered that her sister felt she'd heard quite enough of the wonderful things her younger sister made. When her mother died, she found that all the pieces of weaving she'd given her were in a box. 'She did care! One's parents never gave praise.' Jane, Lillian's daughter, collects fine pieces, but her interests in cloth lean more towards dressmaking.

Cheryl Hannah: *The embroidery, sewing and knitting have come to me as skills from my grandmother and mother, but the spinning and weaving are skills that I've actually taught myself in this generation. I'd like to think that those things of mine were passed to someone who could use them and someone who would also value them because they denote me. I'm conscious of the fact that it's not just a matter of waiting around until someone dies. By talking about those sorts of things, by saying, 'This is mine, and if you love me and care about me, I'd really like you to have this.'*

I don't want to create a massive obligation but, at the same time, I feel very good about having learned to spin. I love my spinning wheel and the fact that it was made for me, and it's the sort of expression of my skill and my ability to see that skill realized. For me, it's important that that not disappear. I'm not going to have any children of my own so I have to give some thought about where I want it to go.

I want the spinning wheel to end up with someone who would love it and use it.

With my spinning wheel I'm generating things in our own time. It was made for me by an engineer who turned spinning-wheel manufacturer in his retirement. Every part of the spinning wheel is hand-made by him. I chose the wood, and it's actually made for my height. It's the Rolls-Royce of spinning wheels. It cost a lot of money, and the thing is that I am really conscious that this is the sort of stuff that in our generation will become the antiques, the heirlooms, in two or three generations' time. If there is anything of mine to be remembered after me, what's important to me is those skills, things like spinning, knitting, weaving, embroidery.

I use both my loom and my spinning wheel, but my loom I see much more as a piece of furniture and my spinning wheel as precious. I want the spinning wheel to end up with someone who would love it and use it, whereas I suspect the loom could simply be dismantled and sold to someone else who was a weaver without any real significance to me.

Mother, an excellent seamstress, reluctant to let her daughter tamper with machine or material when she could do the job more efficiently herself, finds time in her retirement for grandchildren and daughters of friends. But it falls to her daughter to hand sew, and access to the machine is limited, or the activity is too much hard work. It is not unusual to find that good dressmakers come in alternate generations, the intermediate generation specializing in embroidery, crochet and smocking. If there are no daughters, a grand-daughter becomes the focus of attention.

Co-operative endeavours between mother and daughter may draw on different skills. Pip McManus, born in 1952 and now living in Alice Springs, where she has a ceramics studio, and her mother, who lives in Perth, have undertaken several joint endeavours.

Mum is very good with sewing skills. She recently completed a set of small fabric dolls from the commedia dell'arte period of Italian minstrel theatre - characters like Pierrot and Harlequin, which were beautifully made. His Majesty's Theatre in Perth has bought them.

I have not inherited those skills at all. I don't know whether it's a reaction about  something that she wanted me to be good at, and I didn't want to, because I thought it was trivial and messy. I think a lot of it is that it's a medium that I just don't enjoy. It's fiddly, and I don't particularly enjoy that work. But I've never tried or persevered with sewing at all. My mother does beautiful embroidery, and she makes fabric dolls and patchwork and quilting, and that is her greatest pleasure and involvement at night. She always made a lot of clothes for me when I was younger.

I often give her really demanding projects, like knitting a very complicated design. I did one black jumper, which was really complicated, with a gold fleck through it. Into the back is knitted a very detailed picture of the Luna Park face at Melbourne, in St Kilda, with every detail. I worked out every line on graph paper, stitch by stitch, and wrote them down, so it's really, really, difficult, because every line is different. It looks beautiful. She's made things for me. I do the drawings for her.

At the moment, we're doing a joint project. She rang me up a few weeks ago and had this idea that maybe she'd do something for the Bicentennial. She thought she'd do a history of Western Australia, and so she was going to do Governor Stirling, and all those boring men. I said, 'What do you want to do those men for?' She said, 'Fair enough,' so she's doing all those boring pioneer women. She's finished Elizabeth Shaw and doing another one.

Grandma had a good eye for colour. The colour gradations... are more like oil paintings.

The artistic creative flair of mothers and grandmothers is given full rein in tapestries.

There are some beautiful tapestries, needlepoints that my grandmother did after she moved in from the farm. When I was very ill in 1979, and there was a good chance that I could have died of peritonitis, Mum told Grandma that I was very ill, and she sent me a tapestry that had kind of been an agreement between us that I'd have. It hadn't been formally done, and I think some of my family were jealous that it came to me first. It hangs in my bedroom. It's a very beautiful French tapestry, a scene of a river. Grandma, because she was a trained artist

The Fabrics of Life

The collection of silk and cotton threads given to Nina Fletcher by her mother

Ginger's handsewn dresses that were given to her grand-daughter Mary Anne Jebb

The Fabrics of Life

Sarah Jebb and Mary Anne Jebb, Western Australia

Sisters, Cheryl Hannah and Megan Dorrough, O'Connor, Canberra

in her youth, and also worked in oils and watercolours until she was in her thirties, I suppose, had a good eye for colour, and her tapestries are much finer than a lot of other tapestry you see around. The colour gradations are more like oil paintings. She had a better eye for blending colour and worked in a way that the tapestry might have been painted to start off with. They are more like paintings than tapestries. It's very precious to me, and I would want it to stay in my family. It could go to my brother's children or somewhere within the family. But it would have to stay because it's Grandma's.

Elspeth Young has a number of fine pieces of tapestry that link her to her grandmother and mother. It is a tradition she has continued. *The last stool tapestry my mother was doing - it was on her lap when she died - I asked for it, and my sister sent it to me from Scotland straight away, and I finished it. I didn't go home for the funeral, so finishing the piece meant a lot to me. Now, I've finally found the right size stool for it, 1920 vintage.*

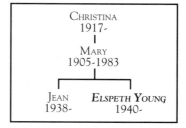

I have lots of different chairs and stools worked by different members of the family, each with its own history. One was my grandmother's, and the tapestry on it was done by my mother. She claimed it for me when grandma died. I was in Australia, and she thought it would be nice for me to have something from her house. Some of my mother's work was done from transfers, but she would make up her own colours. I remember being taught not only to embroider but also to pull a bit of blooming thread out and to use special stitches to sew it all together. I suppose I was about nine or ten.

I set about restoring the tapestry on one of her chairs, but it meant re-building the whole back. The antique restorer I took it to was very excited because he'd discovered it was held together with dowels, not nails, and it had some hand-made screws. He dated it at about 1780. He said, 'It's been made by a Scottish joiner,' without knowing its history.

Elspeth is a geographer, and on the wall in her dining room hangs a cross-stitch sampler depicting a map of Scotland and part of Ireland. Unlike many samplers hung in kitchens, offering words of advice and hope, some general, some personal, this one reflects work interests.

In the corner of the sampler, surrounded by seed pearls, is 'Map of Scotland, Jean Todd 1812'. My sister Jean decided it should come to me - it was, after all, a geographer's sampler. I never found out who Jean Todd was, but it's on the Young side of the family.

Margaret Bates's grandmother, who died in 1966, was part of that generation that was rarely idle. *Nanna embroidered all the time and knitted. The men always knew what they were getting for Christmas: socks. The thing about knitting is that you can take it anywhere - if you're just going for a drive, on the train, or just sitting. My Nanna used to sit with Miss Lowe and darn, knit, embroider and talk 'business'. They were all members of the church group, and they'd be talking about church business. You'd hear one of them say, 'Hang on, I've dropped a stitch', and conversation would be suspended while the stitch was*

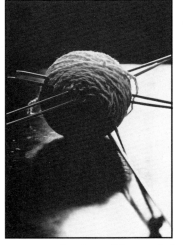

retrieved. Mum complained that she couldn't match the colours when she tried to finish off one piece of work after Nanna died. That was my father's mother. I have one lovely cloth with Australian wildflowers on it. She must have made the design herself.

The next generation learnt with transfers of tulips and daffodils at school and followed the coded colour chart from the Semco range.

In Emmeline Lahey's family, her nieces and nephews worked with an interesting range of materials. *They made beautiful things to exhibit in the local show, although they have children and also help outside. Ruth, my father's sister, knitted bags in leather. We used them as handbags, like dilly bags. Father cut and worked the roo skins, and she did the knitting.*

The fine stitching in embroidery and tapestry gave pleasure, the finished work could be inspected, admired, copied, but not all fine work was to beautify; much was utilitarian. Martha Ricardo recalls the work involved in producing socks for the family.

Mum used to knit our socks, our knee-high socks. They were made in a way where the foot was cut away from the sole and detached. So, when they wore out, you could mend them a few times, and then you'd just unpin them and take them up and put in a new one. Our task was to learn to make that fold in cotton or wool. You make your toes in different colours to match the sock you had. You sewed them on later. I had to learn, and I hated every minute of it. I wanted to go out playing. But I had to do that and my homework. Mum was strict about that. She'd come home and make sure we'd done it. When I got a bit older, I worked in the dressmaker's while we were on holidays.

Learning to darn was skilled work and matching the threads a challenge. *We learned to darn from mother, but I didn't use the mushroom. I did it over my hand. We'd darn silk stockngs and the linen tableclothes and serviettes. I still have the different strengths of cotton from those days. The silk and fine lined threads from thirty-six to a hundred.*

Remember keeping silk worms? You needed mulberry leaves and a callous disregard for your carefully nurtured grubs when it came time to harvest the silk.

I still have some spun silk from when I was a girl. We made the spinner ourselves. I have them as bookmarks. I learnt how to knit, crochet, to make table-cloths, knitted jumpers and, in the evening, when the kids were young, I'd knit socks. I had a knitted petticoat. I remember in the floods of 1926, I fell in wearing that petticoat.

Sometimes it was the headmaster's wife who introduced us to the joys of knitting. On Wednesday afternoons, grubby, sweaty little hands struggled with two and three-ply wool to make a white-ribbed baby singlet. It went home that evening for Mum, Grandma or an older sister to help with the casting off and other tricky bits.

I think it was a way of shutting me up. It was a bit like the same thing with the treadle sewing machine. I think I really wanted to be able to stay up at night-time with her and Grandpa. They'd have the evening meal together, and there would be no more wood put on the stove after dinner. It would stay warm for another couple of hours after dinner was finished. That would be the time when he would get the paper and put his feet up and sit and read, and Grandma would sit in another chair in the kitchen. If I was being a nuisance, I'd be put to bed. Grandma had a creative approach to knitting and gave me my first knitting needles. I still have them. Blue plastic ones, size twelve, bought in a chain store for eight pence when I was five. I knitted a doll's jacket with my grandmother. She did all the ribs, and I did all the straight bits.

The shell ones were heavy and sticky and hard to knit with. The aluminium were quite smooth.

Like Pip McManus, Cheryl Hannah designed her own patterns; a favourite was the rainbow jumper. *I knitted something like twenty-four of those jumpers with the women's symbol around them. And on my thirtieth birthday, there are some photographs of this amazing tribe of rainbow women. There must have been at least ten of them in that gathering in their stripy jumpers. I was a great knitter until I gave myself R.S.I. I don't knit as much as I did. But, yes, I love to knit interesting things and interesting patterns. I still have some of those from my grandmother and my mother from the forties. They are mostly in very fine plys, like two or three.*

I thought I'd lost the anodized knitting needles I had that were my grandmother's. They were probably manufactured in the 1950s, and they came in a full range of bright colours: pink, green, blue, orange. They were light and didn't break. Up until then there were only cheap knitting needles, which were plastic, and they broke, or there were the tortoise shell ones, and they were expensive. The shell ones were heavy and sticky and hard to knit with. The aluminium were quite smooth. I remember my grandmother saying they were beautiful to knit with because you could keep your tension, and they were light when you got 300 stitches for the bottom of a baby dress on the needles. That made a difference. I was really pleased when I found those needles again. They are not valuable in themselves, but they are a bit of a curiosity, and they're nice to knit with.

I put all her patterns into a book, a Standex binder, to preserve them. They're easier to get at, and the silverfish are less likely to lodge in them. They're ones where the photograph is so clear that you can actually count the stitches. If you get stuck on the pattern, you can work it out from the photo. I wish patterns were as good as that nowadays.

Time spent learning about, making and caring for fabric: none of it has the permanence of stone monuments, but all of it is a record of women's lives. *I like to think that there'll come a time when women's domestic skills and women's labour will be something which is treasured and fought over, something that will be seen as a scarce resource. Think of all those things that were produced for an insatiable family appetite; it's all part of women's culture. And it celebrates a time of women spent together, a time when women laboured together, women who were related through marriage and blood, and created bonds. That work should be seen as a celebration of our ability to make beauty of domestic items. The production of memory quilts I see as an example of this. I've made a conscious effort to create heirlooms. I made a christening robe. It was an attempt to reclaim women's knowledge of a generation gone before that knowledge was lost.*

Cheryl's concerns are shared and, in an exhibition brought together for the 150th celebration in Victoria in 1985, an appeal to the public was made to search through old trunks, spare rooms, and garden sheds for souvenirs and mementos of domestic life. A huge number of objects, including fabric and lots of teapots, were lent. At the end of the exhibition they were returned to their owners, to their place in the home.

To be able to sew a fine seam, to embroider or tat while the family relaxed around the fire, was the hallmark of a lady. It showed that free time was available, but that such time would not be wasted. It was a modest feminine activity, quite different from the labour of women in work shops slaving over the treadle.

CHAPTER SIX

FAMILIAR THINGS

I have the old kitchen table, the one we had our nappies changed on. When the house we'd lived in as kids was being dispersed, I needed a table and asked for that one. I saw it as a good writing table and also as part of my girlhood. Mum sat there to breast-feed, and there was a section where she rested her feet. It was important to her, too.

Moving house is great for streamlining your life, getting rid of the junk, the clutter of years: this piece stays, that piece goes. The decisions are not always endorsed enthusiastically by everyone involved, and some pieces are retrieved, some mourned later; others remain contentious. So, how to decide what remains and what goes to whom? What happens when you leave home, or move house, when the big family house is auctioned; the elderly relative moves into a smaller unit, a nursing home?

Old kitchen tables and scrubbed wooden chairs have that wholesome feel, and bring back to me the hustle and bustle of family life.

Large pieces of impersonal furniture may find their way into the hands of dealers in antique and second-hand shops; other pieces are recycled through charities or trash and treasure markets; some go to the tip. It is the favourite and portable pieces that are kept. They recall other places, other people. Taking such pieces from one home to another is not unlike bringing a loved toy on holidays. It is a link to the security of home.

Of all the possible portable pieces, certain special chairs have long histories. There is great comfort in having the chair of a favourite relative in your home, one that is worn in the shape of a familiar body, or one known as 'Gran's chair', its cushions and footrest still ready for her. The imprint of her fingers in the wooden arm is faintly visible, or perhaps the fabric picked where she stuck pins while sewing. Looking at the chair reminds you of her presence. It was her territory, and the times spent in it a special memory of peaceful moments in her busy routine - a time, maybe, to snuggle up and read a book. Vinyl chairs and functional steel may be easy to clean, but they do not give off the same smell, or memories.

Pip McManus is in the process of re-making her house, opening work areas to the light and shading places of retreat. Her workshop, a converted garage, brims with tools, ceramics, poster designs, sketches. The house is filled with art and craft work - some local Aboriginal work, some collected in her travels in the Middle East and South-East Asia. Tapestries, pottery, fabric, it's all there. One chair entwines her Perth childhood to her travels and her interest in design.

```
PATSY
1918-
  |
PIP MCMANUS
1952-
```

On my mother's side, from her father and her brothers, the family had an interest in a number of Perth hotels. I remember when I was thirteen or fourteen, when one of them was sold. There were old chairs, scrubbed wooden chairs around the old table in the kitchen. We used to sit up properly at the dining table, and afterwards we would go to the kitchen and talk to the cook.

When the old Claremont Hotel was sold, one of the things my mother wanted was the old wooden chairs. They went to her new house, and only a few months ago, when I was back in Perth, I asked for this one. I'd painted it a vile orange in the sixties. I'd highlighted all the carvings in brown, or something. Then, I bought this heat-pressure Nefertiti design seat cover in Egypt. I wanted the chair to put the cover on to match. I've stripped it back now, and it's no longer orange. My brothers have the other chairs, so they date back a long time, those chairs. They go back to the family and the hotel context in the 1920s.

Doreen Monro has chairs from her great-grandmother that belong to an era long gone. The folding slipper chair arrived in Australia in the 1860s and has been passed to Patti, her daughter-in-law. The original cane seat, broken when Patti's son sat in it, can no longer be replaced. Its future is nonetheless of interest. In Patti's opinion, it probably should pass back to the Monro line, to Doreen's daughter, because, as she says, 'They're more in the family than me.'

The other chair, still with Doreen Monro, is a cane picnic chair. It belongs to that time when people had large picnics by the river, great events when people, food and paraphernalia were piled on a lorry and driven to the picnic site. Although both the slipper chair and picnic chair are part of history for the Monro family, childhood memories of Goondiwindi, Queensland, before the first world war, are of a similarly stylish, if at times daring, social life, when women worked inside, the men outside, of paid help, and rural prosperity.

On returning home from boarding school in Brisbane in 1921, Doreen, like many of her peers, helped her mother or, on extended visits to neighbouring properties, joined in the social life. There was a well-established etiquette about visiting cards and the integration of newcomers to Goondiwindi.

We did a lot of entertaining. Tennis parties were our main entertainment. Mother would ask friends over on tennis days. They could sit and watch us play and didn't have to sit upstairs. We always had players for tennis. We all had courts. We'd play, have a swim, tea on the lawn and then on to a party, an evening around the piano or perhaps a dance at the School of Arts hall. We'd walk over there in our old shoes and then change into the good ones.

Some of the derring-do has been captured in a photograph of the boys on the top girder of the bridge over the Macintyre River. It is a snapshot that Doreen was warned not to show her mother on any account.

We'd dive in, swim down with the current, run back along the bank and dive in again. Neither mother nor father worried about us doing that. Dad taught us to swim early. We went for a lot of picnics.

Such outings are no more. Work is now mixed: women do jobs that were strictly out of bounds in their youth. The chairs, photographs and writing are the only reminders.

Unlike the forebears of Mrs Monro, with their long-standing association to Queensland, Jane Lloyd has moved many times. Her parents now live in Millicent, South Australia, and it is only recently that some of the furniture and books, in particular, have joined Jane in Alice Springs. Some pieces she chose to move, others were given to her. Having bought a house, having put down roots, she was seen as worthy of holding family treasures. One item she has kept with her all the time is her little cane chair.

It's something I like to have around because it is a mark of a past era of my life.

I kept the chair with me because it was easy to move, and in different places it had different cushions, and that made me feel it was home. I think it was a present from my mother's sister, Ethel. It grew up with me as a kid. It was always in my room. It's something I like to have around because it is a mark of a past era of my life. I have this larger one I purchased in Adelaide as a bit of furniture. It looks similar, doesn't it? Maybe I've progressed to a big chair. I've now given a cane chair to Jessie, the daughter of my friend Isobel. It was a present for her first birthday.

It's not only the chairs we cling to and re-claim but also the kitchen table and the activities and conversation around it. Women had sat around the table to exchange news: men had entered their domain with caution, dismissed the time as 'gossip'. In the galley kitchens of the 1950s and 1960s, the woman became a worker. In the dining room, where the meal was served, she became the hostess. In the bigger new homes, the family room was an all-purpose space in between the large kitchen and dining room. But it was an area where everyone could sit. Women had lost the space that was theirs. With the changes in the design of Australian houses after the second world war, the kitchen, as an area of social activity, all but disappeared. Many women, consciously and unconsciously, have devoted energy to re-making this area: it was where news of 'hatched, matched and dispatched' was exchanged, where women assessed relationships and planned events; the indoor equivalent of magging over the back fence.

Where the table and chairs are not moved, for whatever reason - whether because of distance, quality of the furniture, house style - the idea is often re-worked and the setting recreated. Pat Giles's Perth kitchen is dominated by a table that reminds her of her mother's.

Mother had a kitchen table which everyone lived around, sewed on, worked on, scratched on. So, early in my married life, I suppose, I looked to replace it, and I bought this table for seven pounds ten shillings. It's Australian oak and, even before it was done up, it was really pretty. It was this nice goldy colour. I bought the chairs separately. They were very cheap. And this sideboard still has to be done.

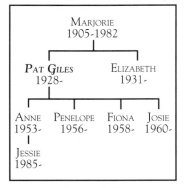

Mother's furniture went to live with my sister, Elizabeth, who is in Adelaide. She had it restored and treasures Mother's furniture. I suppose this table is my compensation for that. We've never really gone in for precious pieces that you polish and don't use. I admire beautifully decorated houses where everything matches. The best we've been able to do so far is this kitchen.

In another family, where precious furniture abounds, a portrait connects one woman to a great-grandmother on her father's side. *I know about her because we have a portrait of her at the age of sixteen, just before she was married.*

Her hair is down, so we know she wasn't married, or it would have been pinned up. It was in 1850. It's something my mother is very fond of, and so am I. It's no relation of mother's, but it is my great-grandmother, and I think it's the first thing I'd save if the house were on fire. I love it. It's a really charming portrait. It should be my sister's; she's older.

Candlesticks, lamps, vases, clocks, all small, all have an association with a particular activity in the home. *Usually I value things for their beauty and interest rather than general family associations, but some have special associations with people I liked. One of these items was a very noisy and inaccurate eighteenth-century table clock, which came to me from Aunt Nan. It is always referred to simply as 'Aunt Nan'. We'd say, 'Aunt Nan lost forty-five minutes yesterday.'*

On the mantelpiece, alongside family wedding photos and the holy symbols, stand the candlesticks. *As children, we'd clean them, and it was then that stories of the family were told. When I set up flat in England, miles from home, the first item I bought was candlesticks. Once they were on the mantel, I felt I was in my home.*

When we went to bed, we went with a candle.

Candle glow is soft, reminiscent of gentle moments. *I used to brush mother's hair and she'd brush mine in front of the fire, and you only had a gas lamp over the fireplace and a candle to go to bed with.*

Some brass candlesticks, like plaster ducks, were promptly given away once the owner died. There was no mantel to put them on, they were tedious to clean, and they were morbid outdated monsters.

As kids we had a small paraffin lamp burning beside the bed. We had electricity, but the glow was gentle like a candle. Katie Wilkes remembers a time when the only light came from candles. She has kept her mother's candlestick holder.

When we went to bed, we went with a candle. After Mum died, Dad was lonely. Well, I understood long before I was a widow, I realized that he wanted to hear a voice in the night. He had a light over his bed. He'd come and wake me at three o'clock in the morning and he'd say, 'What's the time?' and I'd say, 'Oh, Dad.' I was only young, but I realize now that he'd be awake, because I'm a widow now, and I understand that need to hear a voice in the night.

---
*'If you can only get possession of the tools and a
supply of nails, you can be independent.'*

One of the pieces of furniture that seems to have disappeared from women's bedrooms is the blouse cabinet. Made of fruit boxes held in place by a wooden frame, it functioned as a rather rickety chest of drawers. Once painted and decorated with chintz or cotton cretonne, it helped to brighten the bedroom. A piece of dowel across a corner of the room, with masking curtain, provided hanging space. Matching designs or contrasting colours in cheap cotton could transform an ordinary table into a glamorous dressing table. With stiff cotton pleated around the edge, just as the newspaper was pleated around the kitchen benches, it marked out a space as women's, made visible her presence, labour and thrift.

In the bedroom, a shawl draped over a lamp splintered the harsh light into fine shifting shadows; in the kitchen a newspaper skirt above the naked globe softened the glare. The paper stayed there until it yellowed. It was replaced about as often as the fly paper, also attached to the light. The shawl changed with season and mood.

In the 1894 *Australian Enquiry Book,* by Mrs Lance Rawson, there are hints on how to beautify the home: 'There is an old saying that a cook will make dinner out of nothing; it might be truly said of some housewives that they can beautify their homes from the same mysterious source.' She advises her readers that there really is no reason why a woman should not use a hammer as well as a man: 'If you can only get possession of the tools and a supply of nails, you can be independent.' There are instructions on the use of boxes and kerosene tins which, with the addition of cotton-frilled valances, become personal and attractive additions. She recognizes some limitations in women, but encourages them to see themselves as capable of the work.

Some bedroom furniture, especially the dressing table and small chest of drawers, is often coveted by younger women. Before the mirror on the dressing table Nanna sat to comb and braid her hair; little boxes of make-up and jewellery spilled over. Megan Dorrough spent a great deal of time with her grandmother and was anxious to have her dressing table when the furniture was sorted out after her Gran's death. Cheryl, her older sister by ten years, was in a better position to argue for the table than Megan.

It was so significant to her to have the dressing table. I was determined that if

Megan wanted it she'd get it. I was already working and happy to buy my own things.

The dressing table, bought just before the war, is one of Mimi Taylor's treasures and its future a matter of importance. *When Ruby started working, she bought me a canister set, which I still have in the kitchen. But my pride and joy is the silky oak Duchess dressing table. Ruby bought that when she was eighteen at two shillings and sixpence a week. It cost two pounds and fifteen shillings. It has a lovely big mirror. I wouldn't part with it for anything. It must be worth quite a bit now. I want Ruby to have it when I'm gone.*

Annie Gastin has her grandmother's dresser in Alice Springs. *I think it is a really beautiful piece of furniture. I treasure it. It's been stripped, polished, operated on and fixed up. I didn't seek it out. It was sort of an offering. 'Well, look, there's this old chest of drawers in storage, and it's going to cost a fortune to keep it there. Anyone interested? Would you like to look after it, Annie?' 'Oh, yes, that'd be lovely.'*

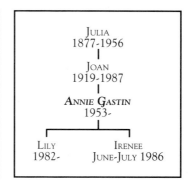

The solid and massive furniture of the old family homes poses quite a different set of problems. *Grandma lived in a big house in Bulimba. There were three bedrooms and a sleep-out as well as a dining room that could be turned into a sleep-out. The Queen Anne rosewood dining table should have come to me, but I left it in the house at Wynnum because I had nowhere else to put it. It's now at the old Court House in Cleveland. My younger brother sold it to them when he re-did the house. He lived in the house after Mum died. It had been willed to him. In Grandma's house, it was kept in the formal lounge room, where no one ever sat. The drapes, burgundy velvet, were always drawn. You only ever saw the little panel of lace in the middle.*

Individual pieces, especially the prizewinning imported chairs, are kept in the family, and their futures hotly debated. They should not pass to another dynasty. But the mid-Victorian cedar dining table, as long as a billiard table, is sold. The wish to hand down such furniture does not appear to extend to re-organizing a house to make room for it. Some pieces have been cut down or re-made - a cedar sideboard becomes a writing table - but many of the big valuable pieces go to museums and dealers; sad but not a disaster.

I would have liked to have inherited more objects that I could remember my forebears by, but it doesn't worry me excessively. It's just as important to me that my children have an awareness and knowledge of my parents and feel that sense of continuity.

*If I see cedar oil anywhere, I immediately think of
Mother... she taught us how to make the wood
come alive.*

We seek out the furniture that we touch frequently, that we were taught to handle and care for. Jo Conway, the seventh of twelve, has books from her grandmother that show where her great-grandmother was born, in Wayford Manor in England. The home stayed in the family for generations. Perhaps this explains Jo's mother's preference for enduring furniture.

My mother taught us an appreciation of fine china, good, well-made, practical furniture. She loved oak and cedar. She always said they had a solidity about them. They would be there for ever, and that's what she liked about them.

She had a great respect for them and said, 'You don't have to be rich and own all those things to have a respect for them and to learn to tell the difference between something good and something that's imitation.' She wasn't keen on imitations. Yet it didn't mean that she had a vast knowledge. It was just something that she had learnt from her parents, and even from what I can remember of her parents. I was very young when they died, but they were definitely like that. They weren't rich people, just ordinary working class.

If I see cedar oil anywhere, I immediately think of Mother and her oil cloth. She taught us how to rub it over and clean it and preserve it; how to make the wood come alive; to feel nice china, good silverware, things like that, but particularly china and furniture.

Louise Moran was also introduced to good furniture and taught an appreciation of fine things by the women in her family. *My grandmother started giving me pieces of furniture on my birthdays, from about the age of eight onwards. She gave pieces to me knowing that I probably wouldn't use them for a long time but, without my realizing I was learning, she taught me about silver and gave me a love of it.*

There's her writing desk, which she kept on using all her life. Every time I open it up, I still have that sense of her smell. It held all the family photographs and other miscellaneous things. She's been dead for nine years, and I've had all my things in it for eight or so years. She gave it to me when I was eight, by telling me that it was mine, but I didn't take possession until after she died.

Many items pass to us for practical reasons. On setting up a new home, and becoming independent, the contents of your bedroom may be transferred. In some families it is a rule: what is in your bedroom is yours to take. In other families, need determines who has what. But mostly subtle choices are made. Is she sufficiently settled to make a home for the dresser? Some annoyance is apparent when a special piece, handed over to be treasured, is not given pride of place. Sometimes it's quite by chance.

When I moved into this house, the house that I now own, I said to my mother, 'I'm going out to buy some brass planter boxes,' and she said, 'Oh, hang on, and I'll go out and have a look in the laundry. I think I've got some of those.' Sure enough, she'd been mixing up the red ochre for the fireplace in these, so I had to clean them all up. I got those, and they were my grandmother's.

The interests of the older generation are echoed in their gifts to the generation that follows. In some cases, it is the books from a library to a woman who has established herself as a scholar; in others, pictures to a painter, or pottery to women who are working with their hands, to the writer, a desk.

The writing desk came with the crystal bottles on the silver swan tray. My mother bought it when she was married, and it was at that table she sat to write letters. There was always the feeling she could have done more in the way of writing. It's still up in Wagga Wagga and, when I began writing, she said, 'That's yours.' I associate my mother's side of the family with writing, but that might be a fabrication in part. I discovered that a poem I'd treasured as written by one of my mother's aunts was in fact merely copied out in her hand.

It is possible to be given small pieces as a favourite daughter, niece, grandchild or friend. But arguing claims for special pieces on the basis of affection from a deceased estate is a different matter.

There was a cabinet made by my maternal grandfather which still houses mother's china. I believed I would treasure it more than my siblings because I am the one who is interested in wood craft and working with my hands. But it will be age and position in the family, reinforced by geographical proximity, that will determine who gets the cabinet. I'm not in a good position because I'm living in the eastern states, and the family home is in Western Australia.

I was away when the home that my grandmother had lived in was broken up. I could recall furniture that was in the dining room, a large room with dressers, settee and table setting. I asked that a small dropside table, dresser and couch be put aside for me, items that I remembered my grandmother telling me had been made for her by her brother during the depression. They've been moved around Australia with me, up and down to Sydney,

Darwin, Canberra, and are now back in Melbourne. The layers of paintwork and fabric in which they have been covered tell of the changes: once the table was painted with a hard enamel, then it was given the antique treatment and later stripped back to the original wood. As with much furniture made early this century, it is made of good Australian timber. Unlike some of the mid nineteenth-century furniture, it was not elaborately carved with motifs of Australian flora and fauna.

From my mother's mother's house I asked for the sewing table, matching bookshelf and small nest of tables. There were other items I would have liked, but I was not part of the process of distribution, which was done by her daughters when they were still in mourning. On reflection, I would have taken the china cabinet. It was the store-house of bits and pieces of her life and travels: her plaster Winston Churchill and cigar, the Dresden china and the Brussels lace doll, the one she had copied for me for my eighth birthday.

Other daughters have shown greater foresight.

The last time I was at home, two years ago, I started making a list of all her possessions of any interest and where they all came from. Not all of them are old, but some of them are of interest to my parents, and I'd like to know where they came from. I hate to think of the knowledge being lost. That something came from my grandmother, or something was a wedding present to my parents, is important. When I'm not around to hear the stories again and again, I'm afraid I might forget. I haven't completely finished the list, but I must, and type it up properly, because it gave my mother pleasure to talk about it, and I'd like to know also.

There're things like furniture which they brought from Ireland. They bought things like a Regency sideboard for twelve pounds, and I remember my father, because it had red worms, squirting Worm-o-Kill into the holes. It's one of my early memories when I was about three years old. There are things that will come to us eventually, but we don't want to take them away from her yet. Occasionally she has fits of cleaning the house out. But no, in fact, she's very fond of her possessions.

The poor piano had a rough time.

Mum and Dad were advised that it would be difficult to replace much of their furniture in Australia so they brought the piano, their brass bed and horsehair mattress, which they were proud of using. They didn't believe in soft kapok or feather beds. They were unhealthy. I think we even brought dressing tables. I know they found we brought more than we needed to, and the freight was more than we could have replaced them with. Not the piano, probably.

Every girl learnt to play the piano, and every middle-class family in England had one, but we were probably lower middle class.

The poor piano had a rough time. It was left out on the verandah (in its piano case with the front taken off so it could be played) in the hot afternoon sun for all the first summer. I don't know why we couldn't get it inside, because eventually we did and had it across the corner of the dining room ever after, with plenty of room. It got terribly out of tune outside. At last a travelling piano tuner came around, and I'll never forget how strange and beautiful it sounded after it was tuned.

| Louisa Anne |
| 1876-1974 |
| Madge Cope |
| 1904- |

We had some good musical evenings at first, with some of the builders who were working with the Midland Railway Company building houses as part of the 'Ready Made Farm Scheme'. Two of them were quite good singers, a tenor and a baritone. Then, later, there were often commercial travellers who stopped for a meal, and if Dad or Mother took a liking to them, they were invited to stay the evening. If they were musical, we had music; if not, there were always discussions or debate of some sort. Although we children were always sent to bed at 8 p.m., we could hear through the thin wooden walls and found some of the discussions very interesting. I remember the religious ones.

This story was recounted by Madge Cope in December 1979 when, to set down her memories of her family, she began a history called 'The Rookes in Australia'. It traces the family's early life in England and its experiences in Australia after arriving there in 1915 when she was eleven.

It was not only to England that the settlers looked for symbols of civilization, status and sociality. Katie Wilke's father had been working on contract in Chile for several years and brought back a pianola.

It was a great thing for us when he brought this great pianola on the boat. I had it for years, and he hadn't died, but I had to get rid of it. I got this piano, and that nearly killed him because it had been in the family all those years. I'd shifted about eight times with the fire brigade, and I couldn't lift the thing, it was so big. The old fellow nearly died when he came to do it for the second time. He said, 'This job again.' We had a good social life and, when the piano was going, we'd pull the carpets up and dance. Dad loved that, you know. Oh, yes, he loved all that.

Pianos deteriorated with moving and in the harsh Australian climate. *One of the things my mother did pass onto me was the organ. She used to play it in church, and it was a great treasure. I've shifted around so much, however, and it has become so battered, that, to my ever lasting shame, I got rid of it.*

In Jennifer Doust's family the piano remained where it was landed. *It belongs to my grandmother, who was born in 1910, and is still alive. But she lives in Queensland, and it wouldn't survive the heat, so it's still in Western*

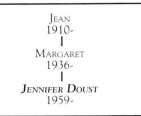

Australia. It's with my parents, and it's unsettled where it will go. It's quite a nice piano. It came to my home after me, so it's not the one that I learnt on.

Another family made the necessary concessions to the dry conditions. *We left our best furniture in Sydney because the climate was too harsh on good antique furniture from England where we live in north Queensland. The only good thing we took out to the country was the piano. We kept two large jars inside the piano and a water plant on top to counter the dryness.*

For some, an evening around the piano was a way of keeping alive the folk music of the country from which they had emigrated. Elaine Aikins' has memories of such times.

All the Lewis clan would congregate at our home and talk in Welsh, and I can remember being sung to in Welsh by my favourite Aunt Catherine, who had had a sad romance and didn't ever marry but lived for the nieces and nephews, and there were plenty at that time. We had great nights around the piano and always played table tennis - what fun.

For others, the piano provided opportunities to meet people their own age. Mrs Mac looked back to this time as one of simple, innocent pleasures. *It was 1916, and Mum wasn't too well, but I could go out with friends where we would all sing around the piano and then have supper. This may sound dull to you, but we were happy in those days and never really missed much.*

Daphne Campbell has her mother's music. *Oh, her music. I'm really pleased to have it, because she learnt singing and, in fact, three in the family, my father and my older brother, would sing. I still sit and play some of those, when I'm nostalgic. Some of the ones she used to play herself, and some she used to sing, I'll play them. Actually, I could have had her piano, but I already had one. It was bought by my father for my mother when I was born. It was a gift for producing a daughter after two sons.*

Lillian Lloyd's mother could sing and play. *We didn't have a piano, but anywhere we went you'd have this feeling of pride because she could sit down and play, and she didn't even read music. We did have a little organ, and my eldest brother used to sit underneath and work the pedals. They were like bellows. Father would stand up and sing; he sang quite nicely. I have these really happy memories of mother and father singing together. It was pieces like 'All things bright and beautiful', not pops or anything. But I do remember there was a record about Amy Johnson, and my mother got it. 'Amy Johnson up in the sky, Amy Johnson flying high.' I can remember her playing it over and over again.*

Some of the stories of piano-playing did not fit in with our view of older

Paula Cristoffanini, Subiaco, Western Australia

Pip McManus, Alice Springs, Northern Territory

Mary-Louise O'Callaghan, Manuka, Canberra

Amirah Inglis with Louise Inglis, Kate Inglis, Deborah Turner and Judy Turner, Northcote, Victoria

relatives as staid. *When grandma died, mother was sent away to be reared by her father's younger sister who ran a guest-house just outside Melbourne. Aunt was seen as a woman of strong character who could rear the children and provide for them an education which would have been impossible in the small town in which they were living. There were stories of her playing the piano and singing for the guests. We thought her to be very strict, and she told the kids that Santa Claus wouldn't come if they were making noise around the piano and disturbing the guests.*

The church, gatherings at a guest-house, and the evening around the piano on a family occasion were ways in which children were introduced to music, and from an early age were made familiar with sheet music, the piano and the care of this prized piece of family property. Learning to play the piano was another thing. Some children were taught by parents, but mostly it was a matter of finding someone outside the home to teach theory and then having the time to practise. Daphne Nash recalls.

I wanted to learn the piano, but it was difficult to find someone to teach me. At lunch-time, and sometimes after school, I would go to the convent to be taught by Sister Mary Michael and Sister Mary Peter. When I was in grade three, I was caned with the rung of a chair for being late. My teacher said I had to decide whether I wanted a career in school or music. Both my parents regretted not having learnt and were determined that I should have the opportunities. My father's mother was musical, and she thought it was important I practise when I visited after school, as long as I had packed the biscuits into the tin first. Practising always reminds me of broken biscuits.

Patricia Richards has her mother's piano. *After she died, and my father decided to sell the house, well, the other grandchildren, they had a piano in their home, and we didn't. By giving it to me, it was a means of having you taught, really. He thought that she would have wanted my children, that's you, Michaela and Rowan, to learn. So I've got her piano.*

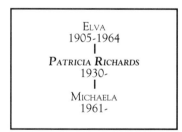

ELVA
1905-1964
|
PATRICIA RICHARDS
1930-
|
MICHAELA
1961-

Not all pianos were passed on as planned or promised. Susan Magarey remembers. *One of the great treats of Sunday visits to the houses of both sets of grandparents was being able to bang away on the pianos they had. At my paternal grandparents' house, the piano was an upright, kept in the sitting room. I remember my own frustration at not be able to make music on it, only noise, and the grown-ups begging us to go outside and play, or do anything as long as we stopped making that racket. When I began lessons in piano playing, when I was eight, I first went to that house and that piano to practise. That arrangement, being beyond the reach of supervision, was quickly deemed unsatisfactory. We needed a piano at home.*

Apparently my mother [Mary] expected to be given her mother's baby grand piano so, until arrangements about that could be made, we hired a piano for us all to practise on. By the time that all four of us were needing to practise, time on the piano had to be severely regimented, and started at 7.30 a.m. By the time that I was fifteen, it had become clear that the baby grand was going to stay where it was, at least for the foreseeable future, and my parents bought a very beautiful upright. This piano moved to a smaller house. Then it went to my brother and, since he was the only sibling who had children at the time, it has remained there. My mother did, eventually, inherit the baby grand, I think at the time my maternal grandfather died and my grandmother moved into a smaller house. But now there is nobody to play it, where it is.

As soon as I was old enough, I was playing the organ at church.

To learn you needed to have a piano nearby. If you had one at home, it was possible to practise more often. Pat Giles remembers that when her mother went back to live at her parents' home it meant resuming contact with contemporaries, Jean Drummond and Marjorie Hartley, who had a love of music.

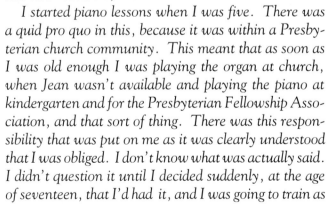

Jean earned her living by playing the piano; Marjorie taught singing. Their contribution to my education and that of my sister was through their skills. Jean taught us to play the piano, and my sister went on to make a career of music education. She's really a very talented musician, too.

I started piano lessons when I was five. There was a quid pro quo in this, because it was within a Presbyterian church community. This meant that as soon as I was old enough I was playing the organ at church, when Jean wasn't available and playing the piano at kindergarten and for the Presbyterian Fellowship Association, and that sort of thing. There was this responsibility that was put on me as it was clearly understood that I was obliged. I don't know what was actually said. I didn't question it until I decided suddenly, at the age of seventeen, that I'd had it, and I was going to train as a nurse. They were both wonderful women, and Marjorie gave my mother singing lessons, and Mother had quite a nice voice. Then, of course, there was the business of being in the choir, and so forth. Those two were unmarried women. Now this was 1928, the year I was born, so these were women who were suffering from the shortages of males in the late 1920s.

Now the youngest of my daughters is making a career out of singing, Josephine, and they're all quite musical in many ways. Penny loves to play. We have three pianos between the five of us, rather, the six of us. That's something we couldn't do without. I mean, it's the reason we couldn't live in a flat. Yes, there is a strong feeling towards music. I don't know to what degree one inherits the capacity for it. I think if you're in a house where there's music from the time you're very small, it becomes part of your life: learning to read music and learning to read your language are happening about the same time, so you tend to take it for granted.

Well, Elizabeth and I had our piano lessons, and I started learning at the age of five and, when my sister turned three, I started teaching her. The first time she performed in public was as my student. I was six, and she was three, and Miss Drummond started teaching her. She really is very talented.

When we set up the house here after I married, I had this upright piano that my husband bought for me, very generously, at the time when we had little money to spend. Then, as the children all started learning to play the piano, and then five of them having piano lessons, we really did need two pianos. I had the opportunity to buy a small grand, and we lived in a big house in Bassendean at the time, and there was room. So, we put the little grand in there. When we moved here, there was only room for one piano in this house. Our baby grand got lent to all sorts of people. It lived with Michele Kosky for quite a while when the children were learning, and I think she learnt to play the piano on it too. It was in four or five different places and then, most recently, with Josephine, when she was living here in Perth.

Then she decided to go to Adelaide and either have to sell it or find another home. At that stage, my dear Aunt Jean, my father's younger sister, had moved to the Sundowner, which is an Anglican home not far from here. She is an extremely talented pianist even at the age of seventy-eight, seventy-nine. She was the youngest daughter of the manse and taught herself to play the piano and, at the age of fourteen, was learning Mendelssohn's 'Songs Without Words', and that sort of thing. She was really brilliant as a pianist and then ran away at the age of seventeen to get married to a farmer. Anyway, she was without a piano down there and had been very sick. She recovered remarkably and just loved the thought of having a piano there for her. So, at that stage, we decided to spend the money on doing it up. Anne and Jean between them had it done up, so that's where it is at the moment. We couldn't bear the thought of selling it, not that it's such a wonderful piano; it's a very pretty piece of furniture in a lovely walnut case. But Jean's having the time of her life, and Penny, who's just now completed her law degree and has been living with me in Canberra while she's studying at A.N.U., will be back in Perth, and she said to Jean last week she could have some lessons, and Jean was thrilled. So Penny will be going there for piano lessons.

Musical evenings with the family provided a rich environment for Annie

Gastin. There were six in Mum's family, and six or seven in Dad's. Mum's side were very musical, and we had these wonderful musical evenings. Sunday night at the Hillmans' was always sort of scones and cold roast and sing-songs around the piano, and all that stuff. Bring your friends home, that was part of our thing. They could all sing - harmonies - six parts. That emphasis on music did bridge the gap.

As a teenager, I decided to become a rock-and-roll singer. I puddled around with the guitar, and my brothers did wonderful three-part harmonies with Seekers songs and gospel stuff. I started with a band called Ready Rubbed. I changed to blues and jazz. I wanted to sing ballads, vehicles for my voice, slow torchy songs.

Learning to play the piano was an accomplishment of a lady, an entrée to different social worlds, as well as a way in which you could earn some extra money. There were even moves to have the piano protected as a tool of the trade like the sewing machine was.

At the turn of the century, the Australian population was less than four million, but there was about one piano for every six people. Little wonder we find many stories of buying and moving pianos; of the problems of dealing with them in the heat and dust; of the trials of learning to play and of pleasant evenings around the piano. The historian Humphrey McQueen, in A New Britannia, has made sure that pianos have a well-defined place in Australian history, but little has been written of women's role as the owners and players of them. Pianos that may have been a gift to a wife became hers to give to the next generation. They are also the largest objects over which women have such control, and it is a responsibility they have taken seriously.

CHAPTER SEVEN

DARYL GOT THE FARM AND MUM GOT THE PEARLS

I don't remember Mum wearing a lot of jewellery but, in photos of her when she was young, she has pieces that match the outfit. I have a necklace from her, but she only wore it when the need arose. It had been brought over from Malaya by her father. Mum always said it was mine, but before my younger brother was married, I had him and his bride-to-be over for dinner. We made a deal and split the jewellery. She took what she would wear, and I kept the rest. I still have most of it because she didn't want it.

In Marguerite Newlove's family, there were expectations about who wore particular pieces of jewellery. There's the gold brooch with a diamond in the centre and a little safety chain. It's about an inch and a half long. Mum got it from her mother. So far, it's been worn by three brides. My sister-in-law has it, and I won't take it back until my own daughters are married. I don't know if my mother's sisters ever wore it, but they were all given a little bracelet by Gran. I have my mother's, and I think the eldest girl in the other two families has hers. I have Mum's wedding rings, which have gone through two brides. When Dad's first wife died, he kept her rings, and when Mum and Dad

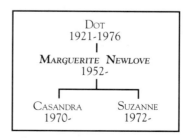

were engaged, the old engagement ring was put over the wedding ring to form a new band.

I've given some of the pieces to my girls. There's a little cameo ring that fits the little finger, which has gone to my eldest. None of it is necessarily worth anything as far as money is concerned, but I don't intend to throw it or give it away. It should stay in the family.

Marguerite's account of the past and futures of the pieces she has from her female relatives is echoed in the stories of others. A remarkable range of small pieces of our mother's or grandmother's jewellery survives, and the way it passes between generations has its own logic. Certain rings, strings of pearls, and brooches bearing a first name or initial have predictable histories, celebrate particular occasions.

The anguish over the piece that is lost, or passes out of the female line into the hands of a grasping in-law, is not about money value. It is about the sentiments, sense of self and all others who have held the piece. We ask, 'If I pass it on to her, will it stay in the family, go to someone who appreciates its significance, or end up discarded? Is she worthy to hold this?'

I don't want it, I don't even like it, but I couldn't tell her that.

Small items of jewellery evoke strong emotions, and discussions about them tell us about the nature of relationships between generations of women. One commented: 'Much of my grandmother's jewellery is still with my mother. She doesn't wear it but shows it to me and says that this will go to you.' Women who disclaim any interest in jewellery or declare that they are not sentimental bower birds still seem to have a brooch, ring, necklace or an intimate item of jewellery from their mothers and grandmothers. *I don't want it, I don't even like it, but I couldn't tell her that. It would be like denying her the right to relate to me.*

Even if families are poor, if there is somebody in the family to whom the piece should or could be given, it is unlikely to be sold. *The ring must have been worth thousands by the time I remember asking my aunt why she didn't sell it. She was really hard up, always scratching for rent and things. But it was all she had of her mother's, and I don't think she ever thought of it as a way of raising money for everyday things.*

Pieces of jewellery form links to the older generation, keeping histories alive and bringing into focus experiences not known to those wearing them. Elizabeth Durack still wears the prayer-holder brooch of turquoise she has from her mother. Inside is the story of the brooch as told by her mother.

For my dear Bet - February 1910. When on our honeymoon in India, we visited Darjeeling at the foot of the Himalayas. On the lapel of my suit, I wore a bright blue enamel swastika. Quite a number were worn at that time and supposed to be lucky. A number of Tibetan women were among the crowd, and one very big woman came close to me and pointed excitedly at the swastika. She gave me to understand that she'd give me this brass turquoise prayer-holder she was wearing around her neck on a cord if I would give her my swastika! This I was only too pleased to do; the swastika was evidently their lucky symbol. I little knew that it was to become the Nazi emblem and hated so much during Hitler's regime.

Some of the jewellery is kept but not worn; not every woman longs to wear the jewellery of her female forebears, and not all jewellery has survived. Sally White, now in her seventies, spoke of her mother's mother's jewellery.

She wore black all the time. She was always in mourning and wore jet jewellery. When she died at eighty-eight, a whole box of it went to my mother, who gave it away.

Some jewellery goes out fashion, is too fragile, beyond repair; some of it is a burden because of its value, but it is always worth worrying about. Years, decades pass, and a comment about 'that little locket of hers' is a spark that can re-kindle bitter disputes. The passion of these arguments lies partly in the understanding, never really made explicit, of the responsibilities of the person who 'holds' such objects. We never 'own' the pieces, merely hold them in trust for the next generation.

Rings, especially engagement rings, pass from grandmother to grand-daughter by way of the mother. Here a particularly interesting set of relationships between mothers and daughters, grand-daughters and grandmothers is set up. A photograph often cherished by the grand-daughter is that of grandmother, hands loose in her lap, displaying the ring that the grand-daughter now wears. Unlike larger dress rings, or jewellery considered to be for a 'mature woman', engagement rings were fine and delicate, intimate jewellery that evokes romance and hope.

The impending marriage of a grand-daughter calls to mind that earlier period of innocence. She, like her grandmother in the photographs, is portrayed as the young virgin. The grand-daughter can bring to life again this age of innocence in a way that the mother, as the holder of the ring, cannot.

To her falls the responsibility of protecting the morals of the bride-to-be, and the engagement ring is an indication that girlhood is ended. The ring binds the grandmother to grand-daughter in a conspiracy against the mother. She is passed over but is the one who must care for the ring. The mother cannot bestow her ring on her daughter because that would invalidate the marriage of which the daughter is a product.

Other rings may be transformed into wedding rings. If the soft gold wedding-band has worn down, the wider keeper ring, the one placed last on the finger to hold the wedding and engagement ring in place, may substitute, as may an eternity ring. *When I was married, my mother gave me her mother's diamond eternity ring. I took it from her when I moved out of the house.*

The original source of the ring may not be in your mother's line, but once it is there, it stays and continues down the generations. *When my mother-in-law was going into a nursing home, she gave me her engagement ring. It had two large diamonds in it, and I told her when I was an old lady I'd give each of my daughters one of those diamonds. I was thrilled because I knew how much she treasured it.*

The one gift my mother really wanted from me was a girl grandchild.

The eldest daughter is in a favoured position to receive the special pieces. The daughter who does not reproduce is likely to be passed by. Not having a daughter for whom she may hold the items in trust, she is not a worthy holder of the rings or the pearls; she will not come into her heritage.

I was very upset when I realized that the one gift my mother really wanted from me was the one I had never given her, a grandchild, and preferably a girl grandchild. My mother always expected that I would have a baby, someone to whom the pearls that she would give me could be passed on. I was annoyed and hurt when I found out that she had given the pearls to my niece and not to me. I probably would have given them to her in the long run, anyway. Instead, I was not consulted after Mum's death, and they were given directly through my brother to his daughter, and I missed out on holding them altogether. It wasn't just the pearls, it was the fact that without a daughter of my own I was not recognized as the legitimate holder of something valued by the family.

To ask about jewellery while your grandmother is still alive may be embarrassing, but the pieces may be the only link with the grandparent's generation. If you wait for a suitable occasion, it may never come.

I think jewellery in our family is not given until you're older, or maybe it's for really special occasions, like when we get married. We are not big on jewellery. Some of my grandmother's stuff has gone to Mum and her sister, but my grandmother only died two, three years ago, so that's still to come down. It's a generation off. Mum's younger sister gave me a jade ring when she came back from one of her trips. She also gave me some blue crystal beads from my grandmother. But no major pieces as yet have been passed on. My mother was given jewellery from an aunt, her mother's sister, when she got married, and I'm sure that will be passed on to me. Now my mother is waiting for me to get married for it to be passed on to me.

The occasion on which jewellery passes to the next or the grandchild's generation is not left to chance. Particular gifts are considered appropriate for the engagement, wedding, first child, or birthday. In many societies, the transition from girl to woman is celebrated at first menstruation and is highly ritualized. In some parts of Australia, Aboriginal girls were decorated by female kin and proudly paraded through the camp. Among the Tiwi of Melville and Bathurst Island, the girl received a special gift of a new name to mark the change; she was no longer *alinga*, a young girl, but *muringaleta*. She was now ready to be a wife.

Although there are no parallels in today's Anglo-Australian culture, young girls are given items of jewellery that are part of the adult female world to show their increased maturity. Those who did not live up to the expectations of the new responsibility remember the anguish. Isobel Skoczek had such an experience.

There was lots of jewellery that Dad gave Mum while they were in India: bracelets and coral necklaces. There is one that was really significant to her. There are some gold bracelets, originally there were eighteen, fine, thin gold, which Dad was buying Mum over a period of time. At some stage in Australia, Mum would give odd ones away to people who had children who were close friends. There were only three left, and a jeweller friend of mine soldered them together, so now there's just three. They're very lovely, delicate Indian gold. I must have been thirteen or fourteen when she gave them to me. It was on a birthday. I guess she thought I was old enough not to lose them because I did lose a lovely heart necklace. I remember the trauma of it. She gave it to me, and I went running to show a friend who lived around the corner and, by the time I got there, I'd lost it. It was terrible. I looked for weeks and never found it.

Girls were likely to be given a watch or pearls after the age of fifteen. A string of pearls would hold its value, was ladylike, virginal, not showy, and could be worn before a girl was allowed to wear make-up.

Pearls are no longer as popular as they were for earlier generations. Pearls as a twenty-first birthday present were given to the generation born during World War II. By the time young women turned twenty-one in the 1960s, Australia was affluent, and parents could afford to give a string of pearls to their daughter. Those who were married when they turned twenty-one looked to their husbands for the pearls. Some of those turning twenty-one in the seventies and eighties, however, found the gift of pearls repulsive.

Dad gave me pearls for my twenty-first birthday, and I was horrified. It took me fifteen years to wear them. I'm not fond of jewellery, and I don't wear it much, but I'm changing on that.

> *My grandmother bought it just because she liked it. It's flawed, just of sentimental value.*

Like engagement, the twenty-first birthday was an occasion for which pearls, a watch, or a piece of grandmother's jewellery was appropriate.

It's an emerald, but it's not a good one. My grandmother bought it just because she liked it. It's flawed; it's not a clear one, so it's not of any value, just sentimental value, but I'm fond of it. I don't wear it very much now because I'm doing things which make it difficult for me to wear jewellery. But it's very important to me. She gave it to me because she knew it would mean more to me than something she bought just for the occasion, and she knew I loved the ring. She wore it often, so it meant a lot to her, and I've appreciated it very much.

A number of women of the generation who turned twenty-one during the war received pearls from their fiancés. These women were given gold watches for their twenty-firsts rather than pearls, which came from their husbands-to-be, or they waited to inherit them. This contrasts markedly with later generations who received a watch when they were younger and could afford their own disposable digital ones.

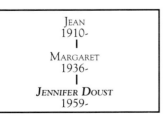

JEAN
1910-
|
MARGARET
1936-
|
JENNIFER DOUST
1959-

One of my twenty-first birthday presents was a string of pearls from my uncle. The pearls had belonged to his mother and had been given to her on her twenty-first. I was not supposed to receive them till I was married. I asked for them for my twenty-first because marriage was likely to be a long time in the future. The pearls had been split into three from a three-strand pearl necklace. One strand went to my sister, one to my mother and one to me. This was in 1970.

Traditionally a groom presented the bridesmaids with a gift to be worn at the wedding. These were often pearls, if the groom could afford them. Those women who did not receive pearls for their twenty-first or as gifts from husbands or grooms had to wait to inherit pearls from their mothers, grandmothers or sometimes from mothers-in-law without daughters, on the understanding that they were held in trust for the daughter in the next generation.

She's wearing the pearls. The photograph is on her dressing table, and obviously it's the image of herself and Dad she loved most.

In the meantime, there is always the possibility of borrowing from a female relative.

I do not own a string of pearls, but Mum has a beautiful string and loves them and wears them. I imagine that at some stage there'll be a dispute between us sisters, because both of us have worn them. We've borrowed them from Mum to wear on particular occasions. I think Dad gave them to her before they were married, but I can't really be sure of that. They're certainly there in the photograph that's taken of her at the time of her engagement. She's wearing the pearls. She has on this rather lovely dress of a beautiful hand-embroidered lavender silk with a sweetheart neckline. She's looking absolutely beautiful standing beside my father looking tall and handsome in uniform. You can see why there was this sort of romantic stuff. That photograph is on her dressing table. It's always been on her dressing table, and obviously it's the image of herself and Dad that she most loved.

Like other valuable and valued pieces, pearls may also pass up the line. Sally White was given a string by Linda, a woman who stands in a daughter-like relationship to her. The gift of jewellery may mark a period of transition or be used to form a link at a time of emotional upset.

She gave me her mother's pearls last year when I was going through a difficult passage in my marriage. I was going to Sydney for an extended period, and she gave them to me before I left.

Not all jewellery follows the path mapped out for it. I have a locket in which my mother has put the photograph of her that my father carried through North Africa during the war and one of her mother as a girl. They're both romantic, whimsical images. The locket was supposed to pass to the eldest of each generation on her twenty-first. My mother's older sister was given it on her twenty-first birthday, but it wasn't until I asked my mother about presents that it came to light. I now have a year before it passes to my daughter. She has other things from my grandmother, so I think I'll hold the locket a little longer.

In many families, there was no particularly valuable jewellery to worry about.

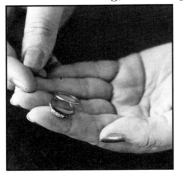

When my parents were engaged, my father couldn't afford a diamond engagement ring, so he bought her a sapphire ring. It wasn't considered to be a very expensive ring, and he did say, at one stage, when he had more money, he would buy her something more expensive. But the children came along quick smart, and that was the end of that. It was the only jewellery she had. I don't think there was any other. We haven't been a jewellery-oriented family, really. In fact, she used to say to me that lots of rings on fingers make them look older.

Some old jewellery presents another problem because it is fragile or difficult to repair. From my mother's mother I have a little late-Victorian jewellery. There's a ruby ring surrounded by seed pearls. It was given to her by her mother on her seventeenth birthday, and she gave it to me on mine. It's broken, so I don't wear it, and the jeweller has declined to fix it. I'm going to have it re-made. I decided that I won't give it to my daughter on her seventeenth, because I'm not having any children. I'll give it to my niece. That is my brother's daughter.

My mother-in-law always thought of me as the daughter she wanted and made it clear that it was me that she wanted to hold the family items.

By giving a special piece to a daughter-in-law, a woman may give her the role of a daughter, so overcoming the drawback of not having one.

My husband's parents were divorced and had only sons. My husband was the eldest, and the only one married to someone 'acceptable'. My mother-in-law always thought of me as the daughter she wanted and made it clear that it was me that she wanted to hold the family items from the English side. The last time I was there, she gave me several pieces of very valuable Victorian period jewellery. I felt embarrassed about receiving it because it was not the sort of thing I would wear, but I realized that it was important for her to give it and for me to agree to take care of it. It was as if I held it in trust for her children's children.

The pieces were far more valuable than anything she could have afforded on a low wage with a big family in England. It turned out it had belonged to one of her mother's sisters who had never married and who had travelled a lot in her youth. There seems to have been some scandal attached to it along the lines of it being an unsuitable gift from men friends of this spinster aunt. The details have been suppressed. It's strange that these gifts, which were seen as improper for a single woman to receive became a valued family gift to be transferred to the only 'legitimate' daughter two generations later.

Jewellery may also be used to establish 'family-like' relationships. *I have a cameo brooch which I wear all the time. It came to me from my father's girlfriend. It was somebody he knew in Ireland before he was married to my mother. She never married, but when he left Ireland they stayed in touch. I have visited her, and I now have it. I think of her as part of my family and enjoy keeping in touch with her.*

> Great-grandfather had been prone to stray, and he usually brought a gift as a peace offering when he came home.

Jewellery has the power to evoke other lives and other worlds. Items of jewellery brought back from the travels of one's grandparents suggest that their lives have not been as staid and conservative as the grandchildren imagined. It may also represent an episode that becomes acceptable as time passes.

Some of the jewellery which she gave me belonged to my mother and grandmother. One that I really treasure is a brooch that's been made from a ring. It's gold, and it has these five tiny diamonds in it, which belonged to her grandmother. I had thought that it was an engagement ring, but when Mother was really quite old, one day, she said to me, 'No, that's not so.' Great-grandfather had been prone to stray, and he usually brought a gift as a peace offering when he came home. This was one of those gifts. So, it is a great deal more interesting than an engagement ring.

The Australian gambling tradition can be seen in women's jewellery. Some pieces celebrate a husband's win on the horses; others may be sold to pay gambling debts. *I have a brooch and earrings from my mother who died in 1920 of cancer. They were given to her after a win at the races of forty pounds. There was a diamond and emerald earring, but I lost one. I gave my daughter the greenstone earrings, and she is having them made into a ring for her granddaughter's twenty-first.*

I always remember there was a gorgeous gold watch with blue enamel around it, and she said that it was mine, and she would have it fixed, and I could have it. I never got it. I really did want it, because I was most attracted to it. But my uncles, I think they were probably gamblers and drinkers, and I'm sure she sold the jewellery to pay their debts. I don't think there would have been much of my grandmother's to give in the end.

Emmeline Lahey has an engraved brooch to celebrate a Melbourne Cup win by Chester in 1877. The brooch, made five years later, bears the date 1882. *My Great-great-uncle James, son of the shepherd James White, had it made up for his wife. It was gold in the shape of horseshoes, with three rows of pearls set in. It was made up for his wife, Emily Elizabeth. They had no children so concentrated on their racehorses. They owned two Melbourne Cup winners and others.*

Lena Kay had the prize from a 'bracelet race'. *It was a beautiful bracelet, but I lost it. My father owned racehorses and, in those days, the prize would be so much money, five pound, or whatever it was, and a bracelet. They used to have bracelet races where they only had bracelets. I had an amethyst one, bigger than a watch, and it must have been when we were shifting at one stage, I lost it. Whether it was stolen, or not, I don't know.*

My sister Edna has the ring. It was a ruby ring. You know, they used to have little settings in them. Not a big stone but just like ruby and pearl. I think Edna had that ring, and my other sister, Ruby, I think she had a bracelet. I don't remember which bracelet it was. Mine was the one with the silver amethyst stone in it. It was gold around the amethyst. I don't have any other jewellery.

The need to recreate, re-work, find substitutes and repair the cherished items is strong. But it is more important to mark the relationship than worry about the actual object. *Mother had a pair of tiny plain pearl earrings which she gave me. I had no idea of what their intrinsic value was, but when I lost one, I was really quite distressed. My daughter took the remaining one to the jeweller to get matched. She discovered they were virtually worthless, but then my other daughter bought me a beautiful pair of pearl earrings, which I treasure.*

Jo Conway, in her late teens, lost her mother's watch. *My mother couldn't wear a watch because it went haywire on her. So it just sat in a watchcase and, at one stage in my life, I was saying about not having a watch, and in those days my job really needed a watch. She said, 'Look, wear this, but do be careful with it.' I said, 'Oh, like a safe.' She said, 'Well, it's just silly sitting there not doing anything.' It had been given to her by my father when my brother was born, I think. It was a lovely gold watch, gold band, and all the works. I was very proud to wear that but, oh, dear, I used to keep company with a lad in teachers' college. Besides being a trainee teacher at this time, he was also an ornithologist. We spent much of our time stalking birds and photographing birds and studying wildlife and, on one occasion, when we were crawling through the undergrowth, I realized part-way through that the watch was missing. It was a dreadful thing to do.*

It took me twelve months to try to get the courage to tell Mother. I went through agony. I knew that the lad I was keeping company with was going to give me a watch for my twenty-first, and I knew I had to tell Mother about the loss of her watch. Eventually I took the plunge and told her all in one breath. She said, 'Oh, dear me, you silly child. You should have told me when that happened instead of putting yourself through such agony.' I said it was an accident, and she said she was very sad about it, and that she couldn't blame me at all because it was an accident.

Some losses were more poignant than others. *She lost her wedding ring the day after she was married while swimming. She was told that she couldn't sleep with her husband. Her mother's mother told my sister about the first night of her wedding, but Mum wouldn't tell her. The ring was replaced by a cheap one, but it was a source of constant humiliation.*

Certainly much jewellery is women's business, but lines blur with objects like watches. Although once it was clear what was men's and what women's jewellery, there are now some interesting variations. Elspeth Young wears the silver chain of her grandfather's watch as a necklace; another has the twin fob-watch chain, which came from her mother's father. *I liked it, and no one else wanted it. He said I could have it. I'm not interested in the silver bracelet from my mother and my step-mother - the sisters can get those - I got the pieces I was interested in.*

Louise Moran has her great-grandmother's hunter watch. *Her husband didn't approve of ladies wearing jewellery, and her children got together and bought her a hunter watch, over his opposition. I have that on a chain. I wear it with great pleasure and often think about its purchase whenever I wear it.*

'Things beginning with ...'

I had a lovely bracelet made of gold and New Zealand greenstone, which was my grandmother's. I've taken the charm off the bracelet and use it as an earring. I don't know where the bracelet part is, any more. It is a little gold envelope with a tiny seed pearl set in the corner. You can open the flap of the envelope and inside is a gold letter with my grandmother's name, Lena, engraved. It was given to my aunt by my grandmother. I was really thrilled that she decided to give it to me and a bit embarrassed because I didn't know whether she was showing it to me or giving it to me. It reminds me that she came from New Zealand.

PATSY 1918-
|
PIP MCMANUS 1952-

This is the voice of craftswoman and traveller, Pip McManus.

We both have names with 'E'. Mum's first name was Ethel, and my middle name is Edna, not one I'd use, because it's so dated, but from Mum I have two pretty little brooches, a porcupine quill jewel case and an ebony 'E' for sealing letters with wax.

This item is held by the generation who still remember when letters were sealed with wax. When it passes to the next generation, however, as did the New Zealand brooch with the Lena stamp, it may be transformed. And in this case the next generations do not have names beginning with 'E'.

The 'Jessie' brooch that has a gold star with pearls belonged to Muriel Armstrong's mother.

It came to my mother who was a Jessie, from her mother, who was also Jessie. Mum gave it to my daughter, Elizabeth, in 1933 when she was born. She would have liked to have been a Jessie, but now her daughter Louisa has decided to put Jessie in her name, so I guess it will go to her. I've never had it. I'd rather gather wildflowers, or make arrangements with twigs.

In another family, a brooch with the letter 'E' was held by the member of the family whose name began with that letter. *I have my grandmother's name and have all the things with 'E' on them, like pieces of jewellery. The wife of my Great-great-uncle James was Emily Elizabeth, another 'E'.*

A first name or initial on a piece of jewellery allows it to pass from mother to daughter without concern about changes of surname at marriage. It is not necessary to cite a 'maiden' name to make the link. The jewellery passes from mother to daughter without alerting others to its history. It is possible to dismiss the histories of these small pieces as trivial and thus deny the significance of the links they establish across generations. But underneath the individual transactions are remnants of the dowry system whereby a woman brought her portion to a marriage. In the last hundred and fifty years, this has weakened as more women have had to rely on romantic marriage to provide once they establish an independent household.

Small pieces were considered a woman's property; they belonged to her body and were not subject to formal rules of inheritance. Little wonder you hear, 'Daryl got the farm and Mum got the pearls.' Pieces of women's personal jewellery were far from equal in value to the real estate that sons could expect from the family estate. Nonetheless, rules did govern the movements of small objects, and breaches were viewed with displeasure. Indeed, rifts over the disposal of these personal items can divide families.

There was trouble over where some of her things went. She'd always said it was mine, but I wasn't there when her stuff was sorted out, and one of the cousins took it.

Marguerite Newlove with her daughters Suzanne Newlove and Casandra Newlove, Rochedale Queensland

Grace Sanders with her daughter Eileen Cronin and grand-daughter Jody Cronin, Alice Springs, Northern Territory

Daryl Got the Farm and Mum Got the Pearls

The watch that Lucy Hanrahan gave to her grand-daughter Becci White

Susan Andrew's teapot, given to her by her aunt

Until special laws were passed in the 1890s, a woman's property became her husband's when she married. She could make no binding rules about where it went after her death; her husband had the right to dispose of it as he wished. Only by remaining single or holding property as the beneficiary of a trust could a woman retain control over property. A father who left property to a daughter was, in effect, leaving it to her husband's line. Personal intimate property was not the subject of special laws of inheritance, and it is particularly interesting that its passage is from grandmother to grand-daughter. It skips the generation that could allow it to move into a new line of inheritance, the husband's, and from there down to sons and daughters-in-law.

Expensive formal jewellery, which is bought to be displayed on special occasions, demands a different set of considerations. It is hedged in by different rules from those pieces that are intimately associated with a woman, worn regularly and her property. The formal jewellery is never really owned by the woman; she only holds it. The pieces must remain within her family's estate. She has no automatic right to pass it to her daughters. If it is engraved, it bears the family name, not just the familiar first name.

If he'd given me a piano, but jewellery - a thousand dollars on a piece. I'd rather a violin, or a piano. He'd always said, 'You won't sell it.' I regarded it as insurance. It's in a safety box. I can't afford to insure it out of the bank. Ten thousand dollars on a brooch. It was bought for me specially, when the second book was launched. He gave me a sapphire ring for the first book. I think he really wanted to give it to his mistress.

He wanted me to dress with style. He gave me objects rather than money. He wanted me to be a different kind of person. He always gave myself, my sister and mother very expensive jewellery as a sign of affection, or as a way of marking some special occasion. It was always his choice, and much of it remains in the bank vault. I wore it on several occasions when Father was alive.

Family jewels such as these are an obligation, binding the holder to the family of the giver. If they were given to a potential daughter-in-law, and the marriage was not consummated, or dissolved, the items had to be retrieved. There is a feeling that the jewellery should and quite likely will be returned to the vault. When such jewellery is given to an in-law, certain undertakings are implicit. *I was given a piece by an Englishman, and although he had his mother's permission to give it to me, my mother was horrified. What if we were to break up? We did.*

GENERATIONS

I value the shell picked up on the beach at Cundalee, not the jewellery.

Some of the women expressed a dislike for old jewellery and its associations with the past. Younger generations of women placed less value on inherited jewellery and more on the modern dress jewellery of which they could afford to buy a number of pieces. Others objected to the connotations of a conspicuous display of wealth generated by a husband or father and displayed through wife or daughter. As one woman said: 'I'd rather have wildflowers. I value the shell picked up on the beach at Cundalee, not the jewellery.'

Of the pieces valued, the strongest ties were to pieces not necessarily worth much, but important as a link to female relatives: a cameo brooch that is now a ring, a little jewellery box, a set of blue crystal beads. It's just too horrible to think of jewellery that belongs in the family being lost or going to the wrong person.

Familiar pieces of pottery, like teapots, move comfortably from mother to daughter. The teapot was always near the stove, but the dinner set was carefully stacked in the buffet. The more formal dining sets, the valuable china, the silver, the serving dishes remain in the estate and pass through the male line. The best china and silver go to the senior son and his wife; the second son and wife get the next in value. Although a daughter-in-law may be named as the recipient, she holds the items on the understanding that they will pass to her sons' wives. If the settings bear a family crest, they are tied firmly to the estate.

These arrangements are left over from the time when the responsibility for providing for a woman passed from father to husband at marriage. The sons retained interests in the property, the eldest being favoured to inherit the estate. As Lillian Lloyd recounts it, only by not marrying could a woman retain a claim on her parents' property.

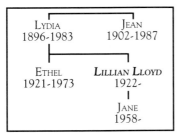

When you got married, you were given some things like a vase or china. The eldest son was left the property and, of course, Dad's brother got the farm. It was sort of ritualized under the Irish system. They weren't too keen on having daughters, and it was important that everything stayed with the family name. If you didn't carry on the name, then you weren't treated with any respect. Now, Mum gave my older sister, who never married, a lot of ornaments and china and linen, things I'd consider family heirlooms. All those possessions belonged to a Payne, and she was the daughter who carried the name of Payne.

144

When she died, she left all those things to the Paynes, so it stayed with family. The tradition was carried on, even though we were now living in Australia.

Within this system, mothers had a call on the services of unmarried daughters. *I always felt that by getting married I was sort of excluded. I didn't have words with my mother very often, but I did on this occasion. I said, 'You'd be happier if I had not married,' and she said, 'Yes, you were born to look after me and your father!' Then when my children were grown up, she said, 'All right, now you can come home and look after me!' What did she think my husband was going to do, chase himself? She was only doing what was done to her. It upset her all her life that all Grandma's possessions went to the sons' wives, and Mother got nothing.*

The bits I have that I've given to my daughter, I got when I'd been married maybe five or six years. I was visiting my mother and said I'd like something for my daughter. She gave me a plaque, which had been a wedding present. What I do have is a tea set from my father's mother's side and a necklace that mother wore when she was married, then I wore it. Before Mum died, she gave it to me for my daughter when she got married.

The good china was only used rarely... it's not the same as the teapot Grandma used every day.

Some china, the mug that fits snugly into the palm of the hand, the Beatrix Potter egg cup, the chipped pottery teapot, is personal. On the bench above the kitchen sink stands a range of sizes and types, a little teapot for the first cup in bed in the morning, a larger one for lunch, one for the camomile, one for the big leaf teas.

There are associations, feelings and values which attach to all of them. It's about the ups and downs of everyday life, but the good china was only used rarely, on special occasions. I continue to feel strongly about it because it focuses attention on the family, but it's not the same as the teapot Grandma used every day.

Penny Peel's recollections of her Gran: *Tea! That woman could drink tea! She said, 'I like coffee, but coffee doesn't like me.' She'd have her first pot when she rose, another with breakfast, one mid-morning, then it would be tea with lunch. There was another pot mid-afternoon, one at dinner, and her pot before bed made seven for the day.*

The pot used for meals was a two-handled pourer, enamel, but her own one was brown pottery, a six-cup pot. It must have been from when she was a young bride. Mum has it, and my sister says it's hers. She thought of it, and that's why she thinks she can claim it. As long as she leaves me the sewing machine, I'll concede the teapot.

In Daphne Campbell's kitchen, there's a little china tea service in the form of dogs. *The teapot is a dog with his paws up begging, and the tea comes out of his little paws. The milk comes out of the smaller dog's mouth and, with the sugar holder, the whole head lifts off the little dog. Then there are cups and saucers to*

match. I played with that as a child, and it's still intact. If my daughter has a daughter, it will go to her; if she doesn't, then I don't know. It will probably end up with my eldest son's wife.

Ann McGrath, not a person who sees herself as particularly domestic, has a hand-painted Royal Doulton teapot. *It has a cute little house and tree behind it and in Gaelic is written, 'Please pass the cream.' It's so quaint and domestic, but I don't use it. It's too good, and I might break it.*

The intimate connection between women and pots is more striking than that between women and the pieces of silver and coffee pots that have survived as family heirlooms. *When I was overseas last year, I picked up a few broken ceramic pieces from old Roman village sites in Egypt and Aswan and a few pieces of Nabatean pottery from Petra. I brought them back and gave them to my aunt who was very tickled and, as a return gift, made me this pot. The patterning was inspired by the pieces I'd given her.*

My one little daughter-in-law is so interested in the meaning of family links.

Once a piece comes into the line from mother to daughter, it is possible for it to continue through the mother's line. A daughter of rural Queensland, born in 1931: *A Royal Norfolk tea set from my father's mother went to my mother, who gave it to me, and I will give it to my older daughter. She knew her forebears and loved being part of this chain and loves china. The Royal Winton tea set was a wedding present, and it will go to the younger daughter, who loves it. My son will also have some of these things, and I really believe the male line of our family should have and needs the continuity of possessions as well. I feel, though, there is a different way of looking at what boys will have. Their wives' attitudes and feelings about things perhaps have to be considered. I'm not sure how to go about it. My one little daughter-in-law is so interested in the meaning of family links.*

I've tried to make it understood to my children that the things that are given to me by parents and grandparents have special significance because of the people rather than the monetary value. Because we have never had an abundance of material wealth, everything we did was done because it was important, and it didn't matter whether a gift was very small or very large or how much it cost. The point was that the people who gave it wanted you to have it.

The large dinner sets, the Wedgewood and Doulton, perhaps nineteenth-century wedding presents from England, are rarely still intact. Like the large properties to which they belonged, they have been split up. The loss of a few pieces of a set makes it possible to give a serving dish to one grandchild and the sugar and cream set to another.

Noticing the break-up, daughters may plead with mothers to keep the set together, to prevent items being scattered through the family. Mothers are prepared to intervene on a daughter's behalf to see that there is a fair division.

Mum has been wonderful in keeping an eye open and saying, 'Look, I think Jane should have this,' because in a sense so much went to the male cousins, and my mother was very resentful of that. The male cousins have done bugger all and don't appreciate things. She stepped in. They've got things like my grandmother's old fridge and electrical things. I prefer the china, books and rugs.

The notion of the 'good china' persists, but it is not the elaborate dinner sets of our mothers and grandmothers. It is not often that one has a meal that requires a matching dinner set for twenty, with gravy boat and serving dishes. In part, this reflects increased mobility and the problem of moving such valuable and fragile pieces around Australia. But anniversaries, too, are no longer marked with formal sit-down family meals as often as they were. *I can remember the times I've used her dining set in the last twenty years. I'm so afraid of breaking pieces, and they can't be replaced because that design isn't made any more.*

Women born before 1930 are likely to have large dinner sets: those born later than 1930 have the pieces of sets.

The tea sets of cups, saucers and bread and butter plates, made of similar designs or on a theme echoed in different colours on each setting, could be divided between the daughters and granddaughters. Many women worked out who would get each piece of china and made it known in their lifetimes. *We used to put a note on the dresser, or write our name under the vase or plate, or whatever, if we wanted it. Grandma said it was too much for her to remember, but she kept a sort of balance sheet in her head, and we only presumed to label something as ours if she'd already given a signal to that effect.*

*When we were getting married, everyone chucked
in for the dinner set.*

Getting together the basics for the establishment of a separate home was a task for which women budgeted; their mothers gave advice and help. It began with birthday presents, like saucepans for the seventeenth. These all formed part of the glory box or 'bottom drawer'.

I think Mum gave me a canteen of cutlery which she had on the lay-by at Edments. I can't be sure. I remember the year was 1939, and we were aware of the things happenings in Europe, and things were not quite normal. 'Peace in our time' was well and truly running out. When I left Brooklands where I was working and where my husband-to-be was also working, we were given a dinner set. I remember everyone chucked in for it, but the management must have added to it, because it was quite an expensive one.

I had a beautiful piece of china on the lay-by for some time. I had seen it on display at Buckley's in Melbourne during one of my lunch-times. It cost sixty pounds, and I paid it off at ten shillings a week. My wages were nineteen and sixpence a week. It was just as well my mother supplied the sheets and other essentials. I was interested in the beautiful items. I remember once I paid three pounds for a pair of shoes, and my mother-in-law was horrified. She thought it so extravagant.

Patricia Richards recalls that her mother helped her with the basics like tea-towels and linen. *The first thing she gave me ever was a little jug; it was the little green one with a flower on the handle. I don't know why it must be a jug, just tradition. I think I gave my daughter a jug from Cuppacumbalong. Mum would say things like, 'Don't pay any board next week, and you can go and buy that, or put it towards something, a piece of music, or something like that.'*

Teapots, familiar routines, the bits and pieces of life shared by women and passed on to other women. *In Nar's kitchen, the teapot sat on the table most of the day and, when there was time, you could prop the book against the teapot and read, mainly magazines; it was a relaxation. It was possible to deal with an article, not a book. They'd cycle through the family and friends.*

There was some white china with a little pattern around the edge. They were Johnson and Johnson's, I think. It's an English china, not a good china. It was just everyday things that you used. The egg cup, you could feel the texture around the edge. There was something else in that dresser that had a texture; it wasn't all smooth china, it was ridged. All the things had a special feel about them. You could feel the tension on the little handle, and inside the dresser there were the egg cups with the ridges on them. They all stood together, all those things, and seemed to fit together: the sewing machine, the dresser, the china, and even that blue cake plate that Edna, my sister, has.

From the migrant and refugee families we heard 'life started here'. Parents did not want to talk about life in Eastern Europe or in Asia and had few records, just some photographs. Piecing together the stories of the lives of one's forebears was not easy. Sometimes a trip home stimulated the memory, sometimes a dying parent spoke of events long suppressed, or an object unlocked memories, provoked speculation.

Myriam Bonazzi was not a refugee; she came here by choice and talks willingly of her life in Australia. But her story is not unusual.

I came here with education and a little work experience from Italy thirty-one years ago. For me, happiness is the most important thing. Our family lost everything in the moves of the border; three times. I've always wanted to help others by facilitating the re-building of lives. The only thing that remains from my mother's side of the family is a dinner plate, which I still have in my cabinet. It came from her mother. It's oval, about fifteen inches by seven, slightly cracked, edged in gold, and it has three fish on it. I had not really thought about it until now, but I've always been collecting fish, and that is the symbol on the plate. I have a great collection of fish: coral, pewter, glass, wood, from all around the world, which has been brought and sent to me. Perhaps the connection is because our family comes from an island in Yugoslavia.

My grandmother is always with me in spirit because we were so close in temperament. She saw personal belongings as giving continuity to our relationship. She worked hard but lost everything.

I was able to tell her things I couldn't tell my mother. It was hard to develop that closeness. She just didn't have the time. She was a tailoress, worked hard and made a go of it. I would like my daughter to have the same feeling for me as I had for my grandmother. I don't want to lead her life for her, but we've always been close.

The relationship between women and pieces of pottery is one that Sue Bellamy has thought hard about. She asks of those who buy her work to consider the future home of the pot.

I like to think that they'll stay with women. I overheard a friend who was buying one of my pieces say, 'This is my first heirloom.' In my mind I heard 'airloom', a weaving together of space over time like a net. I visit my pots in other people's homes. I'm not just making things that don't matter to me. My work is a form of communication, and clay lasts.

Chapter Eight

THE TELLING THINGS

The photographs of us with the family are the 'telling things'. There's all the family around a billy fire or burning down in the gully. There are hundreds with horses, dogs and cats, all in black and white.

Treasured photographs through which links are sought and asserted often enjoy pride of place on the mantelpiece or bedside table, more personal sentimental pieces in the wallet, locket or diary. An occasion such as an anniversary, the preparation of a family history, a reunion, going away to school, travelling, or just leaving home may prompt the putting together of an album.

Like a walk around the garden and a cup of tea, leafing through the album is part of visiting, part of being in a family. The photographs are part of growing up within the web of family and friends. It seems that women order the albums, using them to control the past and impose some order. How many times have we listened to that same story, looked at photographs of times long gone, of grandma as a schoolgirl? This is when a prospective daughter-in-law is incorporated in her new family. She may be shown the embarrassing pictures of her fiancé, and a bond between the generations of women is forged.

The photographs prove we're happy, married.

When my sister was getting married, she was prepared to participate in a romantic white wedding, and I was drawn in as a bridesmaid and had to wear a pink dress. They all thought I looked lovely and said so. Now, instead of the Holy Family, we have the white wedding in a gilt frame on the mantel. It's replicating Mum and Dad. All the photos prove we're happy, married, and that we're particular sorts of people. I'm seen as unsuccessful because I'm not in a long-term relationship and, if I am, I'm wrong, because I'm not planning marriage.

Joyce Caddie: *I have a copy of my mother's wedding photo. It shows a striking aristocratic Scots woman, five foot, seven inches, with red hair. My brother tells me that on winter nights, her long red hair flying, she'd have us skipping around the house to keep warm. In her later years, she grew into a matronly woman, not heavy or big. Some say I'm growing more like my mother. That pleases me. She was a wonderful person.*

| FLORA JOYCE |
| 1898-1972 |
| \| |
| JOY CADDIE |
| 1932- |
| \| |
| JULIA JOY |
| 1955- |
| \| |
| BONNIE JOY |
| 1980- |

Lena Kay: *There were five of us, and I was the youngest. One brother died at three of meningitis. We had a photo of him and, when Mum walked into the room, her eyes would fill with tears. She went out to the cemetery at least once a week.*

I can see myself in her eyes, like a mirror.

Michaela Richard's grandmother died when she was four. *She stuns me. I have strong feelings of my origins when I look at her photo. It's part of history, and I'm fascinated. There is a strong link but, yet, they're of another world, and I can see myself in her eyes, like a mirror; that's part of the attraction. I was close to her when I was little, and we looked alike, so maybe there is a collapsing of images, but it's more psychological than material, because she died when I was four. My mother keeps that memory alive. But I feel I have a relationship with my grandmother which is independent of my mother. What I have from my mother is a sense of my grandmother's presence.*

Jane Lloyd: *There are times when I feel like 'images' or photographs of my mother when she was about thirty years of age. There is one particular photograph taken of my mother at a party in England where she is looking very pensive.*

Jean Mateer, born in Ballarat in 1906, is the only surviving member of her generation. *We went to school at Pleasant Street. Twenty-four girls in our class were in a cantata, and all wore spangled frocks. My mother made my sister's and mine. We were six and seven then. A photograph was taken of us all by Richards and Company. The photographers wanted one of my sister Irene and myself for his window display. When he finished, Mr Richards gave the large photo in a heavy wooden frame to mother. I have the photo now in my living room. I also have the little frock.*

Identifying time and place and keeping alive the special time are essential tasks in compiling albums. Mum reasons, 'If Jack was wearing that jumper, which I knitted when I was at home with you the winter you had measles, then it must be 1953.' The album is an opportunity to order relations, honour friends and family. It's not hard to know who's the favourite grandchild, but it is hard to find out what has been lost or suppressed.

Through the search for photographs and documentation in boxes, desks, and trunks, contacts with distant or estranged family members are made and renewed, lives are put in order, stories are re-told to another generation. Pat Giles and her daughter Anne spread the family album on the kitchen table. Anne's small daughter, Jessie, born in 1985, recognized herself and pointed to her photograph in the album.

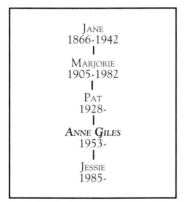

Anne: I think what prompted me was one of my aunts was putting together an album for my father's mother's eightieth birthday, and she'd wanted to include all sides of the family, so she asked for a picture of my brother, Tim. I got to searching our photos for it. I'm glad I have it because it now provides a record for people like my daughter, Jessie. The photographs were just stuck in an old tin, and I didn't want them getting lost, so I put them all together. There were photos of our family, us children, too - there were lots of those - so I picked the best ones and kept those.

My mother had kept every letter I'd written her when I went away from home... I hadn't put on the year.

Pat Giles: *When my mother died, I started looking through her collection of photos, which included some very old ones of her grandparents. I discovered there were no dates, no documentation. My mother had kept every letter I'd written her when I went away from home to go nursing at the age of seventeen and a half. I did write fairly frequently and, although I dated the letters, I hadn't put on the year. It just hadn't occurred to me at that time that it would be necessary. Those letters are in my sister's cellar in her big house in Adelaide now. She has an enormous amount of store-room underneath.*

Most of my grandma's papers are still there waiting to be sorted through. My mother was born in 1905, and I don't think the papers include anything at all about her mother, apart from letters and postcards and photographs of her two sons who were killed during the first world war. As I got older, I realized the significance of the photographs of her sons, who were killed in France, and I used to sneak a look at them every now and then. I don't ever remember discussing them with my mother or with her.

Katie Wilkes had wondered where the photograph of her mother had gone. *I found that Margaret was preparing the family tree, and there was a lovely photo of my mother. She was beautiful, really, although she'd had a hard life through sickness. Too many children, having children, you know, they had children, about ten or twelve of them. She died from pneumonia in the end, but she was very ill all the same. She died of a broken heart, my brother used to say. She hated it in Australia. She was dragged out here away from everyone she knew. She was a real ladylike type and used to say, 'Don't worry about what people say. While they're talking about you, they're not talking about anyone else.' And she used to say, 'Learn how to dance, don't be like your mother. You'll always be left out while your husband's enjoying it.' We used to go to Scottish dances when each family would turn up, and she always had to sit out through the dances. She was only forty-seven when she died. I'm seventy-three now, and I'm pretty good and full of energy.*

Like the cane picnic chair, photographs recall a time and style long past. *The family picnic was a very important form of entertainment. We have photos of large groups of all ages. There are ones of my parents before their wedding, at the wedding, of the house they built, of all its stages, their first car. We used to pore over them as children. I will pass these on to my children along with the portraits of my mother's grandparents.*

Doreen Monro was born in the first decade of the twentieth century in Goondiwindi. As a young wife, with a baby and toddler, she moved to the Gulf country. *Supplies were shipped in around Cape York to Burketown and then overland to the station. They would come with a twenty horse-drawn wagon; later by truck. The photographs of station life at Lawn Hill in the Gulf country of Queensland were passed on to my daughter. Friends don't believe my only childhood playmates were Aboriginal. There are photos of the wagon bringing in the supplies.*

It is not only photographs that provide personal records of the past. Patti Monro's family also kept postcards. *Mum began collecting them, and they date back to 1917. I have Peter Pan in Kensington Garden, and the like. We both have albums and have been able to date the cards. There are some programmes to the ballet and theatre. Whenever Mum would get an appointment for the dentist in the city, she'd try for a time when a show was on. We went to good concerts and theatre that way. We still take each other to concerts.*

Jane Lloyd's postcards, sent to her as a girl, are stored in the trunk with her fabrics. *There's one from my aunt of a girl dressed in a regional folk costume sent from Russia in 1970. It says, 'Dear Jane, This is a very interesting country, and I'm in Leningrad, which the Germans held siege for 900 days during the last war.... See you all at Christmas.'* An interesting card to send to an eleven-year-old.

The collection of photographs made by Marguerite Newloves's grandmother was extensive. *We had photographs going back to before the first world war. I have some, and a couple of cousins have some. We tried to split them up between the families so if anything happened to any particular family, the photos wouldn't be lost. There are only about four we can't identify, and they're on tin plate. There are two with cardboard backing, and we can't read the studio imprint to trace them.*

It's a way of reconstructing history, of learning, of reflecting on special moments.

Elspeth Young found another solution to the problem of loss and distribution. She copied the precious items and now has many of the family photographs in Australia.

Before I left Scotland, we sat down and went through them. They are a source of knowledge for my sister Jean's kids. We used them to trace and locate families. Mother used it as a history to tell us who they all were. The photographs provide highlights and are what is remembered. It's a way of reconstructing history, of learning, of reflecting on special moments.

Pip McManus was aware that memory may be faulty but was sure of the sense of style and personality in photographs of long-gone relatives. *There's a picture of my aunt, an aunt of my mother's, in a Victorian costume with her hair piled up on top. She's sitting in an old cane chair on one of those beautifully lace-work wrought-iron filigree balconies at a hotel. It's hard, I just remember the story but (I mean, I might get some of this wrong because you remember stories very strangely) it mightn't necessarily be the right photo, and it mightn't be the right aunt, but that's what I associate it with.*

This one is my grandfather with this enormous satin tie and stiff collar. My mother was very fond of her father, but a little bit frightened of her mother, I think. She was a very fine-looking woman but quite a severe Victorian lady. She was quite old when she had my mother, and I don't think she was really able to cope with having a young woman in those times. It was the changing times that she used to worry about. My mother always said her mother would die if she was alive today because she used to worry about the problems of the world constantly.

Photographs provide a way of weaving past and present, of moving memories. *A few years ago, when I was in Perth, I went through and took a whole lot, and so I've got my own collection here in Alice Springs. Most of the photos were in my mother's house. She has heaps of old books of family photos in those long, thin, black photo albums, where they fall out with the corners and the tracing paper bit in between.*

There are photographs of my mother as a schoolgirl and in the snow in Europe in her debutante dress. The one that sticks in my mind, in particular, it's one of the older ones, is on the verandah of a hotel which one of my brothers had. As a child we used to go there every Wednesday night for dinner. Mum had a part share in it, and it was our education about eating out. We would get a free meal, and we had to learn how to sit at the table properly and eat properly, with all the proper silver. I used to like going there. I used to chatter madly because I was quite young. My brothers used to say, 'Why don't you hit her?' It was nice being able to go to the hotels. I thought it was special, and during the summer holidays there was another hotel on the beach which we used to stay at sometimes. We could go into the kitchens and into the bars, and that was something really special.

The photographs record another important part of Pip's life: cats. *I have always had long dynasties of cats. There's never been a day in my life where I didn't have two or three cats and, to me, I'm never happy anywhere, unless I've got cats around me. So that's part of the family and the album. My mother grew up with dogs too, but she always had cats, and since I was very little, I had pictures here with just cats and cats and cats, all my life.*

Recording families through photographs depends on your interest and skills as a photographer. Bron Stevens commented that there were very few photos of herself and brother as children until Jim, her brother, bought a camera.

I have some lovely ones of my father which I picked up when my mother died. There is one of him in his tropical rig in Egypt and dressed up on his horse in France. I didn't know they existed, and I really value them. I keep them together with the short stories she wrote. There are only a few letters from Mother, and she wasn't really a great letter writer. She didn't go through the photographs very often with us. She wasn't really into photographs, herself.

```
    DIANA
    d:1914
      |
    'PEG'
   1906-1981
      |
  BRON STEVENS
    1946-
```

Penny Peel: *I think my uncle (my mother's brother) has the photos. She would go through them with me, and I remember one with my mother and father at a Christmas party. He is in a cane chair at the back of the house, and she has a hand on his shoulder. He is in a black suit and tie and upright collar. The studio photographs of the men are all in uniform. We kept those together. She had one of a friend of mine who was in the army and had stayed with her. He'd then gone to Vietnam, where he died. She kept the snapshot of him. It's not a studio one in uniform like the others, but one playing with a dog.*

Refugee families came to Australia with little, but they often held on to a few old photographs. Attitudes to those surviving pieces vary. *I felt inhibited to ask about the times before the war. Then I was doing women's studies, and one piece of work was researching a family history. Mum produced photographs of her as a child and of her sisters. We were able to talk then.*

Another whose parents were refugees from Eastern Europe has a photo of her mother and some taken in Warsaw before the war. *My father was forty and Mother was in her thirties when I was born, so all my memories of her are as old, and here she is young. Mother's got the rest of the photographs which survived. It's not many. She has one of father on the dressing table, and it's been there all her life. I don't want it around me.*

There's a really lovely one with natural light... an early one of my mother and father.

Isobel also has a sparse record of the lives of her parents before they arrived in Australia, but she has a purpose in ordering the material.

I put those together as a Christmas present one year. I was eighteen, I put them all in an album. Now, whenever we go to Melbourne, we look in that album,

> MARISYA
> 1912-1975
> |
> ISOBEL SKOCZEK
> 1949-
> |
> 'NAMPIN' JESSICA
> 1985-

and I have shown it to my daughter and to her father. There's a really lovely one with natural light, which is the reason why it stands out. It's an early one of my mother and father, just after they were married. They are sitting together in a corridor with just one beam of light going down on their faces, it's really nice.

All the photographs are at home with Dad, and he is going through them at the moment and writing down the names of people and dates and things significant that he can remember. He also remembers Mum telling stories about some of the photographs. It was really nice to see photographs of Mum as a young woman dressed up in really nice clothes after the war period, which must have been so devastating. It was also seeing another side of my mother as a young woman before she was married, with all her friends. It was a really high and happy time for her after all the sadness. Just her meeting young men again and going out with friends. You can see in the photos that they are all having a really good time, dressing up, and things my mother really liked to do. She took a great pride in her appearance and loved clothes and jewellery. So it was a time when she could follow through on some of those fantasies.

The desire to reconstruct was not shared by all. *The civil war split people and, after the war, it was like this for everyone; family networks were fractured. I mean, I can't trace family because the records are gone, and the people who knew are dead. All you Anglos really get high on this sort of stuff; family and things. But it's not information that's valued.*

---

*I did ask my mother for a wedding photograph.
She tore... Dad out of it.*

Reminders of dear ones can be too painful, the power to call up the presence of a loved relative damaging to the living. In many parts of Australia, Aboriginal people destroy all personal property, especially photographs, when a person dies. For years the name and all reference to that person is oblique for fear of harm to the living. White Australians also destroy photographs but are not so explicit about the reasons.

I had little from my mother, and my memories of the family focus on the fights, conflict and stress. I did ask my mother for a wedding photograph. She tore it in half, or rather, she tore Dad out of it. She cut him out, and Dad showed it to me, and I confronted her with it. She just said, 'Oh, I didn't want him there,' and I said, 'Well, that was a stupid thing to do.' Dad was upset, very upset. I said, 'That was silly, Mum.' I said, 'You don't do those things.' I said, 'They're irreplaceable.' Mum could be very catty, but she's very bitter now because she still brings Dad into arguments, and I'll say, 'But, Mum, Dad's been gone for seven years.' I think she's never really forgiven Dad because she didn't get to see her mother before she died. He didn't come home until late and, by the time they got to her Mum's place, she'd died.

Bushfire, cyclone and flood may destroy records. Jane Lloyd: *I think it was the books and the lost photographs that I grieved for after Cyclone Tracy. We've still got some of them, but the ones of us when we were children, they went. Some of the ones of my mother's girlhood were okay. I tried to re-do my mother's photo album and started putting together ones of my father. I was about fifteen or sixteen. I was really into constructing and putting together their lives and history. My mother's was much more interesting, much more easy, than my father's. It was very hard to find out much about him. Mum's got those albums now. And, yes, there is conflict over who has the photos and who doesn't.*

Lack of interest may account for some loss. Or it may be that constant talk of family becomes an occasion for 'switching off'. Jenny Doust, born in 1959, comes from a well-established and well-documented family. Photographs and information about the Doust side of the family appear in histories of Western and South Australia.

All except one of my great-grandparents was born in Australia. The family books and photographs are important, though ours is not a family for 'passing things down'. I regret how little I know of the family history.

For some, there was literally nothing to be passed on. The rigour with which documentation was pursued was not motivated by curiosity or whimsy; it was a search for self.

My mother [born in 1904] was reared by two sisters, English spinsters. They were my 'grandmothers'. They ran a private school, which I gather was phased out when state education came in. They took in welfare children, twenty-six over the years, and my mother was one of those. They took her out of the orphange in Brisbane when she was three and reared her.

The women who reared her were fine Christian ladies, Plymouth Brethren, actually. They'd educate their charges to sixteen, to be able to stand on their own feet, and then they'd find board with a Christian family. They sent Mum to a business college. The aim was to make her independent. They also had her taught music. They were very old ladies. I still have a photograph of them. Mum stayed in touch. She was very fond of them. Mum was very practical and would say, 'Don't go overboard about anything, not even religion; just keep a balance.'

My mother's great dream was that one day someone from her real family would come and claim her but, of course, they never did. She was a state ward and, at the age of sixteen, they called her in and gave her some information. So she knew her grandmother was a hotelier, and her mother had been a schoolteacher. I have her teaching record from the Education department in Queensland, and she had a year off in 1904 because of her illnesss. I could tell you what the illness was!

Somehow or other one of my father's brothers knew she was a schoolteacher, and one of them got a photograph of her, which I now have. For many years she had this photograph with 'My Mother' written on the back in shorthand. She forgot that I had learned shorthand and could read it. She didn't ever tell me, but I could read it. She's a very strong-looking woman, a sort of Miles Franklin type. We found out more about my grandmother. She had another family, so my mother has half-sisters. We contacted the daughter of one, and she knows, but it's hard to tell someone their mother had another child unbeknownst to them, in this case, seven years before their mother.

Some of the information I got from Dad because Mum wouldn't talk about it. She'd burst into tears and leave the room. My brother told me one night he was singing around the piano:

Vi Cay's collection of wedding photographs, Whetstone Station, Queensland

GENERATIONS

The Telling Things

A family's history on Nina Fletcher's dresser

Isabelle White with her photograph as a flapper, Coolbellup, Western Australia

The Telling Things

*My Father was a Spanish Captain
Went to sea a month ago
First he kissed me, then he left me,
Oh, no, John, no, John, no, John, no.*

Mum jumped off the piano stool and rushed out of the room in tears. He didn't know why, but the story was my mother's name was Spanish for ship, so that might be in the meaning.

Among my mother's belongings I found this poem from The Australian Journal. It says:

*Judge not though clouds of seeming guilt
May dim thy mother's fame
For fate may throw suspicion's shade
Upon the brightest name,
Thou can not tell what hidden chain
Of circumstances may have brought the sad result
That takes an honest name away,
Judge Not.*

Underneath she has written, 'All right, we won't.' It went very deep.

Putting the fragments together, a sketchy image of her mother's family emerged. The need to know was strong. *It was part of my identity to trace her family. It has to do with who I am. My poor husband can't understand it. He thought I was crazy that I would want to know. But it had something to do with me because there was my mother, and nothing, a blank wall, just a couple of cuttings, ones she copied or had been sent to her.*

---

*I kept old family correspondence. I hope my
children will value it.*

The letters written home from school, while travelling, once married, always contained more than news; they were full of feelings and opinions. The S.T.D. phone call home on Sunday, which has replaced the letters written between family members, does not provide the rich record and access to the past. Gone are the days when the family clustered around the radio to hear the news from the front and anxiously awaited letters from loved ones in the war zones. Letters, when they did come, were heavily censored, and the rare photograph of the troops in action that survived is cherished.

I have all the letters written by my Uncle Frank from the trenches during the war

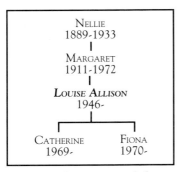

in France to my grandmother, Nellie. I'm torn between depositing them in an archive or keeping them in the hope my children will treasure them, too. I have the photograph books and letters. I want to keep some integrity of family history alive for my daughters. They, however, are quite cynical about it. I hope in time they will come to appreciate why I chose to keep things like the letters. When I was divorced and having to split all the property that I had owned in common with my husband, I re-assessed the importance of material possessions and wanted to retain some documentation for my children.

Muriel Armstrong: *I have every letter written to me from my brother during World War II. I belong to the historical society in Queensland and feel that these documents should be saved. I saved some of the documents from my husband's family as no one else wanted them.*

In some families, the letters have long gone. We sent lard sewn in calico packages to the English relatives. None of their letters telling of conditions in the old country just after the war has survived, but I do remember the emotions engendered by the readings. We'd sit around and Nanna would say, 'Ah, a letter from home.'

Daphne Campbell: *I've been deciphering the letters of my great-great-grandmother, on my father's side, which were written to her daughter about her daughter again, who was my grandmother. In one of the letters she says, 'I'm sorry to hear that little Lizzie isn't strong. Little Lizzie has her babies too quick.' This is my grandmother, and she had ten babies, my father being the youngest, and she lived until she was over eighty, but little Lizzie wasn't strong. Grandmother was one of eleven, and six died at birth. She came out from Northern Ireland in 1887 on a trading ship called the* Scottish Bard. *We've done the family tree, and it goes back to Matthew Stewart, who died in 1827.*

Penny Peel's great-grandmother was determined that she would hear from her family. *She loved to get letters but hated to write. 'Just a line, saying I'm fine, how are you, that will be sufficient,' she'd say. She was known to send a self-addressed envelope and blank sheets to recalcitrant writers. Under her bed she kept letters and photos - some were kept and some not. She had letters from her brother from World War I. When my father died, she gave those letters to her brother's descendants.*

Prolific writers generated a rich resource. *My mother was a great correspondent and wrote to her four surviving sisters every week of the year of our childhood. Their link was strong, and they all spoke of their mother and father with such affection. My mother and her family put great store by family china, pictures and silver being spread among the children. We still have things from my mother's family home, all of my cousins and we three daughters.*

'I have tried to live my life as my beloved mother would have liked me to,' Mabel MacKay wrote to her grandchildren over the Christmas and New Year of 1982-3. At the time, Mabel, born in 1900 in Albert Park, Victoria, just two years after Mimi Taylor, was the last of her generation. She died in 1986. Her letter recalls the exuberant games of a child and playing at being a housewife - a job she declared she still enjoyed, 'except for the venetian blinds'. She describes her apprenticeship, various jobs, court-ship, marriage and family life. 'Don't think I don't understand affairs of the heart. I also was young,' she assured her grand-daughter.

In clearing and sorting, the desire to protect a name and reputation may mean lost letters.

In my aunt's stuff, there's all these wonderful books on Persia and bits of Persian art. When I came back from my trip to the Middle East, I learnt that there had been a beautiful letter from an Iranian man to my aunt. She'd had affair with him, but the letter was destroyed by her sister. She didn't want anyone to read it; too personal. I was so disappointed. I would have loved to have read it and sort of captured something of it and also explained her interest in things Persian.

Another told a similar tale. *I didn't realize until too late that Father had thrown out all Mother's diaries and medals - she was a nurse with the R.A.F. and worked as an air photo plotter - in his anxiety to clear the house of everything to do with her. She'd been an alcoholic for years, and he couldn't cope. So when she died, it all went.*

One generation may feel shame about what another treasures. In certifi-cates of birth, death and marriage, 'facts' are recorded. *I have my great-grandmother's wedding certificate. She eloped with her husband and got married at Gretna Green. What I have is a xerox, but the real one is here with her belongings. The interesting thing about it is they couldn't write, so put x's for their names. But then later he learnt to write because there is a letter saying how he is looking forward to coming to Australia. That was nine years later. He immigrated here in about 1875.*

The faith placed in these records was not always justified. Even 'official' documents could lie. *My grandmother insisted she'd been born a day earlier than the date which appeared on her certificate. The birth had been registered by her father, who had to make a trip into town to complete the formalities. It was some time after the event, and he couldn't remember whether it was the twenty-*

second or twenty-third when his fifth daughter had been born. It was not a mistake his wife would have made. It was Tuesday, the day after washing-day.

Their words have driven me to show education wasn't a waste.

Joyce Caddie's aunt did not mince words. *During one stay with my grandmother and one of her sisters, I saw a letter written by my aunt to one of my family. I can see her words now: 'I don't know why George and Joycie are trying to make ladies out of their daughters. It's just a waste of money.' Their words have driven me to show education wasn't a waste.*

That faith has been vindicated. In 1987 Joyce completed a degree, but getting an education had been a struggle. *To go to high school I had to board with a private family. Mum wasn't happy with the situation, but her big ambition was that none of her girls would go into 'service'. Three of us girls became schoolteachers and one a nurse. None of the boys went to high school. One would have loved to, but my parents thought it was easier for him to get a job. Dad was a farmer, and there was no traditon of educating the children further than primary school.*

I went to high school under a system where the Education department paid an allowance. I was bonded and went on to Teachers' Training College. I was very young and living away from home . Mum would have died had she seen some of the places I lived in. It was probably more by good luck than good managment that my chasity was preserved.

Other sources kept in family archives are school photos, reports and records.

Jane Lloyd: *Mother kept them until probably the last seven or eight years. They used to be in a file in their filing cabinet, and the file was marked 'Jane Lloyd'. That was my file. I've had control of it, I suppose, for the last ten years. It's been up here with me for the past three years since I've had this house. Having a base to keep these things in has been very important.*

```
BEATRICE
1892-1973
    |
UNA VON STURMER
   1915-
    |
   PAM
  1934-
    |
  VICKY
  1955-
```

Una von Sturmer's mother died in 1973 at the age of eighty-one. She had led an extraordinary life, and in the trunk, which was brought down to Una's home after the funeral, they found the banking records from the business she had run. After her partner had been lost at sea, the boat they had jointly managed was sold because fishermen wouldn't take orders from a woman. In her papers were the certificate of registration for the boat, her union membership book and a letter dated 15 July 1946 from a journal called *The Fisherman*, acknowledging her application and cheque.

Dear Madam,
I am in receipt of your short note and application form with cheque attached, for which I thank you.

As you realize, women are by no means in the minority in the fishing world, and it is our aim to make this journal of interest to them as well as the male members of the fishing community. Noting that you signed yourself 'Professional Deep Sea Fisherwoman', I feel sure that you would be able to help us to further our aim in this respect.

As it is impossible at this juncture for us to send a representative to interview you, I thought that you might possibly be able to supply us with some story or article of interest to the women readers. You may not be a writer yourself, but this does not matter. No matter how rough your copy is, we will put it into shape for publication at this end. Any photographs which you have had taken of yourself while on one of your trips would also be greatly appreciated.

Trusting that you will give this your due consideration.

There are photo albums and postcards from the various trips that she made. The Hong Kong photographs were taken in the 1960s. She won prizes with her photographs. There is one with an eighty-pound mackerel. Also in this collection are numerous news clippings.

No one knew what became of her; she just disappeared off the family tree.

Joyce Caddie has kept 'The Three Little Graves', a poem written by her grandmother, Annie Macfarlane. The accompanying letter to the editor in 1906 reads: 'The enclosed verses I wrote several years ago in memory of the time we had lived in a sparsely settled and lonely part of Queensland, where we buried the three children on the selection, reading the burial service over them ourselves, and making the little coffins ourselves out of cases.'

The poem was Grandmother's favourite, and Mother's, also. The dead children were my aunts and uncle. Mum was from a large family, but only four survived childhood. Three died of diphtheria.

A long-term resident of Longreach, Queensland, told of a letter written by her great-grandmother's sister to her family in Scotland in about 1840. *At the age of about twenty, she had come out to Australia to live with friends at Duntroon, where Canberra is now. She was very lonely and, in one of her letters, it's one of the saddest things, I think, she said, 'Please remember me to everyone who might know me.' The part that moves me is that last sentence. The letter came back to Australia about fifteen years ago when one of the old family houses was finally sold up. It is now owned by my aunt, and I'd love to have it. She is single and says she will give things to me. The letter always moves me when I think about it. No one knew what became of her; she just disappeared off the family tree.*

I would love to have heard stories of the pioneer women who had no one to share their anguish with.

More recently women have begun to write a different sort of history. They are reclaiming, through oral history and the documents that women wrote and saved, those women who 'fell off the family tree'. But it has also been necessary to find ways of writing and thinking about women's past that allows continuity of experience between generations.

I would love to have heard stories of the pioneer women who had no one to share their anguishes with. Often they did not know where their men-folk were, or whether they were safe. What of those women who went up north and saw no other white women and only had Aboriginal women for company? I have great admiration for them. A lot of our history is not yet written.

On marriage, the documentation of another family becomes important, regretfully so.

I didn't realize until I parted with the photographs and diaries how much they meant to me. When women change their names, they can't tell children, 'That's yours,' because it's not their name. Once you lose your name, you can't tell you children all about the family because that is not their name. Then, to make matters worse, some fathers, the ones with the name, don't pass on the family history to their children. You couldn't expect sentiment from the men, they had such a struggle, and the diaries record that. No doubt the men were busy with the sheep and the cattle, and what little survived is recorded on the flyleaf of the family bible.

The Telling Things

Compiling family histories is a middle-class preoccupation for they have the time, interest and ability. Welfare records contain the histories of many working-class families, who have little control over how they are represented. Frequently, their accounts of their past are different from the records. It is oral history, not a search for documents and written proof. To be sure, public libraries, Freedom of Information and photocopiers allow more people to have access but, as several women commented, 'There is a strong sense of the family being its own network.' So while written accounts may exist, the family can maintain its own history. This may give rise to a sense of satisfaction at each generation level, but ultimately these accounts are vulnerable and may be dismissed in a way that written accounts may not.

Women keep the 'stories' of their relatives alive, gather and hold the precious documents, but the 'history' passes through the names attached to the properties; the 'family bible' is passed from male heir to male heir. Thus the continuity that women seek in their exchange of family news is constantly fractured. When the documents are finally ordered and placed in an historical society or archive, especially one in the family home, the possibility of establishing links between women becomes remote. The written accounts, by and large, are about links traced through men.

From the records of the company for which James White worked, we can reconstruct his story, the shepherd who brought out seventy-nine French Merino sheep in 1826. Fifty-nine survived. We know little of his wife who accompanied him on the voyage, however, and their baby who died on the trip. We know his wife Sarah bore him ten children, the first and last called Jane and that, between 1839 and 1842, they owned their property and had some support from his sister Jane and brother-in-law Edward. James died young, leaving Sarah with ten children, the youngest of whom was fourteen months. Sarah lived into her seventies. Did she re-marry? Stay on the land? What of the children?

We know from the diary of his son, James, of women's presence, but their actions were not recorded in any detail. In his diary, an entry reads: 'Mrs White had a son today.' Mrs White, of course, was his wife. The next day the entry reads: 'Mrs White felt indisposed and did not come to church.' A person needed to be really sick to miss going to the church in the buggy. The diary contains detailed accounts of calving, an occasion on which, unlike the birth of his son, Mr White was obviously present

---

It might have been called gossip... but it was their history.

Dissatisfaction with the lack of knowledge of women's activities and the poor understanding of women's contribution to society comes in a number of forms. It may be a complaint that we know 'so little' of our female forebears, or as one daughter of the Western Australian gentry commented, the public history was at odds with her experience of the family's history as told by female relatives.

It was strange to become a history student at university in an era when the history of the gentry was being contested. The push was to write history from the bottom up in order to reclaim the other side of the history of the establishment of the state. From my knowledge of the 'hearth history', however, I already had a counter to the history which they were rejecting and wishing to revise. I'd hear them talk about gentry families, or any family, in that informal way, of the 'other side of the blanket', of the renegades, the hasty marriages and the relationships between Aborigines and whites on the colonial frontier. And I was doing that history course, and I could see straight away that the anti-gentry analysis was necessary. But to make it work and give it a future, it had to be more sophisticated. People had to see that individuals were reacting and responding; that within women's culture, they did know what was going on, and they did sit around and talk about it. It might have been called gossip - it was a lot of gossip - but it was their history.

Distinctions between that information and sense of self based on shared experience, gossip during an afternoon of 'needle and tongue' and the 'real stuff' in the museums and public libraries removes women from history written with a focus on events and individuals. 'Gossip' does, however, leave women in control of how certain family experiences are related. It is possible to adjust and re-arrange, to emphasize the motivations of one against the behaviour of another. In these settings men, where men are present, listen rather than recount. Of course, young boys hear much of this and, in their later years, ask their mothers, in private, to clarify family details.

Much of the information is in the hands and minds of the females of the family. It is they who remember the birth order and dates, the costumes worn. But, when the official history of the trials and tribulations of the family is written, when the material is structured for the benefit of an audience beyond the family, a curious ordering device is evident. The family becomes those who bear the same surname. The wives belong to another line. Their documents are sought by their brothers. Mothers find they have been incorporated into the family of another and their children may no longer draw upon the stories of mothers' mothers and trace the changes of name and residence. The family tree has a name: 'McDonalds in Australia'. Those who attempt something more complex find that once they have gone to the four grandparents the tree needs a prune, it is too top heavy.

CHAPTER NINE

A FORTUNATE LIFE: MIMI TAYLOR

It was winter, just two days after my sixth birthday, and Mum was sitting at the open fire. My two sisters had gone to school, but I was still in our bed. Mum said to get up and come over to the fire. So I sat up and I said, 'Oh, Mum, my arm's funny,' and she said, 'Come on over here, and I'll rub it. You've probably been sleeping on it.' I got out of bed and fell over. No pain, not a bit of pain. She knew there was something wrong, of course, and I was put in hospital. I was in the Children's Hospital for nine months, and the only treatment I got was a hot water bottle, a metal one.

Mimi Taylor had contracted polio. The 1904-5 epidemic left many victims severely handicapped, but Mimi was lucky: only her right arm and leg were affected. Mimi's uncertain balance and numerous falls caused problems: she has broken many bones. Once when a clothes prop slid along the line and knocked her over, she broke several toes. Another time she bent her boot back on her toes. Mimi found it difficult to lift and carry her children. While her first two daughters were young, their father took work that allowed him to be with her. And when Mimi's youngest needed regular hospital visits, Mimi's second daughter took her.

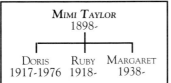

Negotiating steps always presented a problem. It was a relief when, in her later years, Mimi and her second husband lived in a house built to accommodate her special needs. It is the one she calls their 'dream house'.

In the early twenties, Mimi used her daughter Ruby as a prop, then relied on a stick, later on crutches; she didn't wear her first surgical boot until 1967. In the 1970s, she agreed to try a wheelchair, which she now describes as 'the best thing I ever did'.

My first boot was made by a friend who was not a bootmaker, and I still have the mark, the size of her thumbnail, on my leg. I used to sit around the corner and take my boot off on my way out. Then I'd sit and put it back on when I came home. In the years before I got a proper boot, I walked with just a stocking on the bad foot and, gradually, it went over until I was walking on my ankle, and I got two big corns on the side of my foot, and if I trod on a stone, the pain …

None of the doctors I had seen over the years had ever told me to get a boot and a leg brace. It was only when I fell over and damaged my other knee that the doctors suggested they could do something for my bad leg. I now have a plate in my foot and a pin and plate in the side of the bad leg.

As Mimi tells of her ninety years, we learn about two world wars, two visits of Halley's comet; we can trace changes in welfare policies for orphaned children and single mothers; learn of improved health care; and document the struggle of a young family to survive through the depression. Mimi's account is fleshed out with photographs and other personal and familar objects that are touchstones for her descendants. To her they are 'dear things' that allow continuity with the past. We may check details of her story, ask Mimi what she was doing on a particular date. The answers will take us beyond the written record and give us that feeling of being there. But it remains the story of Mimi's life and is told from her perspective. It is a story in which her descendants have begun to take an interest.

When Wanda decided to work on a family tree, she approached her grandmother, Mimi Taylor, who was born in 1898, for documents. A mid nineteenth-century wedding photograph of Mary Anne Lupton and John Hodder Needell, Mimi's grandparents on her mother's side, bore the stamp of Hodder and Stoughton, publishers of London. The great-great-granddaughter pondered the possible relationship to the house of Hodder.

Mimi knew something of the life of John and Mary. They had lived a comfortable life on their English property: he was a gentleman, said never to have worked in his life; she was a lady with maid servants. Of their eight children, a younger daughter, Connie, became a nurse, worked during the Great War but never married. The second daughter, Ada Phoebe, born in 1864, did not get on particularly well with her mother. After the death of her father and, with a little money from the property, Ada set sail for Australia, at the age of twenty-four, to fulfil her ambition to become a governess. The year was 1888. British settlement in Australia was one hundred years old.

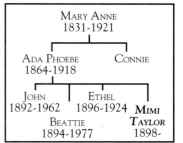

Ada worked as a governess on various stations. It was in Queensland, shortly after she arrived, that she met and married Mimi's father. It was a match between an educated girl with no domestic skills and a clever but illiterate sailor from Devon. After the marriage, Ada taught him to read and write and continued to work until the birth of their first child in 1892.

Links to the home country were maintained in letters between Ada and her sister Connie. Mimi still has one in which the nursing conditions in the black-outs during the first world war are described. Mary, their mother, wrote books, and these were sent to Mimi, who has a list of the titles. When Mary died in 1921, at the age of ninety, her books fetched fifty pounds. The comfortable existence of which Connie and her mother wrote to Ada contrasted starkly to her life in a tin shed in Australia with her young family.

Eight years and three daughters later, Ada's husband was drowned when the boom of a ship knocked him overboard. Mimi, the youngest, was eighteen months old. To provide as best she could, Ada went back to work, and the four children were put into an orphanage, where she paid five shillings a month for their keep. The Commonwealth of Australia was one year old, and there were no widows' pensions. Ada had no extended family to whom she could look for support.

It wasn't a happy life, and Mimi remembers sitting on the step in a red dress when she was three. Her only contact with her mother was covert and traumatic.

Mum would come on and off when she wasn't supposed to come and meet us. I was going to Sunday School, and she'd waylay me, and I remember her picking me up under the arms. I had to go past a hotel to get to my Sunday School with one of the girls. I didn't go by myself. I remember her picking me up in her arms, standing under this hotel and, of course, then she had to put me down and let me go.

They stayed in the orphanage until Mimi was four. *I went out of that orphanage on my brother's back. He was ten or eleven. He carried me and held my two sisters by the hand. We were found and returned. Then we were boarded out with different families. Because he was old enough he was sent to work, he went cane cutting at Mackay. He was belted and changed families. He never had a childhood.*

The first foster family received two shillings and sixpence a week in keep for Mimi. The family argued so badly, however, that after crawling through the hedge to refuge with the neighbours, she was moved to another place where she found some stability.

The woman lived in Balaclava, Rockhampton, near the creek, near the Kanaka town. The house is not there anymore. She had four 'state children', and we worked very hard. The four of us would sit at the kitchen table and take the stalks off all the currants and sultanas for the Christmas pudding, and we wouldn't dare eat one. I was belted once and can't remember why, but I remember Davie [one of the wards] came and sneaked his crusts through the door. I'd been sent to bed with no food. I think it might have been because I let Davie cover me over with mango leaves. It was our job to scrape up the leaves for Saturday, and I laid down, and he covered me with leaves.

An inspector used to come around and speak to the children about the care we were given. She wasn't cruel to us. She belted us only as a mother might. She did belt me one day for walking home with a little black girl from school. That was Frenchman's Creek school, now Frenchville.

In 1903, Ada re-married. Earnest Steel had deserted from the Navy and taken the name 'Sam Jones'. The family was reunited. It was a happy time for them. Then, in 1904, Mimi went to hospital with polio.

Visiting hours were strict, just two days a week. My mother walked up that Denham Street hill Wednesdays and Sundays for nine months to see me. She'd bring some pineapple cut in little squares in a paper bag. That was as much as she could afford, I suppose. She had to walk past the orphanage to the hospital.

A photograph that survives shows Mimi's sister in a cashmere frock sent from England and the other two sisters in hand-made flannelette dresses. Mimi is wearing her first boot.

Mimi left school when she was twelve and in grade six. Then the family moved to MacKay.

We were poor and couldn't afford fares of any kind, and my stepfather was a wharflumper. He didn't get very much work on that wharf 'cause he wasn't real strong, but he got to know somebody on this cargo ship, The Gabo, and he talked to him and they said, 'Pack up your stuff, and we'll take you.' So we all put our goods and chattels in a tub, a big galvanized-iron bath tub, the biggest one you could get, and covered it over with hessian, and all the rest of it. I can remember watching the sling take it on board and down to the hatch.

Mimi's daughters knew the tub well. It was the one Ruby and Doris had sold.

Ruby: *If we hadn't pushed, Mum would still be sitting beside it doing her washing. She used to sit with this big tub where she soaked the clothes and then another tub beside it to rinse them. There was a wood-fired copper. Mum would be washing when we went to school and, when we came home, she'd still be washing. We had baths in it when we were about five, in front of the stove.* According to Mimi, it was slightly mis-shapen from the way it had been slung on the boat, but it was a good tub. It never leaked, and she held on to it like grim death, and then they got rid of it.

Well, we went to Mackay on this cargo ship among monkeys. I sat and watched them. Mackay had a sort of a zoo, and the monkeys were going there. We were only there a couple of years before we went back to Rockhampton. We paid our fare on the S.S. Peregrine.

Before we went to Mackay, we lived in a very little old house with no verandah. You just had to stand at the front door. It was 1910, the time of Halley's comet. My mother said, 'Come on, out of bed. Halley's comet.' Of course, at my age, then, Halley's comet didn't mean much to me. She said, 'Come on, get out. You might never see it again.' So I got out, and I saw this beautiful ... it was so beautiful. Now I think, Why didn't we have a picture of it? It was this long, over in the sky like that, all full of mist around it, with a big long tail. Three nights running, she got me out of bed. 'Course, I wanted to get up the other nights, I think, to see this funny thing. So you imagine all these years when I knew it was coming in 1986. So they got me out there, and I didn't even see it. I saw what was supposed to be it, but I couldn't think that it could be what I had seen in 1910. I can see it in my mind. Beautiful. I won't see it again.

When Mimi left school, she worked for two shillings and sixpence a week to nurse children at a hotel. Like Mrs MacKay, she would do her mother's bit of work at home and then go to work . Then life changed. In 1911 her step-father died suddenly of pneumonia.

He was only forty-six. He had been out working as a cook at Blackall. The last few years of Mum's life after her husband died weren't as happy as they could have been because she didn't have much. She used to walk (like from here to Sunnybank station) about three miles, to save threepence. She'd walk that distance to get her issue of two pounds of sugar, two loaves of bread and a bit of meat for the week. That was rations. There was nothing else, like pensions; there was nothing like that. Mum would do some tatting for sale. One of her sisters can do it, but I can't. I do remember a little cigar box that was padded and covered with tatting. Also a little powder compact.

In 1915, at the age of seventeen, Mimi married. She and her husband worked on stations in the area. By the time she was twenty, Mimi had two daughters, Doris and Ruby, sixteen months apart. When she was first married, her husband had a job at Blackall on Terik Terik station.

He was a boundary rider. We had a little house with a dirt floor and a board where you put the bed. I used to sit on the phone to a lady on another of the Terik Terik station substations to get the war communiqués at night at seven o'clock. That's where I got news that a boy I'd been fond of had been killed. It was a party line that went through the main station. They'd get the news and relay it. I got five shillings a week for attending the phone. It was a very lonely life. The woman I used to talk to on the phone, Mrs Brooks, was there for about ten months, and I didn't even meet her; we'd talk over the phone. I'd sit, and Mrs Brooks would play her gramophone to me. We were only about ten or twelve miles apart, but we never met.

Mimi's mother died of consumption in 1918, aged fifty-four, just six weeks before Ruby, Mimi's second daughter was born. *She had been caught in the 1918 flood. She was sitting on a table, or something, waiting for them to come and get her and was taken to hospital. I went up. I know I was very fat, and I had a little short smock on, and I stood beside her. She looked at me and smiled*

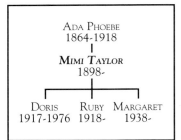

and rubbed my tummy. I always say to this day that she put her looks into Ruby. She's so much like her - she's tall, dark hair, and she's getting more like her grandmother as she gets older.

When Doris was four months old, there wasn't much work. My husband had been working at the gas works, but because of my leg, I could never carry my baby with safety. He left his job to be home and look after me. Work was scarce, and he met a chap that was going out scalping, shooting kangaroos, to sell the skins. He asked if we'd like to go to make a partner. So the other chap did all the buying, and he hired a dray and horse, and I think we helped buy provisions. So, we set off from Rockhampton. This is 1918. The horse's name was Toby.

We got as far as Stanwell, and we had to cross the deep creek. The horse wouldn't go, but we managed it and camped the night on the side of the creek. The other chap Bert had his wife Molly with him. They could see a house in the distance, and they went over to ask if we could cut saplings for the tent. It was blowing like mad, and the man told them they were going to get caught. There was supposed to be a cyclone coming. He let them use the old humpy to camp in for the night. That night the cyclone came, and Doris slept in the hamper basket.

They had to stay there two days 'cause they were marooned. Two little bodies had already floated down the creek. We forgot the scalping business and came back to camp in the hut. Our provisions ran out. The men shot a kookaburra and made soup from it for me. Some people nearby heard there was someone with a baby and came across to see if I'd like some milk. Those people stayed bosom friends for years. We stayed in the little hut for a few weeks. The other couple had left.

When we were still at Stanwell, my husband got into the railway. The people who had come over with the milk helped us get a little house. It was all wallpapered and had been torn and like that. And when I disturbed it, because there were cockroaches, I pulled a lot of this paper off the wall. And one morning, when my husband had gone to work, I got up, and I threw the blankets back off, and in the bottom of the bed there was a little snake curled up. So, he'd gone to work, and I'm there with my baby in the bed. I got the roller from the blind, and I stabbed it. I had it in spirits for years till it disintegrated, and we threw it out.

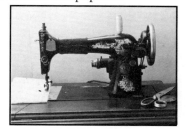

I was a gatekeeper for the railway lines, and my husband was a lengths man. Railway families got a market pass once a month to go down to Rockhampton to do the shopping. I had to wait until one o'clock in the morning to catch the '51 down' to come into town and then went back on the '10 up'. They used to go from Walton, that's the siding, to Bluff on the pumper to the races and then to the ball at night. Then, with a lot of drunken men to pump them home, they'd be ahead of the '51 down' at one o'clock in the morning, and the women would be scared stiff.

Then we were transferred to Yamba, and we bought a piece of land and built a home. The land was right near these MacDonalds, their land joined ours. Doris and Ruby were five and six, and the gate that led into the MacDonalds' property was on the main road. There was a place called Canoona that had been a great gold place in the early days, and they held races there. One of the times, there were cars going through, and my kids ran out and opened the gate for this car. The man gave them sixpence or threepence, or something like that, so, from then on, whenever they saw a car coming, they ran and opened the gate. We bought them a money box each and, as time when on, they went and opened the gate, and most of the time they got something.

One time we got a telegram from the taxi driver in Rockhampton that some club was going to the races and would the little kids have the gate open 'cause there would be a lot of cars. They got everything. They got biscuits. They got a cabbage. They got a pumpkin and plenty of money. Their father had put up a bit of a lean-to. It must have been hot. They'd sit there. They made a lot of money and soon had their money boxes filled.

During the depression, my husband only worked three days a week, and I had to be very careful not to overspend. We had a book for the corner shop where *we could 'tick things up'. She'd write down everything I spent and keep a check on it all. My husband was on four pounds five shillings a week, and that went back to three pounds a week. We had good landlords at the time. They did reduce our rent.*

When Ruby started working, she bought me a canister set, which I still have in the kitchen. But my pride and joy is the silky oak Duchess dressing table. Ruby bought that when she was eighteen at two shillings and sixpence a week. It cost two pounds, fifteen shillings and has a lovely big mirror. I wouldn't part with it for anything. It must be worth quite a bit now. I want Ruby to have it when I'm gone.

Mimi's third daughter, Margaret, was born in 1938 when Mimi was forty. It came as a surprise to Mimi and her doctor. Doris, her first daughter, had had her first child just two weeks before Margaret was born. It was Ruby who helped her mother to bring up the child, although she was rather shocked at her mother having a child so late in life. A number of people believed it was Ruby's, not Mimi's child. It was a breech birth, and the instrument delivery left one of the baby's arms paralysed. Mimi was not told straight away, and then the condition was diagnosed by her doctor as being 'hereditary'. As her own polio had been contracted in the epidemic of 1904-5, she rejected this idea and sought a second opinion. The treatment required visits three times a week for six weeks to a clinic but was successful. Margaret played the piano and hockey.

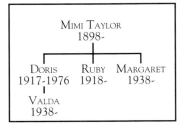

Then, when the baby was only two, Mimi's husband of twenty-five years died. He was only forty-six. It was 1940 and hard times once again. Mimi made jam, and Ruby would sell it for her. Mimi had bought a house but only had nine pounds in the bank. Ruby, newly married, gave up her flat and moved back in to help her mother with the re-payments. Mimi tried to get a pension but was knocked back.

The man said to me, 'Couldn't you get a job?' and I said, 'Well, who'd employ me? Now I had a fall just before I came down here as you can see.' 'Well,' he said, 'Couldn't you save yourself on the other leg.' I howled. 'I just fell stepping off a step. How can I get a job?' He said, 'Could you drive a lift?' I said, 'There're no lifts in Rockhampton.' But I had admitted that I could, and I didn't get that pension. I did get a pension, but it was because I had come out in big blotches, and the doctor told me to put in for that.

During the second world war, Ruby was in Sydney. It was before Bob, Ruby's son, was born, and her husband was in the army. She was staying at Woollahra in a block of tenements. One night she was home alone and heard the siren go. She thought they were practising, but it was real.

Mimi Taylor holding a photograph of her mother

Mimi Taylor's silky oak dressing table, bought for her by her daughter Ruby

Mimi Taylor with her grand-daughter Valda Livingston, her two daughters Ruby Davis and Margaret Ryan and her great-grand-daughter Michelle Livingston, Sunnybank Hills, Queensland

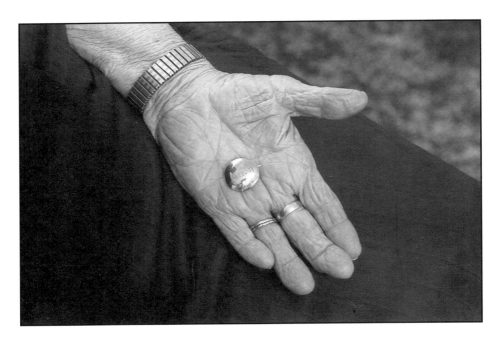

The brooch that Mimi's mother gave to her

Ruby: Next morning I went down to the butcher's and heard them talking about the shells that fell in the harbour. That was very close to where I was, so next day I moved to Marrickville. Mum says that some people dug shelters in their yard in Rockhampton, but they weren't well constructed. The first lot of rain, and you'd be drowned.

In 1948, Mimi married again, to Alf Taylor. It was a happy time but, as they aged, Alf began to worry about who would care for Mimi if he died. They sold the home they'd had for eleven years and built a flat on to Margaret's place.

He was happy there, but it almost broke his heart to sell our dream house. It was his suggestion to move, and he was sensible enough to know I'd want to be near my girls. I had plenty of grandchildren and Ruby, my second daughter, is a mighty girl.

Alf died in 1985. Mimi has the first ring he gave her. *It's very worn, but you can still make out the coin it's made of on the inside. It did have two hearts engraved on the outside, but they're worn away. Someone made it for him. I love this little ring because it was his.*

The small pieces of jewellery that link mother to daughter in Mimi's line are also treasured. *The other day I heard that my great-grand-daughter is getting married to a doctor. She's a highschool teacher. Interesting isn't it? My grandmother came here as a governess. Well, Wanda phoned me to find out if I had an old brooch that her daughter could wear at the wedding. I asked Ruby about it. Ruby had the little brooch my mother had bought for me. It was real, round gold with the mizpah - the Lord watch between me and thee when we are absent one from the other. I had lost this brooch, advertised and got it back. Later the pin had broken, so it had been put among a lot of stuff and, going through this, I found it and gave it to Ruby. She got the pin fixed and really liked it, but she wouldn't let my great-grand-daughter have it.*

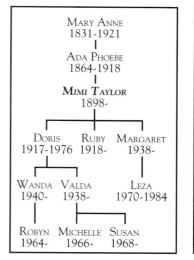

Mimi recalled that one piece, an entwined brooch passed down to her from her Aunt Connie, had been borrowed and lost. She was reluctant to put the mizpah at risk. Then Ruby remembered the 'Doris' brooch.

My first daughter had been given a silver brooch, an inch and a half or two inches long, with 'Doris' raised, not engraved, on it. Ruby's giving it to Wanda whose elder daughter is getting married. She can keep it and lend it to each daughter for their wedding. Then Wanda's sister, Valda, that's Doris's children, who has two daughters, can borrow it, but it must go back to Wanda.

These pieces may be held but are never owned.

Once begun, the momentum of Mimi's story carried the teller forward, but the tale weaves events past and present in a unique design that belongs to that life alone. Mimi told her tale in a series of cross-references that moved back and forth in time, followed one theme until it was played out and then began again. Imposing a rigid chronology would help put order into the tale, but it would then no longer be Mimi's story.

Nina Fletcher also grew up in Queensland and is not much younger than Mimi. Major epidemics, in Nina's case, the Spanish flu epidemic of 1918-19, are remembered because of the way in which they touched their lives.

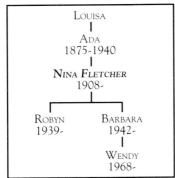

During World War II, we spent eight years in Sydney because mother was not well. We rented a house at Randwick and later bought there. We had a nurse, chauffeur, and left Sydney when I was ten to avoid the pneumonic flu. We spent weeks in isolation at a camp on the border at Wallangarra. They were attempting to stop the spread of the flu to Queensland. Do I remember that time? Eight children with a nurse; of course, I do.

The stories of Nina and Mimi take us to the limits of memory. It seems we only begin to record, only come to understand the value of such knowledge when it is almost too late to record from those who were there. It is as if we fear by asking for a life history that we suggest that that life has been lived out.

Recurrent themes in the accounts of older women were premature deaths from illnesses that are now treated with antibiotics. If it was infant death, a mother mourned. If a mother died, was ill or in need, the family could help but, increasingly, it has been agencies of the state that have intervened. Mimi struggled with various bureaucrats: as a child in an orphanage, as a mother in need of support, and then as an invalid pensioner.

Other women found a lack of sensitivity in dealing with their needs. Unfortunately that experience is not part of the dim past.

In a life history we hear the voice of another; we identify; we distance ourselves; there is an invitation to go into more private realms; to see childhoods and explore personal relationships of the rich and famous who are the subjects of many biographies. But the fascination extends beyond the public figures. We all have an interest in and know something of the biography of our friends. We look for shared experiences and respond, 'Oh, did you do that too?' Of course, there are a number of filters on what we are told and what we hear. We all embroider our stories to present different accounts for different purposes.

CHAPTER TEN

A LITERATE TRADITION

It was quite strange to read about the marriage of Josephine to Henry Prinsep. In the 1860s, Australian society was not extensive, and the marriage was always presented as an arranged one. It was a famous match, really, and I didn't know about it as that until I read Stannage's The People of Perth.

The Brockmans, Prinseps and Bussels are part of the history of the settlement of Western Australia. Mary Anne Jebb confronts the history of her forebears in a number of sources, such as in this love poem.

Josephine

J ust at the hour when dusky twilight fades,
O n me the dearest eyes of love incline,
S erenely calm above the darking shades,
E ach peeping star on my delight doth shine,
P indaric ode or Spenser's flowing line
H as not the voice to sing the joys I mean:
I ne'er can tell how sweet a lot is mine,
N o words for me can ever paint the scene.
E nchanted, I can utter naught but Josephine.

Few women find their histories in print. But, from the way the surviving documents and family histories are preserved, it is clear that some see their past as worth salvaging and savouring. That we need pieces of paper to prove our identity partly explains the interest.

A Literate Tradition

Diaries and photographs are critical for the family historian. For a family reunion or an anniversary, an interested family member may put what is available together, but name changes at marriage can frustrate attempts to trace links between mothers, daughters and grand-daughters. And, because women leave the family home when they marry, much of the information they hold is lost. Ways of dating photographs and letters, of identifying individuals, remain locked in the memory of women no longer living where the documents are kept.

A family history compiled by Joyce Fuller confronts these problems. Beginning with Margaret Fraser, the mother of Marion Sutherland, who was born in 1808, Joyce traced through eight generations of mothers and daughters from Scotland to Australia. The documents and objects that Joyce relied on include photographs, pencil drawings, letters, maps, shipping records, postcards, reports of inquests, wills, newspaper reports, school photos, christening robes, and clothes. She lives near her mother and daughter, sees them every day and is very close.

I am like my mother in that I use older things first. My daughter is the same. I have a love of garden, plants, country and have an interest in family history.

Janet Shaw (née Douglas) also has an interest in family history. In researching the history of the Douglas family, she found documents in some unexpected places.

MARGARET SUTHERLAND
(née FRASER)
|
MARION POLSON
(née SUTHERLAND)
1808-1893
|
JANE WARD
(née POLSON)
1838-1923
|
SARAH ANN TAYLOR
(née WARD)
1864-1921
|
ETHEL HARRIES
(née TAYLOR)
1889-1979
|
JOYCE FULLER
(née HARRIES)
1920-
|
BRONWEN ROBINSON
(née FULLER)
1952-
|
PENELOPE ROBINSON
1982-

The earliest letter we have is dated 1803 from my great-great-great-grandmother, born about 1770. It was found in a shoe box by my cousin. The letter refers to her husband as Mr D., illnesses, people met. Communications were slow, and letters were important. They're significant simply because they had been kept all these years, but they also contain insights into the character. The writers were well educated, cared about family; they mention nieces and nephews and don't complain.

The 'Mr D.' is Robert Douglas, of whom there is one in each generation, just as there is a Mary. Distinguishing one from another was hard. *The eldest son was always named after the father's father, the second son after the mother's father and the third after the father. Daughters were named in reverse to this pattern. The first daughter was named after the mother's mother, the second daughter after the father's mother and the third daughter after the mother.*

Because the family was still following this strict Scottish system of handing down names, there were whole families of cousins with the same name, and several infant deaths confused it further. In 1980, Janet helped to write a book on the Douglas family. *At the launch of the book, three hundred were present. The personal response was gratifying. There was a service at St Mary's Anglican church, Kangaroo Point, Brisbane (the first Douglases went there), and three christenings at the reunion service.*

Reflecting on her life, Janet said: *I know where I am not going rather than where I am going. At our stage of life, we've probably come to terms with what we are, and who we are, and what we've done ourselves, our family, generally, and life the way it is. We can accept changes for what they are because we can recognize them. It takes great intelligence to enjoy simplicity.*

> CHRISTINE PAULINE
> 1897-1985
> |
> CATHERINE MARY
> 1918-
> |
> SUSAN MAGAREY
> 1943-

Susan Magarey is another who finds her family in a number of sources. About the Brownes and Gilberts, her maternal ancestors, it is possible to consult the new *Social History of South Australia*, and two books written by Peter Verco contain a great deal of antiquarian information about the family. Surviving records are a rich source for Susan, but what of the documents that have been lost?

My maternal grandmother said, for some years, that she had written a biography of her ancestor John Harris Browne, who came down the Murray with Charles Sturt. I believe that she did; she showed me a bulky handwritten manuscript once. But she would not let any of us read it, promised it to all of us one by one in her will, and since she died I have seen no trace of it. My mother believes that her brother threw it out, in the process of cleaning out their mother's house after her death.

From one of her great-aunts, Susan sought an account of growing up on Pewsey Vale, a property at the southern end of the Barossa Valley, which she describes as 'an almost feudal environment'.

My maternal grandfather had three sisters who never married and lived together all their lives. I prize the essays my great-aunts wrote as historical documents. One of them was used by a historian reconstructing childhoods in the past.

I'm a custodian of family history, and I've done a lot of researching.

Bev Dinn's family reaches back to the Chinese on the goldfields in Ballarat and the first Jewish convicts in Tasmania. Documents have been hard to find, and she has needed to do more research to understand them; she is still working on it.

I'm a custodian of family history, and I've done a lot of researching. I've got everything, and everyone's given me things. My grandfather, Lew Din (that's how he spelt his name then), was born in Canton in 1878. He came to Australia when he was fourteen with his uncle. His mother died when she swallowed a fish bone, so the story goes. I've tried to check his arrival in the shipping records, but the European passengers are listed and then it says '12 chinese'. He worked with his uncle on the goldfields in Ballarat and also as a gardener on the Manifold property in Camperdown. I have some records of that. In Little Bourke Street, which is Chinatown now, there were a number of little stores each representing a different clan. The mail would go to the particular general store, and the family would know to get it from the particular store. I visited a number of them looking for records.

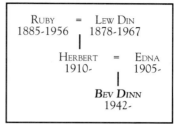

I know that in 1903 he was baptized in the Presbyterian Church in Brighton. That's where he met my grandmother, Ruby, who used to run the Chinese school. She was a missionary. There was a number of schools to teach the Chinese who were coming down from the goldfields to speak English and Christianity. I traced information about her, my grandmother, back to Kent, England. Her grandfather, Juda Solomon, arrived in Tasmania as a convict in 1820. He later presented land for the first synagogue in Australia. He and his brother were very smart and became wealthy merchants but, when my grandfather met Ruby, she was a Presbyterian missionary.

On the wedding certificate my grandmother is listed as a dressmaker, and he as a gardener. He was eight years older than her. Then, in 1913, six years after they were married, she applied for naturalization. She stated she was Australian by birth and had lived in Victoria all her life but was applying because she was married to a Chinese subject. The Naturalization Act of 1903 explains why.

The Act set out the conditions under which 'aliens' could become naturalized. They had to live in Australia for two years, or have appropriate papers from the United Kingdom. Explicitly excluded were 'Aboriginal natives of Asia, Africa or the islands of the Pacific, excepting New Zealand'. No doubt, Ruby felt threatened by the anti-Chinese sentiments but her status was secure. A wife did not lose her citizenship when she married.

Because I was adopted... I feel like someone from outer space.

The need to document the past is greater where there is no known family. *I was adopted when I was three weeks old, in 1952. My younger brother is the only natural child of the family. But, if I go back through the papers, my adopted father was my real father. My aunt couldn't wait to tell me that after my mother died. She had always been jealous of Mum, who was the favoured child. She contracted polio when she was two years old and always got a lot of attention. One day, at lunch, my aunt gave me the adoption papers and announced my mother wasn't my real mother, after all. It was something I already knew, anyway. Dad had given me the papers before he died. I don't know if Mum knew the real relationship between me and my father. She may have, but it was never spoken of. I was told I was adopted when I was about ten or eleven. I was told the name of my mother, and I know where she lives if I ever want to get in contact with her. Things were fairly open in the family.*

Because I was adopted, there are things I don't know about my medical history. It's embarrassing and frustrating to have to tell people that I don't know - specially as I have an epileptic child. I have a problem with my eyes, and my record says 'no information' in the part for family history, and I feel like someone from outer space.

Mimi Taylor's mother had a similar experience. She saw a girl passing by in the street. She knew it was her daughter, who had been sent to live with another family, but she did not have the papers to prove it.

Without the ability to read and write, we are worse off. Mothers, grandmothers, and aunts often go to extraordinary lengths to ensure that those in their care are able, at least, to read and write. They have struggled to provide an education and made sure that we developed a love of reading.

Joyce Caddie and other women who grew up during the depression remember books as scarce but a joy.

Mum didn't marry until her late twenties and then had nine children. She'd always had a hard life and was determined her daughters were not going to have as hard a life. She was very proud of her children's ability. At one time, she had five children at the little one-teacher school, and each came top of their class. Books were given as prizes, and I still have all those books. One I received for not missing a day at school. We read them over and over again.

There were not many women writing and publishing in those days.

Some of my books belonged to my mother and my aunts. We were read to when we were little; Dad read to us from the paper. The travelling library that came around the schools brought other books. The love of learning and books came from Mum's mother. We have a book of poems written by her which were published under her name in local papers. I think Dad's family might have been a bit jealous. There were not many women writing and publishing in those days.

The books awarded on prize night, or for best attendance at Sunday School, were an important source of literature. With them came not so subtle messages: adventure books for boys, the lives of the saints for convent girls. Our responses to the carefully chosen awards differed, but we hung on to the books. The illuminated sheet glued on the inside cover paid tribute to our success. Ros Fraser was given *A Town Like Alice* for academic achievement; the 'Most Improved' in her class received an Enid Blyton book.

I really loved the smell of that shiny paper.

Marion Black's prize began something. *I had glasses right from prep, and I felt different. Then I got this prize. I took my glasses off to get the prize, but that book got me interested. Every spare penny I had, I'd buy those little Br'er Rabbit books. I really loved the smell of that shiny paper. They've come out recently, and I was going to buy them for my kids, but the smell was different, and the shine wasn't there. They've made a real botch of the reprint, and it's on thin, horrible paper.*

Books were given on occasions such as birthdays and at Christmas; a birthday wasn't a birthday without a book. It was then that a favourite aunt could single out a niece for attention, a close friend became 'family'.

Mother had books from her mother, and they were cherished because they were old and part of the family, especially the family ones inscribed by the forebears. I had four grandmothers: my real two and my Nanny and the artist J.H. Hiller's sister, who was known as 'Hillah'. Mother's mother's love of literature came from Miss Young, a Scottish teacher at boarding school. She was there from 1928, for forty years or so. That love of literature has been handed down to us.

The childhood books that survive are read to the grandchildren when they visit and form a link to their own parents' childhood. 'Tell me about the time Mum won this book, Gran,' they ask. One favourite is *Coles Funny Picture Book*, which grandparents seem to have kept to read to their grandchildren. These collections of old books - originals of *Milly Molly Mandy*, *Snugglepot and Cuddlepie*, *Blinky Bill*, the Billabong books, *Winnie the Pooh*, Hans Andersen and Grimm's fairytales - tell us, among other things, that Australian children enjoyed stories set in Australia and in other countries.

My childhood books, which had been read to my children by my mother, had stayed in her house for the other young children who visited her. When my daughter wanted to claim these books, we found they were missing. My mother had cleaned out the house and garage after the death of my father and had not thought it necessary to consult me on my books. I'm still not sure what happened to them. She says that at the time she 'went funny', a common expression for those in mourning. We pay so little attention to those who are grieving, after our initial offers of support.

She knows what books are for, and 'ck', which means book, was one of her first words.

Pat Giles has kept some of her mother's teaching materials, including the hand-copied illustrations of Shepherd in A.A. Milne.

There weren't many books. As soon as I was old enough, I joined the local lending library, and that was my recreational reading. I just read and read and read. I was never involved in sport. The only thing I ever played was the piano.

Now Jessie and I read together every morning. I started it off as a way to preserve the newspapers so I could read them and to allow Anne time to shower. She knows what books are for, and 'ck', which means book, was one of her first words. She has a bundle of books, not all of which she recognizes and, as I said, she doesn't tear or chew anything.

Books recall happy memories of the times spent cuddled on the couch, or snuggled up in bed. Lena Kay in the early thirties: *Mum used to make toffee and coconut ice, we'd go and sit around the fire, and they'd read to us, and then Dad would make the coffee. Then there was radio, and we used to listen to 3SH, Swan Hill. They'd have request programmes, and we'd write in, and the night your name was called, you would have the programme for that night.*

For a number of reasons, perhaps because women were too busy with younger children, or just plain exhausted, it was not always our mother who read to us. In large families, there were other people.

I did like being read to, but the most enjoyable reading that was done was by my brother, not the eldest one, but the one who's five years older. He used to make up stories rather than read, and we have this tale about Willie the Seagull. My mother is a very good storybook teller, too. Probably some of it is due to her theatre training. For years now, she's done a lot of reading for the blind. She records books. She reads novels as well as the academic stuff, and she used to read the news on the radio at university. She's quite good at it. I'm not. I don't like talking much.

A Literate Tradition

For country women, the library was very important. Nina Fletcher remembers: *Mother did a lot of reading, but not to us. She'd had measles, and it affected her eyes. We had Dymock's library books sent up. I don't remember any state library facilities. The books came out by train. I loved reading and would tuck in behind the door in the dining room and read a book. I thought the Girls' Own Annual was a bit sissy, and I liked Chums' Annuals, which was for the boys.*

The only accounts that my family ever had were with bookshops.

In those families rich enough to maintain a library, a love of books meant that books were often bought.

Both parents read to me during the day, my mother especially during the day because Poppa was out. By the time I went to school, I was reading. The only accounts that my family ever had were with bookshops. The only thing I've ever been allowed to put on account has been books. I grew up in a family who could not walk past a bookshop without going in and coming out having bought something.

Books open up new worlds of travel, of little known relatives, special moments and interests. Whether or not a parent had time to read to a child, the number of books and those that were kept tell something about women's lives and their knowledge, values and aspirations. Some books have survived, some have been destroyed or lost, others are being re-bought and reclaimed.

Women have been important as the 'keepers of knowledge', the 'holders of books'. It is a tradition that reaches back to medieval Europe. There, women promoted books in the common language of the land. Books in Latin could only be read by the educated. Laywomen were important in making sure that books that could be read by the literate layperson were available. In the same way, our mothers, not literary scholars, shaped tastes, encouraged reading and left libraries to a favourite relative.

As young children she always gave us very good books.

Well, my mother's older sister had lots of books, just, like, bookshelves of books and books. She was involved with the book world and was manager *of the Workers' Education Association bookroom at the Adelaide University. As young children she always gave us very good books. There were ones written by this Englishwoman about India. They were very good traditional tales. When I was ten or eleven, it was the most recent Australian books for children, written by Australian authors, that she gave us. At Christmas and birthdays it was always books. Unfortunately most of them were destroyed by the cyclone in 1974 in Darwin, so I don't have any of them any more.*

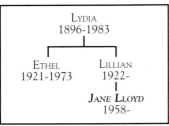

It was very distressing because I lost that link to those items of the past. We were in England at the time, seeing my father's mother for the first time. We flew back to Sydney, to Adelaide and finally to Darwin in early February. I remember walking around the house because we were staying in a flat. It was basically just a big sundeck, and part of my room was only just there. Mum and Dad had actually cleared out most of it, but there was my Pablo Picasso poster, which was hanging off the wall. The books were still on the shelves that were wet. I just remember throwing them around and being very distraught. My brother was extremely upset too. That was the first time I actually learnt about how people react differently to traumas and tragedies.

In Jane Lloyd's family, the books were to come to her because the library was her special field. *I have my aunt's books, but they are ones she had and were given to me after she died. I was fourteen when she died, and I was doing Indonesian and getting very interested in people from other places. When we visited her, we'd just poke around and pick out different books and look at them. All her books went to Pat - she's the younger sister of Mum and Ethel - and my grandfather put all the bookshelves in her house. Some went to Mum's younger brother. But since I've been to university and with what I'm doing, it was a decision by Pat and Clarke that I should have those books, and I was welcome to take them any time I wanted to, because it was now my area. Now that I have this house in Alice Springs, I had a base myself, and I could bring them back, and I was given them. I understand that in Pat's will, all the books, hers and Ethel's, are left to me.*

In other families, daughters have inherited books that enhance their choice of profession. For many women, this has meant taking on books from their fathers - especially where their chosen field has been medicine or law. From mother came the love for books or the artistic flair for writing and drawing. From mother came a thoughtful book on a birthday or special occasion. For Pat Giles it was a birthday present, her seventeenth: the Scottish Psalmster and Church Hymnal on which is written, 'Patsy with love from Mother 1945.'

Books may be a way of saying something or broaching a topic indirectly.

A Literate Tradition

This is particularly so of the gifts from daughters to mothers.

I hear a book reviewed, and I think, Mum would like that, and I chase it down. I gave her Kate Millet's Sexual Politics years ago, but she found that heavy going. And since she'd never read D.H. Lawrence or Miller, it didn't make much sense. She likes reading biographies.

In some families, there is a treasured book that is inscribed and links the holder to the past generations. Wendy Wright has one such book from each side of the family: the poetical works of Alfred Tennyson and a bible. The large leather-bound family bible was presented to her grandparents on their wedding day. The inscription on the fly-leaf reads: 'Presented to Mr and Mrs W.C. Gallagher by the Trustees of the New Methodist Church of Lancaster on the occasion of their marriage - 18 April 1906'. Pressed in cellophane and attached to the endpaper is a pale green fern frond from the bridal bouquet. The poems were a gift to Wendy's paternal grandmother from her parents on her twenty-third birthday. This book is one of Wendy's treasures and was only given to her a year ago. *The bible and the book of poems are not only mementos of my grandparents, I do read them from time to time.*

Family bibles, with the family history in copperplate on the fly-leaf, were not in as much evidence as the prayer-book. This small item could be kept by the bedside table - not always read but comfortingly close. Women were called upon to read prayers, especially if they lived some distance from a clergyman or church. To them also could fall the task of reading prayers over a dying child.

Patti Monro has a little prayer book with a silver angel cover design: It was from the clergyman who married her mother's parents in Johannesburg in 1906. Patti's grandmother had been a choirgirl, and the clergyman had later run a soup kitchen in St Martin in the Fields.

Sue Andrews asked her grandmother for a set of encylopedia that she loved reading as a child.

I thought I would like my daughter Jane to have them. They're an historic curosity more than anything else. They're falling apart. I'll get them re-bound one day. For me, like my father, the passing on of knowledge, the acquisition of education and the fight to increase opportunities for the ordinary working people are far more important than material objects. The most important legacy I can leave Jane, my daughter, is the confidence to believe in herself as a woman and the courage to fight for what is right.

EVA
|
HILDA
1920-
|
SUE ANDREWS
1948-
|
JANE
1976-

For some women, access to books led to an interest

in writing. Where Patti Monro lived, there were few children to play with, her father was away at the war and her brother at school. Her communications were with Argonauts on the A.B.C.

I didn't win anything for writing. We always had to write home from school. Our letters were read and censored if we criticized the school. My communication is by written word, and I feel comfortable with that. I always had the story in my head, but I have a filter on speech, and I edit myself. I don't have that facility to engage people in conversation with, 'Guess what?'

Now I have my parents' library. I had no idea of the extent of my mother's interest in music. She had booklets on how to listen to music and had made notes in the margin. There was an undated song book with sea shanties, Negro spirituals and lullabies. There were four beautiful books of songs from Britain, Wales, Ireland and Scotland. They came from my mother's aunt to me, because I played the piano.

Michele Kosky: *I read* The World of Suzy Wong *when I was thirteen,* Peyton Place *and* Kings Row. *They were all very risqué. I read ferociously. I once had twenty-six library books in my desk and was taken by Mother Dolores to the science room and ticked off soundly.*

I read Time *magazine and used to subscribe to it when I was eleven. My aim was to become a journalist on* Time *magazine. Then when I was fifteen, I started getting* New Statesman. *I realized where I had gone wrong, and now I wanted to work for the* New Statesman.

There was a section in the school library where the big girls (over fifteen) were allowed to sit to read. It was where they kept books like *War and Peace*, unedited volumes of Shakespeare and Chaucer. The books fell open at the pages we weren't supposed to read. In the threepenny library in our local shops, there was another section that was restricted. There I found authors such as P.G. Wodehouse and Arthur Upfield. I read, in binges, everything by one author until I'd finished that section and I could copy his or her style. My English teacher thought I was a hopeless case. I submitted some pieces to Argonauts and had no success under my own name but had the stories read when I used a boy's name.

Dad read to us when we were very little. Then, when we learnt to read, we read to Gran.

Penny Peel found books a treasure. *When I was young, there was enough money for necessities and, when things got tough, books were an escape.*

They were a luxury, but we always had them. Dad read to us when we were very little. Then, when we learnt to read, we would read to Gran. Dad read the newspapers to us. The cricket scores and local football and politics, if an election was on, that was what we heard. I grew up with an attitude to Bob Menzies that I find hard to get rid of. 'Oh, him,' I say, when I hear his name.

We got books for birthdays and Christmas. There were no paperbacks in the house then. There was a series of classics, and we didn't get another one until we'd finished the first. We were never bought 'improving books', and comics were spurned. We were encouraged to read, and there was no T.V. in North Queensland until the 1960s. We listened to radio serials with Gran, like 'Blue Hills' and 'Portia Faces Life'. I re-read my children's books now that the ones that I love are back in print. I bought some for the girls and re-read them - things like Anne of Green Gables. I read everything, except the telephone book.

Some books were given to us to build character.

Without easy access to books, it was difficult to learn to read and understand different styles.

We didn't have a lot of books. We had our prizes from Sunday School. Every day, mother would sit me down with the Advertiser *and make me pick out long words and look them up in the dictionary and write them out twenty times. I always felt in doing that I became a proficient reader and speller.*

Muriel Armstrong's mother was an avid reader and borrowed from the New South Wales State Library. *She read Shakespeare to me at the age of six, the myths and legends of Norsemen and Romans. Both Mother and Father read poetry to us, and both of them were storytellers. Some books were given to us to build character. Mother always honoured a promise and would save to buy a book if we wanted it.*

It was always, 'Go and get the Pears.'

Lillian Lloyd: *Mother was well read, and I used to go to the library to change books for her, and we used the library so much my sister and I were allowed to get books for free. That was wonderful because there wasn't much money. We had* Black Beauty *and* What Katy Did *and the* Pears Encyclopaedia *in our family: that was like the bible. Being an Irish family, there were always arguments, and they were solved with, 'Go and get the Pears,' from Mother. We had a lot of political arguments. They'd left Ireland because of unrest between the Catholics and Protestants. I was well informed on Ireland, and I remember getting top marks for an essay I'd written on the topic and being quizzed about whether someone else had written it!*

For those whose books were seen as un-Australian, the ramifications were drastic. *I knew that friends of his were involved in the socialist club at the university, and that he'd been delivering* The Tribune *as a student, but it hadn't really made much of an impression upon me. My knowledge of politics was vestigial. I was a conservative person, and I was probably voting for Menzies, or whoever the conservative candidates were. At that stage, I had two small babies, and we were actually living in Katharine Susannah Prichard's house - she was in the eastern states trying to sue Wentworth for libel - it was a dreadful shock when I realized that those country trips that my husband had taken meant that our car had gone to meetings which were for the Communist Party. This was at a stage when there was a real McCarthyist sort of feeling around [1953-4], and all I could see at first was a dreadful threat to the security of my precious little family.*

I realized my worry was that he'd be taken off to gaol. His friends used to joke among themselves about their mail being opened, and people turning up and searching through their papers and books, and that sort of thing. Irene Greenwood's papers and books were hidden in the Presbyterian vestry during that time by a minister who didn't particularly believe in communism, but who believed in her right to have those ideas. It was very very frightening, and I was pretty stupid, I guess. I also felt very vulnerable, and I don't think he understood, and I don't recall really talking to him about it.

Other books from that era were lost when the party bookshop was burnt in 1985. Madge Cope particularly remembered *The Socialist Sixth of the World*, which she'd given to the party bookshop with a number of other books.

I didn't hold on to them for my children because they wouldn't have been interested, and all my friends were in the party, and they'd go to the bookshop to get second-hand books if they wanted them.

My father threw Animal Farm in the rubbish
because the word 'communism' appeared
on the cover.

Censorship took a number of forms: *There were no books in the house, only Alice in Wonderland. We had little Golden books, which could be purchased with the groceries, and a prayerbook. My father threw Animal Farm*

Jane Lloyd, Alice Springs, Northern Territory

Susan Magarey, Kent Town, South Australia

Isobel Skoczek and her daughter 'Nampin' Jessica Owens, Alice Springs, Northern Territory

Michele Kosky and her daughter Anna Kosky, Hollywood, Western Australia

in the rubbish because the word 'communism' appeared on the cover. One of my cousins gave me Ginsberg to read, and he hit the roof. I went to the library to read nihilistic ideas - those sorts of exciting ideas were forbidden. In a way, my Catholic upbringing backfired because it was after Vatican II, and we were introduced to other religions, and I got to reading about other ways of thinking. We had good books pushed at us - about the lives of saints - not bad books. My mother's father gave me a dictionary, and I learned from that!

At the other end of the scale are the women's magazines, which were passed from one woman to another, read, clipped for recipes and knitting patterns. Eventually they disintegrated and were thrown out. Reading back copies of these journals, we glimpse images of Australian women, the images our mothers and grandmothers perused. Remember that photograph of the young Princess Elizabeth in a boiler suit, part of the war effort. Then in the fifties, the models of the young royal mother and boys had their hair parted on the right just like the young Prince. Not until the late seventies did the image of a woman in a boilersuit, as a trade apprentice, become acceptable.

Books were a luxury for some women; for others, tools of trade. Access to a public library and cheap paperbacks extended the range available. Habits established as a child, encouragement from a teacher, special interests are all reflected in our collections of books. What was available at home was the first opportunity to know print and, from what is remembered, locally produced material was popular. Those reading to the children, the mothers and grandmothers, rarely had a classical education. They bought and read books that felt familiar to them. Like the medieval book owners, they were essential to a literate tradition.

Chapter Eleven

EVERYTHING A WOMAN OUGHT TO KNOW

My Book of Household Management contains everything women ought to know about running a house, cookery, children, home doctor, business, stress, society, career and citizenship. The book was a present to my grandmother, born in 1866, for her twenty-fifth wedding anniversary. The inscription read, 'To my dear wife Janie, 11 August 1911'.

It contains recipes and all sorts of stuff about how to furnish your house, how to deal with your pets, and your servants. It has home nursing, first-aid, physical exercises, home-gardening hints and lots of good advice about budgeting. It is progressive and even talks about women being involved in community activities and projects, that sort of thing, but when it comes to anything to do with reproduction or the intimate side of marriage it is silent, quite silent. There is good advice about how to actually bring up babies and look after your health during pregnancy, but as far as the actual process ... that's left to the imagination.

Pat Giles assures me that she has read the full seven hundred and twenty pages of the book. It is not, however, where she learnt the facts of life.

Living on farms, women had opportunities to observe animal behaviour but, even there, girls were sheltered.

My parents were unenthusiastic about my studying. In their view, clever women go mad and end up fat and disgusting, with scabs. They would tell me about Bea Miles and how eccentric she was.

Ideas of what a girl could witness made first-hand knowledge of anatomy, even fowls, difficult. *Making mush for the pigs, feeding the cats, chickens, turkeys, goats, calves, dogs, all fell to mother, and I helped. It was women's work. When the turkey was gutted, I was asked to leave the room, but I would be there for the plucking.*

But there was nothing about feelings, or how it might be to enjoy sex.

To find out about our bodies, we turned to whatever was available: household manuals, mysterious medical texts and true-love novels.

My grandmother gave me a book called On Becoming a Woman. *It had pictures of brides and advice on how to be 'popular' without being a 'sinner'. It had a fairly detailed anatomical drawing of the male and female reproductive system. Suddenly, it all fell into place, and I understood about menstruation and pregnancy. But there was nothing about feelings, or how it might be to enjoy sex. I got practical information about tampons, and things like where my vagina was, and how it was different from the urethra, from a girlfriend who had older sisters who presumably had lovers and knew heaps. You didn't just explore that part of your body then.*

Questions about our bodies were kept private, even from other women. 'Don't talk about that!' or 'Thank God, that's all behind me,' were common responses from older women.

It was all invisible... No sympathy. You'd be in agony.

For a growing girl, there was abundant homely advice on health and the making of nourishing soups for invalids. There were descriptions galore of coy behaviour, but nothing on sexuality, nothing for dealing with menstrual cramps.

It was all invisible. We had our monthlies, and I'd get a backache; my stomach would go, too. It would just be, 'Get out and walk, go on, go on.' 'Here're these tablets.' No sympathy. You'd be in agony. I didn't talk about it with other girls. I was too afraid, too embarrassed. We were separated from each other by that, and this is the fifties.

It was not only menstruation that was hidden; even pregnancies within marriage were denied in public. *Pa was a councillor, and we were invited to all the royal functions. He said I would be his lady, and that I should 'look after myself' and not get pregnant for the next year. I did get pregnant with the fifth, but I went on a diet and didn't tell him. He was of the school of thought that you didn't appear in public when you were pregnant.*

In a country town in the thirties, husbands were not seen with their pregnant wives. *We went walking after dark. I'd be waiting for the cool and the chance to stretch my legs and talk to him.*

Rather hazy clues about how our bodies worked were in some popular magazines. *I'd been to mother-daughter nights and knew how chooks and rabbits got pregnant, and somehow you were meant to extrapolate to humans. In the back of the English* Women's Weekly *were letters which were an endless source of fascination to me in late primary school and early high school. There would be this letter, 'I think I'm pregnant,' and a long answer in equally euphemistic terms, but at least there was some information.*

'You think you'll enjoy it, but you won't; it's your duty.'

Sexuality was too close for our mothers to talk about or, when they did, it was in a distant foreign language, not really part of our experience.

One of the few girls of the time whose mother was prepared to talk about such things called her first period 'the flowers', like in the bible. To acknowledge the emerging sexuality of a daughter was to invite her to acknowledge a mother's sexuality - a difficult task for both. How do we come to think of our mothers as sexual beings?

I think Mum remained basically ignorant and embarrassed about her body. One night I remember Dad got a bit pissed, and we were talking. I was at university by then, and he said, 'I tried to teach your mother a few things, but she wouldn't be in it, wouldn't learn anything.' She used to say to me, 'You think you'll enjoy it, but you won't; it's your duty.'

A mother's responsibility for a daughter was clear: protect, control, create good women. For those taught to hide menstruation, and even pregnancy, open discussions about sexuality were almost impossible. You didn't need to know about pregnancy if you 'saved' yourself for marriage. Information was not even shared among peers. Sometimes an older sister, cousin or friend would help out with details, but the anguish arising from the fear of pregnancy from an innocent touch or a kiss was real. Sex belonged in marriage, and pleasure arose from the arrival of children, not from knowing how one's body worked. We were also fed a number of myths.

My first child was born within a year of being married. It was a bit of a shock. I'd always been led to believe, by my mother, particularly, that I was not feminine enough to fall pregnant - so I didn't worry about it when I got married.

In the *Illustrated Family Doctor* of 1935, there is a wealth of information on the diseases of the penis and vagina, but nothing on sexuality. There is, however, a fascinating entry on masturbation, which suggests this form of self-abuse is the result of irritations caused by threadworms or 'the decomposition of discharges owing to lack of cleanliness'. To avoid it, children are to be encouraged in 'vigorous open-air exercise and an ambition to excel in games'.

This fellow kissed me, and I thought I was pregnant.

Contraception, abortion and sexuality were not matters about which a girl should burden herself, and certainly not ones a mother was in any position to talk about. Sessions with experts, such as doctors, were not always helpful. Other avenues for finding out were heavily moralistic. There was little in most homes to which girls could turn; little outside the home.

I remember, after a dance, coming home in the moonlight, and this fellow chased and kissed me. I thought I was pregnant. I nearly went mad. I had no one to talk to about it. I had read all sorts of novels, a bit spicy, but really very innocent.

Instead, we received not so subtle indications about what was proper behaviour for girls. *I remember the day that I realized the difference between boys and girls. I was about six or seven. On moonlight nights, every evening after a meal, in the early evening, us kids would go out to play hide and seek. My brother said he was going, and I said, 'Me too.' I was told not to go. I went. I came home and got a strapping. I'd never been belted before.*

If contact with boys was so dangerous, and pregnancy out of wedlock such shame, how far could youthful play go? I'd stayed overnight at a friend's and *slept outside on the verandah. One of the boys got up and threw water over me. I got angry. He was in his pyjamas, and he got me at the back of the tank stand. I felt his body against mine and got so frightened. He kissed me. I got my sister down the river with me and asked her if I was pregnant. I was fifteen, and she was sixteen, but she didn't know, either. It was something to do with the body, but I didn't know.*

Confusions were inevitable. *I remember asking for the meaning of a four-letter word I had seen written on the back of a public toilet door. We didn't have a car, so we were always sent to the toilet, with strict instructions about not actually sitting on the seat, before we boarded the train. I laboriously sounded out the word, which was illustrated with a crude sketch of male and female genitalia, and proudly pronounced it in the clear voice of a five-year-old. I was given 'that look' and told it had to do with bodily functions like going to the toilet. It took me some time to understand why other toilet doors told me, 'Jamie' did it to 'Leanne'.*

At what point did the magic moment come when we could be told or be allowed to read about 'it'? Madge Cope, born in 1904, remembers: *Mother always insisted anything to do with your bottom was rude. A man exposed himself to me once. He undid his fly and said, 'Feel this.' I could see he was drunk. I knew what it was, but I didn't know what it was for. I turned and walked away. I wanted to run, but mother had always told me not to run away from a dog. I told her when I got home.*

In the sixties and seventies, conditions were tougher. *I mixed with a pretty rough crowd. We were drinking at thirteen. I came out of it without getting into too much trouble. Most of the others were pregnant, or finished up in gaol. One was killed in a car accident. We were helping our girlfriends get abortions at thirteen.*

The messages a girl received when her period first began were ambiguous. On the one hand, she was told this had to do with achieving womanhood and, on the other, she found menstruation hedged in by a number of taboos. There was no celebration of her new status, just new rules and a new vocabulary: what amounted to a woman's slang about a secret matter. Men did not hear it; they had their own language, which was crude and derogatory.

Protecting others from the knowledge that menstruating women lived in a house extended to keeping sanitary napkins out of sight in a linen press, or underwear drawer. They were not kept in the bathroom or toilet where they were actually used. Dispensing machines were visible in the 'ladies' rooms', but only very recently have napkins and tampons found a place in shared toilets and bathrooms. Keeping menstruation invisible included shielding even the males of the family from evidence of it at home. It was quite a feat. When menstrual cloths had been washed, they needed to be off the line before the men came home.

Wash them, don't show your father. You can't wash your hair, you'll go silly; all those myths, and this was the fifties. You were told, 'You're going to get this every month, just keep yourself clean.' But you couldn't have a shower, you couldn't bath or wash your hair, you'd smell yourself.

The task of making the menstrual cloths was… like my initiation to womanhood.

Each of the older women we interviewed had memories of the problems of menstruation, but none had discussed these with her friends. In their view, 'the curse' was just part of being a woman.

Part of reaching puberty was the making of these cloths. Mum sat me down and had a very straightforward conversation about what was happening, and then set me the task of making the cloths. It was like my initiation to womanhood. The material was soft winceyette, with the double blue line down the side. I sewed a loop on each end - that went flat against your body - and a tape which went around you was threaded through the loop. We couldn't change at school and wore dark pants in case of flooding. The cloths chafed my legs. What a bonus when Modess came on the market. Kotex came first, but they were too expensive.

Acknowledgement of menstruation, when it came, was of a practical nature. *I remember one poor girl at the boarding school. She knew nothing about it. She just started menstruating, no information, but all the gear was in her case.*

It was women who dealt with menstruation but at a practical level. *I never had any of the facts of life. I woke up one morning, and the bed was all blood. My mother was dead, and Dad said, 'Oh, look, you go to the lady across the road.' She fixed me up, and it was never mentioned again.* Few, it seems, learned much from Mum. *She said, 'You know that bleeding, it will happen every month!' I said, 'I know all about it.' I'd read an old medical book at home. I knew what happened with the cattle, but I didn't connect periods with having a baby. There was only one young woman I knew who had a baby out of marriage. She was naive. She had to do agriculture work that men wouldn't do, like picking turnips in the frost.*

Isolated and ignorant, women lacked someone who could inform them. *I found out about periods from*

everybody else, not from Mum. She told me to expect it to come. She was probably terribly embarrassed. Her mother didn't tell her. She only had grade-three education. What we did learn were attitudes, and that these could be exploited. I consciously used this thing. I said to Dad, 'Don't hit me. I'm bleeding.' I knew he didn't hit Mum, and I thought it must have been because she bled.

By the sixties, there was an increased openness in discussing sex. *One of the really important things with Mum, which we both felt proud of, was that we were open about our bodies. I saw blood in the toilet, I asked her, and we had this really big conversation. I kept it under the hat for a while because most of the girls didn't know. I think she was careful to talk to me about sex because she didn't find out about it until she was married. It was progressive but, to her, these were things that were for marriage. That came from the Catholic Church. I've been antagonistic towards the church because I see it as being the greatest impediment to a perfect family.*

We'd do what the men had done all these years and play the field.

By the seventies came world-weariness. *When I was living in Canada, my girlfriend and I decided we'd do some research. We'd do what the men had done all these years and play the field and pick someone up and use them for sex. We decided while we were doing it we might as well be constructive, so we'd keep a record and write a book. We got up to twenty-six nationalities. The next morning we'd say, 'Well, piss off now, you're chapter six!' They nearly died. It was just what they'd been doing all these years. I stopped when I met this Indian guy. He taught me there was a spiritual side. He wanted to get married, but I've stayed single.*

Sharing across the generations opened a new world for one mother. *I really admire her because she hasn't closed her mind. When she was visiting me in Perth, we went down to the beach, and she met a number of my lesbian friends. They were sunbaking in the nude and, when they saw Mum coming, said, 'Put your knickers on,' but they didn't put on their tops. It was a really hot day, and Mum went back with them for a cup of tea. I followed and, when I got there, they were talking, quite engrossed, and Mum was saying how she'd never had a room of her own, and she wants to transform the laundry into a room where she can sew and do yoga and write. And they talked about female spirituality. Next morning, Mum says, 'That was one of the best days in my life. All my life I've walked around hunched up.' She's really heavy breasted and embarrassed by it. 'But there were those women, proud of their bodies. It's a lesson I'll never forget,' she says.*

The literature written about sexuality since the sixties, especially that inspired by the women's movement, has put women in touch with their bodies, removed fears about pregnancy, provided information on disease and treatment, removed shame about our bodies and their functions. We no longer need to see ourselves reflected in the male gaze.

From older woman we heard of family-planning dilemmas.

I'm not married five minutes, and I'm pregnant. It was war time, and my husband was granted compassionate leave, for neither the baby nor me was expected to survive. It was a very dramatic time for us as a young couple. We came through all right. But he said, 'If that's having children, no more.' But when it came time for him to leave, to go up north to New Guinea, and it was the last night, 'Do you think we'll take a punt?' 'Oh, all right.' That's the next one. I lived with my parents and my little family till he came home. Then we resumed. I finished in 1962; nine children we had.

He gave me a book on the ovulation method... I thought it was an insult.

One couple married young and had children before the husband had finished school. Constant childbearing created pressures with no easy solution.

We lived with my parents, but when I was pregnant again, we had a big ding-dong. Dad stormed out, and then came a knock on the door, and a man had a subpoena for us to force us out of the house. So we went to live with the in-laws. Then I was pregnant again. My father-in-law said, 'One more, and you'll have to go,' and he gave me a book on the ovulation method. I didn't take any notice. I thought it was an insult. The next one, my husband delivered it. I'd taken castor oil to move it because Mum was coming to mind the kids. Then my husband had a really bad car accident. Then I had another one, five in all, in six years. Then I realized it wasn't fair on me, the kids or my husband. The priest said it was my duty.

Bearing children was a full-time job for those women who saw themselves as vehicles of God's will. *It was a terrible struggle rearing us all - seven boys, five girls and numerous miscarriages - but she wouldn't be without any of us, and that, of course, is the most reassuring thing that she can say to us now. But it's taken its toll of her, and she has a certain faith which I both admire and am cynical about. That's what got her through, but I can't believe in a church that requires that of me.*

Happy families? How many of us went in search of a relationship as an escape, to duplicate our parents' marriage, or to create a different unit, the one we'd always longed for?

They used to fight over religion. Dad was an alcolohic, and he used to have epileptic fits. She stood up to him and nagged, but no communication. I left school at fifteen. I wanted to get married and have twelve kids. Well, I did get married, at twenty-one, to a boy of eighteen. I was pregnant, and that was that. We didn't have nothing. Six kids later, he left me for another woman, but he still was always around us. Then he ran out of money, and she left. I took him back, and he's been out of work for seven years now. I work, clean, that's all I'm really fit for. I haven't had much education. I'm after something, but I don't know what. I have one daughter with me now, with her baby; her boyfriend left her. At least I know she's getting a good feed.

Fights had as many causes as solutions. *I always thought I was to blame in fights. He'd rant and rave and tear his clothes. His best effort was pyjamas. He'd rip them off in a fit. I'd patiently sew the buttons back on and darn the holes. Then I woke up to myself. I bought him ski pyjamas.*

There were, of course, ways around the problem of contraception, even in the thirties. *After the third child, I told the doctor I didn't want any more. He said he could do an appendix and tie my tubes. You were allowed to do that but not have an operation on your tubes. For fifty years now, I've been working for women to be able to have some control. It seems like as soon as we get a victory, it's lost. Now I'm more concerned with the elderly and with the right to die with dignity.*

Reliable contraception and the possibility of pursuing a career while married, or independence from the family, brought new choices for a woman. You can stay single and not rely on family, marry but not reproduce, divorce and sustain life as a single mother. But higher education and building a career take time. And although child care and maternity-leave provisions help, women are still faced with hard choices.

With my second child, I took leave, and being with him has been important, but at times it's hard to maintain my confidence in regard to work. You lose self-esteem at home, and there is no feedback from the outside world to you as an individual. With my first, I had no choice. I was a single working mother, and I had to cope. I had to manage the domestic side efficiently or go mad. Mum wasn't much help at that time. She criticized rather than supported - brought me down a peg. When my parents helped, there were always strings attached. Now I have to decide if I will risk another child. I'd love a daughter, but I'm nearly forty, and it would mean more time out of the

workforce. My husband helps, but there is little impetus for fathers to change their habits while there is someone at home.

Some choose not to have children. *That's my preference. I think I'm too selfish to have children, and I've seen what it did to Mum and to my friends. There was no peace in our place. It would have been far better if they'd compromised. In one situation she's the bully, and then he's the victim, then he'd get the upper hand, and she's the victim. If that's what marriage is for, forget it. Anyway, it's too late now without taking big risks, but I have god-children and, at the end of a lovely day, I pack them up, and they go home.*

It's a very female-oriented culture... what would a son mean?

In lesbian relationships different questions arise. I'm in a long-term relationship with another woman, and we were talking about having a child, and how we'd do it, and who would have it. I'm older, so it makes sense for her, but then I'm Jewish, and it's the first time I've thought about that aspect of me. I do spend a lot of time with my friends' daughters, and that's important. It's a very female-oriented culture we live in. What would a son mean?

Having children imposes a routine, 'the internal clock' as Annie called it, but in the view of one country mother, city women handicap their children. *They take away the challenge from their children by presenting them with opportunities. They are rushed off to obtain skills. Everyone has to have time to sit down and watch the clouds, have time to dream; you don't have to do something physical every minute of the day to be productive.*

Other older women recognized the changing nature of the responsibility in rearing children. *There are more pressures now. I see my daughters; they are servants to their children. She drives them, here, there. I think, I didn't do that. My kids would set off in the morning. I can see them with their little blue berets and white shirts. The roads weren't dangerous. It was more peaceful.*

In these 'good old days', young mothers turned to older women for advice on child-rearing, but the emergence of books dealing with scientific methods in the 1940s, followed by others on the need for natural motherhood in the 1970s, left mothers bewildered.

I remember John Bowlby's Child Care and the Growth of Love, wretched book. I was convinced that even leaving the child with grandmother for an hour while I went to the dentist was going to do the most dreadful things to the child. Now, with my daughter's children, I'm relaxed and think it's important she has time out, and they learn to deal with other adults.

Trusting your instincts and knowledge of your own childhood was discouraged. *Always us kids slept together. I don't remember many nights when I slept on my own. If they woke in the night and were cold, or wet the bed, I hopped in. But with my first child, I wouldn't let him in bed with us. I was too much taken in by theories of 'raising your child'. Now, with my second family, this is my first experience of shared parenting; some nights the baby comes with us, some not.*

Doctors don't always encourage women to be well informed about their bodies. *I had multiple sclerosis diagnosed. I had to fly back to Australia. I was very ill and had a lot of trouble sleeping, and the doctors prescribed sleeping pills, willy nilly. I became addicted, and it was a major health problem getting off them. I went to health centres, ones for women, but there wasn't any information, no pamphlets. I found a book later on, the first one published in Australia about the long-term effects of tranquillizers, but none of the doctors, and I'd been to many, had been able to tell me anything.*

A psychiatric patient who sought information about her drugs and requested fresh fruit but was given mush, who took on the authorities and was labelled 'trouble', had books withheld on the treatment of women as psychiatric patients. She was drugged into submission. Now, with self-help, fellowship through the church, exercise and a good diet, she lives at home and helps others who have been through similar experiences.

Religion emerged as an important part of women's lives, one that offered security in simplicity. One woman described how hard work, sharing life with others and having children were basic to the lives of the Brethren, a Christian sect that shares the values of the Pennsylvannia Dutch. Grandmother had worn the uniform of the Brethren: bonnet and long pinafore in dark colours; Mother had taken a less than strict interpretation of the code, and her generation, born in the fifties, was encouraged to pay attention to their appearance. Their hair was curled, and they wore softer clothes.

For some women, religion provided guidance on issues such as contraception and abortion; for others, it was an impediment to a happy family. Some daughters followed their mothers and found strength and fellowship through participation in church activities; others rebelled against their early religious training. Nonetheless, religion was important in women's lives, whether in total rejection or as the active keepers of the faith.

I still find myself going, 'Hail Mary.'

I'*m not a practising Catholic any more but, in times of crisis, I still find myself going, 'Hail Mary.' When I can't sleep at night, I say a few.*

When asked, Where is your rosary? the answer was prompt even among those claiming to be lapsed Catholics. To be sure, we talked to more lapsed than practising Catholics, but they all admitted that their early training had an effect on their careers and identity as women.

My Catholic girls' education taught me a sense of social responsibility but, at the same time, it limited the manner in which I might respond.

Others trusted that their faith would provide in hard times as their families grew and the income remained static. Religion was a comfort in times of crisis, especially for those in violent or alcoholic homes. *I took it one day at a time and said, 'If you'll get me through today…'*

For many women, religion was interwoven with family, special food and visiting on Sundays. *I loved Sunday afternoons. We'd go to Sunday School, have dinner, and mother would sit on the verandah, or inside if it was cold. We were allowed to get sixpence worth of sweets. We'd bring them home, put them on the table, and you could take your choice.* In Lillian Lloyd's family of ten, this was quite a treat.

If church attendance was difficult, as in Jo Conway's family, Sunday School came to the home. *We were living some distance from the church and, as the family increased, it became more of a hassle to drive the family to church on Sunday. Mum was afraid we would all end up as heathens if we didn't go to Sunday School, so we had it at home in the afternoons. The little ones and the older sister would play hymns on the piano, and we had to learn the words and sing those hymns. She'd give us a text each to learn for each Sunday and explain the meaning. We'd have to be able to stand up and recite it. She'd do a bible reading and tell us a bible story. This was the Sunday thing after lunch, on Sunday afternoons. I can still see us as a family sitting around in the lounge room.*

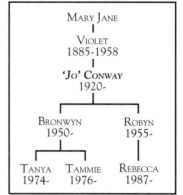

In Jo's mother's family home, religious observances were strict. The prayer book was in constant use. *In grandmother's family, they had prayers, in the morning after breakfast, straight after breakfast. We used to visit, and we had to participate, too. At the evening meal, my grandfather would have a bible reading and prayers. It was normal procedure in that household. It wasn't in my father's household, but they would have been seen as heathens. They thought it was sufficient to do your praying at church and before you went to bed at night.*

Responses to parental regimes were anything but constant. For some, strict religious codes engendered disenchantment and rebellion; in others, obedience and subservience.

After Vatican II, some of the schools became more liberal and taught things like philosophy, and that's where I found out about other religions. I was cross to find so much had been hidden from us.

Another complained: *I didn't believe in things like papal infallibility. We weren't taught about theology or the history of Christianity. We didn't even encounter Martin Luther because it was dangerous. One of my brothers lent me books and so, privately, I decided I had my own concept of good.*

I used to count the white spots on my nails. They said all of them were lies I'd told.

Martha Ricardo had a concept of good imposed. *My grandmother told me, 'Every time you look in the mirror, you're vain, and the devil will walk seven steps towards you.' I was terrified. I used to count the white spots on my nails. They said all of them were lies I'd told. I had quite a few when I was little, probably something with my diet, but the guilt! I was six or seven and worrying about sin.*

Others remained puzzled. *I knew Catholics looked like me, but I thought there must be something under their clothes.* Some mothers gave up. *When I was going overseas, Mum sent me a St Jude's medal - St Jude for lost and hopeless causes.*

Younger women reacted strongly to what they saw as coercion. *Mum used Catholicism to back her up, and she called the tune in the household. She was relentless about getting her own way. Dad influenced her but more by gentle persuasion. She'd often feel we weren't grateful enough for her mothering. I think she was probably pretty dissatisfied with her role. She'd play the martyr if you went against her wishes. She can still get a big reaction out of me, make me feel guilty.*

She rings me every Sunday and says, 'Why aren't you at church?'

The generation gap between mothers and daughters is nowhere as clear as in those families who settled in Australia in the forties and fifties.

Still my mother rings me every Sunday and says, 'Why aren't you at church?' Because for her it's not just religion, it's part of your culture, your upbringing, everything. I think she understands my rejection both of the culture and the church; you can't separate the two. She has never absorbed any Australian values and is quite critical of them. She has her own stereotypes of Australians, quite racist ones, too.

Until I was about twelve, there was a very strong emphasis on Sundays being the day for church, saying your prayers, knowing the bible. But it was all unintelligible to me. I mean, it's in ancient Greek, and no attempt was made to reach my generation. They couldn't hope to reach us, gain our allegiance. Being in Australia is so different from in Greece, but my mother didn't see it that way.

For Isobel Skoczek, also the daughter of post-second world war immigrants, the experience of the rituals of the family, religion and Sundays was very different. Born in 1949 of Polish parents, Isobel grew up knowing little of Australia beyond a close group of Polish friends.

I went to Catholic primary and secondary school, and my weekends were spent with my parent's friends and their children. They were like cousins. It was like growing up in part of Poland. We spoke Polish, and I went to Polish camps from the age of about eight. The last time was when I was about nineteen. There was a strong emphasis on Polish culture. We celebrated the name days, heard stories of life in Poland, went to European films. I was shocked when I found out about the way people ate and talked outside our little Polish community.

```
       MARISYA
       1912-1975
          |
    ISOBEL SKOCZEK
        1949-
          |
   'NAMPIN' JESSICA
        1985-
```

It was not until she left school, trained as a nurse and travelled that she moved away from the family circle. *When I went overseas, I was someone who was strongly moulded by my family, because that's where all my influences came from. Even during my school years, my influence from home was a lot greater than from school. Socially it was not really a lot from school, either. Then going nursing and overseas and coming back, having experienced and met different people, I was a very different person.*

There was this feeling that a girl's good life came to an end when she got married.

For Isobel, the Polish community provided models for the proper, young Catholic woman.

Mum was very strong on religion and she even talked about becoming a nun. At the least, it was expected I would marry a Catholic boy and settle into a traditional role of wife and mother.

Paula Cristoffanini, of a similar age to Isobel, also came from a strict Catholic background, but she had grown up in Chile. When she arrived in Australia in 1970, she had no instant family, and she could not speak English. According to Paula:

It was really interesting for me to look back into my life. I grew up in a woman's world; everywhere there were women. There was my family which was important to me. Other than my father and my grandfather, everyone who was important to me on a daily basis was a woman. So I grew up in a woman's area. I was taught by the Sisters.

> GABRIELA
> 1900-
> |
> SOPHIA
> 1928-
> |
> PAULA CRISTOFFANINI
> 1951-

While I was growing up, there was this feeling in Chile that a girl's good life came to an end when she got married. So you really had to enjoy yourself, and you had to be spoilt as a girl child. Your good life was going to end and your hard life would begin.

My mother would get up in the morning and make herself beautiful and then take us to the park and do some knitting and sewing. She is very artistic and used to draw and paint and have hobbies. She used to make our dresses. We were absolute dolls, absolutely beautiful, she was a beautiful wife and mother, and her children were beautiful. I was the ugly child of the family, and she used to make me beautiful by giving me beautiful clothes.

Life in Australia was not easy. There were problems with accommodation, health and child care and no extended family as back up. *I arrived here as a new bride. I was eighteen and a half. I'd gone from a household of women to a man's world and, worse still, I was a foreigner to my husband's friends, because I was Italian Chilean and didn't cook Chilean food. I had to learn. He was proud and didn't want me to work. He wanted to support me. I went to the employment office with my broken English and letters from the Australian Embassy, and I was so determined - they got me a job in a government department as a tracer.*

Both Isobel and Paula deviated from the expectations of their parents about what a Catholic daughter should do; both sought education and training that has kept them working with women: Isobel in nursing, Paula in Women's Affairs. In 1987 Paula became the president of the Women's Advisory Counsel to the Premier in Western Australia, having completed a university degree in 1982, and worked with migrant women for the Multicultural and Ethnic Affairs Commission.

Isobel and Paula thought it important to maintain knowledge of the culture of their parents. *I'd really like to keep my Polish background strong for my daughter, even as far as learning the language. I'd like to teach her Polish words and for her to understand how I grew up and something of her grandparents. But it's up to her. She was born in Alice Springs in the Northern*

Everything a Woman Ought to Know

Phyllis Christie and her daughter Mary Christie, Glen Osmond, South Australia

Mary Christie and her daughter Amelia Dickens, Hackney, South Australia

Everything a Woman Ought to Know

Barbara Bishop Hewitt, O'Connor, Canberra

Anne Covernton with her daughters Mary and Helen Covernton, grand-daughter Alison Wigg and daughter Christine Wigg, Unley Park, South Australia

Territory and has the opportunity to grow up knowing about aspects of Australia I didn't discover until I came up here nursing in 1979. I still see family as important, but it's not a Catholic family, and it's not bound by expectations that I be a certain sort of person.

It was very important you grow up to be well spoken.

Mothers invested a great deal in the religious upbringing of their daughters. Going to church often at the insistence of mother persisted through childhood and could consume a good deal of Sunday. Choosing the right school was not only about scholarship.

It was very important you grow up to be well spoken, a well-behaved young lady. I think a lot of people sent their girls to that school for the same reason - to know how to behave as a Catholic and learn to marry young Catholic boys. My mother's mother was not a Catholic, but she was the upholder of religious, moral domestic standards, and she made sure my mother went to a young Catholic girls' school, and my mother insisted I go to mass and communion every Sunday. The day I stopped going, when I was eighteen, my mother stopped too. I realized my mother wasn't the centre of the universe and didn't know everything. So I could make decisions. I came across books on other religions, and I was furious there were these religions I'd been told nothing about.

She thinks my unfortunate politics and feminist ideas are creating the problem.

If mother was a staunch supporter of the church, great stress was put on daughters staying close to the family. For those who had left home, completed tertiary education, married and sought a career, the gap between mother and daughter was a cause for chagrin.

Mum just wants me to be happy, and somehow she thinks my unfortunate politics and feminist ideas are creating the problem. For her, life was much less complicated.

Rather than looking to religion for models of womanhood, many younger women drew on a different set of principles. But the same fervour and the commitment to shaping values was evident.

One thing I definitely will pass on to my daughter is confidence in herself, a sense of worth. I have to be careful not to stomp on her prissy elements, frilly dresses and fairy rings, and things. I think my notion of feminism has helped Mum articulate some of her feelings or has given some sort of comfort, put words to some deep feelings she hasn't expressed or realized before. She'd say she wasn't a feminist, but she doesn't see herself as any man's servant either.

Despite their lives having being ones of independence and adventure, a number of women denied that they were feminists. *I've had a number of jobs: jillaroo, art teacher, kindergarten assistant and director, real-estate salesperson, art-gallery guide. I was brought up more as a boy than a girl. I'd go out to the camp mustering, horse breaking, branding. But I couldn't be a burden. I had to keep up with my brothers. I had to cope. I couldn't just be a girl along for the ride. I'd come in from the cattle yards and there'd be a ball that night. I'd have to scrub up, look beautiful and be feminine. I lived two lives, a dual role. You can still be feminine. I'm not a feminist, but I believe in women's rights. There is no need to come out in public and make a big issue about everything.*

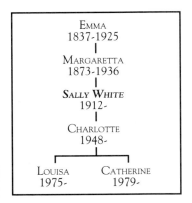

Sally White, in her mid-seventies, said: *Three things are important for women. The right to work. The right not to be exploited. The right to a career.*

It took a personal experience for some women to begin to examine their standing in their society. *I always assumed that I was as good as anybody else, and nobody ever told me I was different because I was a girl. It took me years to understand women who had not been brought up like that. Then, when I was twenty, and I was working in the public service, I was incensed that I was paid four hundred dollars less than men, for no apparent reason. Equal pay didn't come in till the end of 1969.*

Women in their thirties expressed concern. *I've grown up with all the advantages of equal pay, but I know what it was for Mum to earn less than the male wage and have no career prospects, no maternity leave. I worry a lot about younger women. They don't seem to understand how fragile the gains are. They think the battles are won.*

A ten-year-old, reviewing her mother's involvement in politics, observed: *Mum goes to the Women's Advisory Cuncil, and they sit around having meetings and they say, 'Women are having babies', and those sorts of things. That's okay, but I don't think it's important. They should be doing something different, something sportish. They can do political things if they want to, but Mum shouldn't.*

Madge Cope, in her mid-eighties, has long been politically active, but it was not until the 1970s that she began to examine the nature of sexual discrimination.

There was the apron case, that was about peace. A few of us made calico aprons with slogans on them, 'Ban the Bomb' and that sort of thing, and marched down the street until we were arrested. On our fifth time around the park, a couple of police motorbikes pulled up and bailed us up. 'Hand over your slogans.' 'What slogans?' we said. 'They're aprons, clothing, not slogans!' 'You know you're not allowed to carry slogans in the street'. 'We're on the footpath!' We had to go to court, and we were fined, appealed and got off and a lot of publicity. My husband was furious. Our photos were in the paper.

The first women's organization I joined was the Modern Women's Club started by Katharine Susannah Prichard in the late 1940s. It set out to educate women and get them out of their homes. Then the Union of Australian Women started and, at that time, Irene Greenwood was broadcasting. She always called herself a feminist. I wouldn't have said we were in those days. We had no idea of the discrimination that went on between men and women. We thought women had achieved equality in Russia, and it was only later that we found out that they were still doing housework. It was really the peace movement that drew me to socialism.

Our best effort was our magazine. It was to interest people at their own level in cooking, sewing and fashion, and all that sort of thing, and insert politics gradually, to get them to realize there was something beside their home. This was before Women's Liberation or when Pat Giles brought the Women's Electoral Lobby to Western Australia.

Pat's commitment to women's affairs is of long standing. *I've always maintained that for a feminist there is nowhere else to go but the left. I am convinced that women must be prepared to identify with other women and show that women's issues are serious. Just look at the way the 1975 Conference in Mexico was reported: 'Mum's the Word as Big Yak Yak Begins.' Taking the long view, the advances are remarkable. One of the things about the Nairobi conference in 1985 was that we were using a newly coined language, like 'sexual harassment', despite the fact that it doesn't translate readily into some languages. Of course, the practices are not new.*

Pat, admitting she is an optimist, recalls a favourite line from a New Zealand colleague, Anne Hercus: 'As a mother who has taught her children to walk, I have never denied the value of small steps.'

Chapter Twelve

SOMEONE'S DAUGHTER: SOMEONE'S FRIEND

Sometimes I've been jealous of Mum's relationship with my daughter. When we moved up to Alice Springs, Mum and I hugged, and she said, 'She's part of me too.' They have this very strong link.

Memories of happy hours spent with grandparents, reading, sewing, learning the piano, visiting the zoo or gardens, sharing experiences beyond the ken of the grandchild abound. The boys played outside, the girls built card houses and listened to tales.

I was sent off to my grandmother's to be good for the weekend.

While my grandparents rested after Sunday lunch, we played card games in the vestibule. It was often patience set out on round stools. I longed to be old enough for Grandpa to teach me. If I looked, he'd laugh and say, 'It'll be very easy that way, but that's not how it goes .'

Often the bond between grandchild and grandparent is built on indulgence. *I used to go and stay with her when my mother got absolutely fed up with me. Apparently I was a ghastly kid. I was sent off to my grandmother's to be good for the weekend, which was one of the rare times that I was good. I just thought of her as a much loved woman and very exciting. When I went to stay with her, she bought me a dress. She took me to Thompsons, which was where all the 'best' Perth women went to buy their dresses. Then she took me to King's Park for lunch on the Saturday morning. Then we went home, and I sat and built card houses while the ladies sat and played bridge. And then she gave me supper: South African fillet and eggs. By Sunday I'd had enough, and Mum knew it, and she'd come and collect me. I'd be good for thirty-six hours, and I couldn't stand any more. I'd had a lovely time.*

Among Susan Magarey's earliest memories are visits to her grandparents' houses on Sunday. Her father's family lived nearby, but her mother's lived in the Adelaide hills. Visiting was as an exciting expedition.

On the property, there were more exotic things to do. As a very small child, I was put in the bales of wool in the shearing shed to jump up and down (they told me I was helping pack them down). Not much later, when they were building a dairy, I was given a toy saw to help with sawing up the timber and was humiliated when, after sawing away furiously at the fork of a felled tree, one of the men came and pulled off the bark, which included all of the hole I'd sawn.

The weekend visit, especially a family meal on Sunday, brought generations together. *For us, the family was the centre, the primary focus, of sociable activity. When I was eight, my paternal grandmother died. After that, family gatherings in my paternal grandparents' house occurred very seldom. At Christmas time, for instance, both sides of the family gathered at our home instead, for many years. But family gatherings at my maternal grandparents' house continued until I was grown up and had left home, indeed, until my maternal grandfather had died. I was in my late twenties, a time at which most of the grandchildren had grown up.*

CHRISTINE PAULINE
1897-1985
|
CATHERINE MARY
1918-
|
SUSAN MAGAREY
1943-

With relatives, especially those without children of their own, visiting could be special, an opportunity to be humoured.

Lillian Lloyd: *Aunt Jane and Uncle Sam had no children, and he ignored us, but she was a lovely person. She had a tin on the mantelpiece, which was always decorated with lace, or something like that, and she kept special biscuits and would give us some. I can remember she used to wear button-up boots and had this special hook to do the buttons. My sister and I would sit down, undo the buttons and then do them up again.*

> *Mum's besotted with Emma, and it's a chance to get closer to me.*

In retirement, grandparents usually have less demands on their time and money than when they were parents. Lavishing care on a grandchild may give a grandmother an opportunity to compensate for lost times with her own children.

I lived in Wollongong as a child. At twenty-nine, Mum had three children under five and no help from any relatives. It was very lonely and isolated. I've only realized lately with my own daughter, Emma, who was born in 1984. Mum's besotted with Emma, and it's a chance to get closer to me.

As times changed, families spread out, children had greater autonomy, the nature of the Sunday visits changed, and these occasions could become endurance tests. 'When are we going, Mum?' Mother hoping her children would visit her when she was old said, 'Show some respect.'

According to Gertrude, Meg's mother, the problem now is that children expect to be entertained. 'In my day, they amused themselves,' she said. When you left home, it was possible to avoid the gathering, but once you had your own family, you were called back to the fold for 'the family dinner', or to become the focus of a new Sunday ritual.

No doubt, for many, Sunday visits were a time of celebration, of family unity, an opportunity to read Grandma's books, play the piano; for others, it was enforced conviviality.

Every Sunday we went visiting. We'd be all dressed up and bundled into the car and go visiting. Grandma never wanted to go. No one ever came to our place on Sundays 'cos we were always out. It was not done for pleasure but because it was the done thing.

A daughter of an Eastern European Jewish refugee family that had come to Australia in the forties has been able to build a network of friends in a number of places. *Occasionally, I felt envious of kids with grandparents, but all the kids of our school were in the same boat. It makes me feel very cosmopolitan, and I could settle anywhere. It's arbitrary where I finish up, and that's part of a long history. I can settle wherever there is an urban culture, an intellectual climate. I felt more at home in New York than in Israel, but when I was in England I developed an Australian accent.*

Those with no grandparents recognized the loss. *I was always envious of other girls who talked about and visited their grandparents. Mum was an abandoned child, so we had no one.*

When we become mothers, we begin to understand the endurance of our mothers. *It was only with my own family that I've come to know what it means to have the cake tins raided regularly. Mum never complained.*

We look back, forge links and find ourselves in verbal and visual images of our female forebears. In times of stress, or perhaps just out of habit, we repeat the exhortations and admonishments of our mothers and grandmothers. In casual gestures and studied moments, we reflect their presence.

All her friends called her Ginger, and she was very special to me. I look very like her, really. As a child, I was the only one with red hair. I don't have it now. She died when I was fourteen, and I was terribly upset about it. My mother sent me away to be with a family friend to work on his fishing boat because I was so upset.

```
BESSIE
1863-1951
   |
'GINGER'
1891-1969
   |
MALCOLM  =  AILSA
 1922-       1927-
   |
MARY ANNE JEBB
    1955-
   |
  SARAH
  1977-
```

We know certain facts about the lives of our relatives: their birth place, religion, educational standard. Of Ginger's life, Mary Anne Jebb can say: *I never met my grandfather. He died when my father was a young man, approximately 1944. So Ginger was always a single woman to me, living in a flat in West Perth. She'd done a very traditional Western Australian professional thing. She had met him in Egypt, she was a nurse and he a doctor; they'd gone back to England and got married. She had her first child in England and then came out here and had my father and aunt. They had mixed in 'the society', and she was a society lady.*

I heard stories of her from her friends after she died that changed my childhood image.

As we grow, we hear anecdotes told of and by our grandparents, but we also come to interpret these stories in new ways. We see grandma in a new light and judge her by standards measured against our experience.

I've begun to realize that, yes, she was fairly selfish. She and my grandfather had taken off to Hawaii to look for a cure because they knew that he was dying. They put my father into a boarding school at five. As I began to hear stories about her and about her life, I realized she was quite a selfish woman and, when I think about it, I was terribly good. I sat for four hours while they played bridge and built card houses. The gift, of course, was tremendous coming from a family of five. I really enjoyed that single focus on me. But I heard stories of her from her friends after she died that changed my childhood image.

There are stories of her as a socialite dancing on the tables of the Palace Hotel. She used to race up to the second floor and change all the shoes that were outside the doors so that people didn't know where their shoes were the next day. She'd fly bowler hats into the kitchen from the top of the stairs of the entrance hall. All of those things. But she really was a great woman, and when I went to stay with her, keen on having fun, she would often have a bath full of champagne. It was wonderful. One time I remember waking up late at night when Ginger had just returned from a party. She had wet hair having decided to take a dip in the pool, scanties and all. She was in her seventies then.

I used to be fascinated by her morning ritual - preparing to face the world. It took two hours which, as I grew older, began to try me. She was transformed from a pale eyebrow-less woman into a well-groomed, pink-cheeked lady. The various powder boxes, lipsticks, etcetera, were beautiful, with their inlaid butterfly wings and what seemed to me very exotic colours. These have been given to my aunt and will be passed to her daughter or to me.

My grandmother brought me up, actually.

When mothers worked, child-care arrangements could include time with grandma.

Our mother was one of the deserted wives of the depression, and she had to go home to her parents to live. It was a dreadful disgrace to the family, awful. Mother had been trained as a schoolteacher, but she couldn't be employed by the Education department in 1931 when they were putting people off. It wasn't until 1936 that she got back to schoolteaching. In the meantime, she was doing all sorts of work, digging potatoes, and cutting up fruit, and housekeeping for people, and so forth. So, she just wasn't around during those years. My grandmother brought me up, actually.

For a grandmother who had reared a large family herself, however, the responsibility of a new young family was not necessarily a joy. *She didn't talk, really talk, to us younger children much. She'd brought up ten children of her own well into her sixties and, to be lumbered with two more tiny babies, it must have just been very difficult for her. Mum was the second youngest of ten, but she's the only one of that family to have had a post-secondary education. I think some of the others resented that. I didn't know them all because a number had died before I was born. Of the ten, I think only five reached adulthood.*

SOMEONE'S DAUGHTER: SOMEONE'S FRIEND

For Gran it was part of her girlhood, for my daughters it was history.

Penny Peel speaks of her Gran, her mother's mother's mother. *She was a wonderful, cranky old Gran, who would tell stories to my daughters when they were young about people they might have known, like my father, and also about what it was like growing up in a world without cars, electricity, trains and frozen foods. She ruled with a rod of iron, and there were few things she couldn't do. She would have stand-up fights with you, but you could argue. She didn't suffer in silence. I don't think she was one off. There were plenty like her. My mother's mother died when Mum was very young, and I was raised by Gran, her mother, a woman sixty years older than me.*

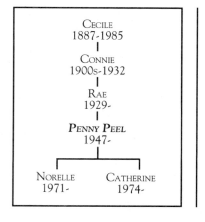

In Penny's family, the gap between generations is not great. If, as in Penny's family, mothers and grandmothers had their children young, it is possible that a child may know both grandmother and great-grandmother. My daughter did, and it gave her an experience that she treasures. She saw her own mother as a grandchild.

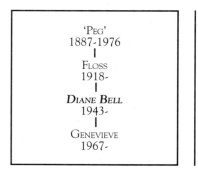

In Lillian Lloyd's home, the stories her mother told in the quiet of a Sunday linked generations across continents and gave her a way to know her grandparents. *She'd tell us stories about Ireland. She was homesick all her life for Ireland and, when I was thirty-one and visited Ireland, I took the walk my mother had talked of so often. Up the brays, down into the square where she'd worked. She'd tell us what it was like when it was snowing, how to hold the rails when the streets were slippery. These were vivid stories. And when I went for that walk with Aunt Jean, she said, 'I didn't take you for a walk, you took me.'*

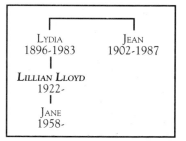

Unlike the relationship of parent to child, the behaviour of neither grandchild nor grandparent reflects on the other in a way that gives rise to guilt or shame. Both have some obligations to the generation in between: a grandmother to her daughter and the grand-daughter to her mother. But neither grand-daughter nor grandmother is bound by ties of authority or deference. It is a relationship in which friendship and ease in exchange of ideas may occur.

For many reasons, it is often the maternal rather than the paternal grandmother with whom a close link is established. The age gap between mother and daughter is often less than that between daughter and mother-in-law. Women tend to become parents younger than men, and a woman's mother is often closer in age than her husband's. Because daughters tend to look to their own mothers for support with child-rearing, they try to live near each other. Our mothers teach us much of our early understanding of family relations and, if we spend more time with them, it is not surprising that we have a deeper knowledge of our mother's relatives than of our father's.

They viewed children as imperfect adults, and all you needed to do was treat them with discipline and respect, and you would get disciplined and respectful responses back from them.

Grandparents offer a buffer for both child and parent but set up other tensions. For the child, an extended visit with grandparents offers an opportunity to be a 'small adult'; for the grandparent, it is an opportunity to help her daughter and come to know her grandchild; for the mother, it can be an occasion for guilt and confusion. She feels she cannot care for her child properly and resents the relaxed approach of the grandmother.

Mum had miscarried with twins and was very sick. I got packed off to my grandmother in the country where they were living on a dairy farm. Living with my grandparents was the period in which I learnt to read and became more self-conscious of who I was and what I was in the world. I arrived back living with my parents and my younger brother, and obviously Mum would have been pretty shattered by all the things that have been happening to her, and then she was confronted with this very, what she thought, sullen and withdrawn five-year-old. What it felt like from my side was that I'd gone from being spoken to as an adult to as a child again. I wouldn't have been able to articulate the distinction, but I knew what it felt like from the new style. I'd been able to ask questions of my grandparents, and they'd answered them. I'd ask questions of my mother and be told to shut up and get on with whatever I was doing.

My grandmother had been born in the late 1880s and my grandfather in the 1890s. They viewed children as imperfect adults, and all you needed to do was treat them with discipline and respect, and you would get disciplined and respectful responses back from them. In my case it worked because I was terrified of their displeasure but, at the same time, I really enjoyed their company and would do anything to be allowed to stay up and listen to them talking, or whatever, at night-time. Back at home it was a matter of being put to bed with the baby.

First of all, my stay was to be for a short time while Mum recovered, but it ended up being about a year. Mum says it wasn't as long as that. I certainly remember coming back late for school. Apparently my grandmother missed me a good deal and wrote to Mum asking if I could stay. She said I could go to the local school, but Mum panicked and brought me home. I suppose she thought she wasn't being a good mother.

Echoes of our relationships with our mothers create double binds. *She didn't have a good relationship with her mother, and I think at some level may have been a bit jealous. Somehow, I was going to get the kind of time with her mother that she never had. I don't know; we never talk about this. This is one of the topics on which Mum says, 'Oh, you exaggerate how long you were with your grandmother.' She won't talk about it.*

But it may be that awareness of conflict between mother and daughter allows bonds of different kinds to develop. *She didn't have a good relationship with her mother, and it's been of great concern to her that she have a good relationship with me. In a sense, she's come to grips with her mother through our relationship as mother and daughter and has tried to build ours as a very different experience.*

Fear of pregnancy created such awful tensions.

The difficulties of developing an open relationship with our mothers are apparent when it comes to matters such as sex. With grandparents there are not the same considerations. It is sufficiently distant to be discussed.

Grandma talked about it years later and said how much she'd loved her husband. The only thing she regretted was that she'd let passion get away with her one time, and that resulted in a child they could ill afford to raise. Fear of pregnancy created such awful tensions. Mum was horrified after I reported this conversation back to her. She said Grandma had no business having such conversations with me.

I can remember waking up in the night and being scared her heart had stopped beating and wondering what life would be like without her.

With our mother we are of the same body, needing separation but fearing separation.

I think of my mother as warm but very strong as a Christian. She'd had seven children and was a sort of a matriarch. She brought us up in her own way because Dad was away at the war. He was in the permanent army and didn't return until 1950. He was a sort of shadowy figure who arrived in the night. I used to sleep with my mother during the war to keep her company. He would arrive and put me out of a warm bed. I can remember waking up in the night and being scared her heart had stopped beating and wondering what life would be like without her. When I stand up for things that are wrong now, I see her in myself.

Some offered wholehearted support to their daughters in pursuing careers and more honest relationships, but others expressed bitterness and thwarted their daughters' progress.

I used to bring lunch to school in newspaper, and I didn't have any socks. Mum had such a terrible time herself as a kid when her family went broke, and I think she was terrified that something like that would happen again. Her philosophy is, 'Give them nothing', and I hate her for it. I try to re-educate her now and, through my children, I give presents so she can see what that means. Maybe I learnt to stand up for myself through that. I don't know.

We found it was the daughters, especially those who had been part of the resurgence of the women's movements from the late sixties on, who puzzled over their relationships with their mothers and who had worked on ways of finding common ground. These women recognized that humour in exchanges between mother and daughter fed on certain ambivalences towards each other. Mothers were proud of the accomplishments of their daughters but also resentful that their daughters were enjoying opportunities that had been denied to them. Ultimately, we know ourselves as women through our mothers.

I left school, and I got my results for matriculation. Mum took me to a restaurant in Collins Street, which was terrific. I had a vermouth and dry, and that was terrific, and then she told me I had holes in my stockings, and that was a bit bad. There you are, suave, just matriculated, and a hole in your bloody stocking - so you aren't the perfect woman, are you?

Someone's Daughter: Someone's Friend

*I think my mother was determined that our lives should be based on reality. It was so harsh that...
I married a fantasy.*

The relationship between mother and daughter is fraught, too close, there are too many moments of tension for friendship to develop easily.

I think my mother was determined that our lives should be based on reality, hard, tough reality. It was so harsh that, when I married, I married a fantasy. I went from one extreme to the other, and now I'm back to the middle ground. My husband's life was the exact opposite of mine. I also think that while I am still not brave enough to confront my mother, as we were brought up in an authoritarian society, my children and I do see ourselves as people of different ages, experiences and not as 'perfect' and therefore questioning is not a challenge to defeat a system but a learning process.

She'd had a terrible time herself as a kid. Her parents had gone broke on their farm in the Mallee, and they were destroyed. She says that her father died of grief. And then there was the depression, and I think she was really terrified that something would happen, so she started to save pennies. She couldn't help herself, and that's had a profound influence on me.

In illness, in old age, the daughter becomes the mother and cares for her mother as she was cared for. *My mother is now ill and requires daily care, and I'm no longer able to deal with her by avoiding conflict or contact. It's been a time for revelations for me, coming to recognize many of her characteristics in myself. I have to struggle not to betray her. She's old and vulnerable. Once she was elegant and poised, but her sickness has taken that away to a large extent.*

Recognizing our mothers as people can transform the relationship. In finding common ground, we see our mothers in ourselves. *Mum had just been to Alice Springs and seen something of the Aboriginal people there. She realized what was behind land rights and why it was important. So we were having dinner and sitting together as colleagues and fellows in arms against a table of her friends. That's the first time that's happened for us.*

A reticence to look critically at conflicts and tensions between generations was manifest among the older women interviewed. Most often the relationship was recalled in terms of happy times, of mother the hard worker, perhaps eccentric but not neglectful or malicious. For those whose mothers were dead, she was 'a dear thing', just the memory the daughter hopes to have. But this group of women also recognized subtle changes in their relationships with other women.

When I was younger, I was always happy in men's company. I was competing with other women for their company. But now I really enjoy women much more. It's easier to talk to them. I've got males in their perspective now. I find my daughter's friends so refreshing and honest.

The closeness continues but is expressed in different ways as we each live out our lives. *My mother and I have always kept in close contact with one another - relating what we're doing through letters and phone calls, and I think we've become closer as we get older even though we don't live in the same towns. I also feel it's my mother's influence rather than any religious education which instilled in me a sense of responsibility and perseverance - to stick at something if you can do it and to stand by people you respect and who have been good to you.*

Mothers were required to cope, to stay on an even keel. The primary responsibility was theirs, and it was enormous. *When she was a baby, we were told she was probably brain damaged - it's pretty obvious she's not. She's gone on to complete her professional training and is doing well. I always believed in her. I think I went into this little cocoon for a long time and dealt with it completely by myself. I think that is the inner strength women have.*

I can't remember seeing Mum lie down. I remember a period after Dad's death when her defences were down. It was a shock.

On the whole, mothers kept a tight rein on their emotions. *Mum worked very hard during the depression, but we were lucky. We were on the farm and always had vegetables and eggs and killed our own meat sometimes. I can't remember seeing her lie down. I didn't think she could ever be not fully in control. I remember a period after Dad's death when her defences were down. It was a shock. She stayed with me for a few weeks and seemed to get herself together again.*

The bonds of family are strong. But new family-like webs are created by increased travel and expanded opportunities for women. *It's the people with whom I share the same ideas and values that I feel a bond. It's those people who are family. There is this sense of global village for students who travelled and lived away from home in their early twenties. I know that might change if I marry and establish blood ties to the next generation of my own children.*

The group of lesbian women we inteviewed were most explicit about what it meant to choose 'family'.

I think of my network as 'elective kin'. I've chosen them, and they are family in a real sense. My parents have difficulty accepting my sexuality, and that's why I live at such a distance from them. Things which I have from them I feel should stay in the family, but things I've bought with my own money I can leave to my chosen family, my sisters, those women who are important to me and who care for me.

Those who have not had children pass to their nieces and the daughters of friends that which would go to daughters. Often it was our unmarried aunts who provided role models of independent women and who were able to extend our worlds beyond that of family life.

My mother's mother has five sisters. There were two brothers also, but they were not part of the history. Lizzie, one of the younger ones, born in the 1890s, was my favourite. She only died in 1985. She and Mary, the youngest of the sisters, lived together for years. Then in their sixties, they married. To me, as a child, visits to their house in Mosman were a treat, a break from routine, a time to do special things with the maiden aunts. Mum and Dad would bring us down from the country and leave us with them. We'd go swimming at Balmoral, play in the overgrown backyard. They sent us wonderful presents in beautiful wrapping.

Mary Anne Jebb compared her family to that depicted by Randolph Stow in *The Merry Go Round In the Sea*.

Everyone who is older than you was an aunt or uncle, and everyone who's equal is a cousin, and everyone who is in a chair was a great-aunt or uncle. The family was very matriarchal, mainly women, and they lived a long time. So there was an aunt at a hundred and her sister who is ninety-four living together in the farmhouse. They owned land and probably wielded the power of propertied women.

We look back to mother, grandmother, aunt and ask, Who am I? We see ourselves in her and are reassured we are individuals with a past. In recounting our stories of our experience of her we focus on the relationship. In passing on objects connected with her life, we seek ways of representing that link in a concrete and enduring way. Meg Sekavs:

It struck me while I was interviewing Mum, and I could feel it, this feminist allegiance. In re-telling the stories to each generation, the older speaks to the younger. We study oral histories in other cultures, but there it is in our own society, and it was asking her about the treadle which provided the stimulus.

The objects are given new meanings and values: a work tool becomes an occasional table, a shawl serves as a ceremonial object, a family bible a rare book. It seems there is a need to see ourselves as having connections, as being the inheritors of certain traditions, even if it is only to rebel.

Pat Giles and her grand-daughter Jessie Giles, Nedlands, Western Australia

GENERATIONS

Sally White with her daughter Charlotte Palmer and grand-daughters Louise Palmer and Catherine Palmer, Lyneham, A.C.T.

Someone's Daughter: Someone's Friend

Vu Thi Diu, her daughter Pham Thi Thao and her grand-daughter, Tran Thi Thuy Tien, Collingwood, Victoria

Muriel Armstrong and her daughter Elizabeth McKenzie (right) and grand-daughters Charlotte McKenzie, Emily McKenzie, Jane Armstrong, Louisa McKenzie (back) and Meredith Armstrong (front), Anstead, Queensland

Chapter Thirteen

HEIRLOOMS AND HAND-ME-DOWNS

I place value on things from friends, objects which reflect the relationship and moment and therefore have a powerful meaning. I resist and even refuse gifts from my mother. My daughters understand it is a desire to free myself of many of my possessions. They've begun asking for things to ensure that I do not throw them away. I treasure the ability to be able to walk away without even a backward glance.

What we have from mother and grandmother, what we pass on to friends and to family are surviving records of women's culture. In stories told of the histories and genealogies of the objects that pass from one to another and in the changes in their use and value, we can read much of women's experience, of their relationships with other women, of their attitude to and rights in property.

When we look at the range of things that women have the capacity and interest to pass to others, we find it is not real estate, not the stuff of which wills, bequests and trusts are made, but rather the personal and particularly female items. The largest appears to be the piano. To play it was the sign of an accomplished woman; the pious practised and played at church; the gregarious were the focus of the family gathering; those on hard times could earn money by giving lessons or playing in public.

The smallest items passed from one woman to another appear to be rings and lockets. These personal, intimate objects provide ways of maintaining links between generations of women that are otherwise obscured at marriage. In between, we find books, papers, diaries and photographs  being gathered and ordered. Fabrics, fine work, pots and plants retain the essence of home from one place to another; the old treadle, however, has a central place, recalling women's work in the home and workshop.

Because the things we are dealing with are under woman's control, a woman may do with them as she pleases. In passing them on, she has the capacity to demonstrate a preference for one person over another, the power to share her achievements and passions. The objects, like the items protected under the laws of Distress for Rent, and the dowries of old, are women's property. Although these are no longer the result of a formal exchange at marriage, or the subject of special laws, there is still the sense that to establish and maintain yourself independently, you need a basic kit.

Although on the surface the traffic in the bits and pieces of women's lives may appear haphazard, patterns do emerge. Women work to create ways in which their experience may be given some continuity. The passage of personal treasures from one generation to the next is hedged in by a number of expectations on how and to whom these items should go. If fulfilled, these expectations give rise to feelings of order and satisfaction; failure to comply sets the stage for bitter family battles. In deciding who has rights in things such as embroidered cloths, teapots, christening gowns, initialled jewellery and collections of postcards, we do seem to follow a set of rules.

An important one governs a woman's tools of trade. Sewing machines, patterns, recipe books, libraries, and writing desks go to the next worthy woman in the line with an interest in the field. Certain objects pass directly from grandmother to grand-daughter or through the mother, who then holds the objects in trust for her daughter. Whether the passage is from mother to daughter, or by skipping the generation from grandmother to grand-daughter, the things are being kept within the matriline.

The mother with only sons faces some difficulties in passing on some of her cherished possessions. In many cases, it will be appropriate to give them to a daughter-in-law, on the understanding that the objects pass to her daughter. But in others, they will pass to her sister's children, or perhaps out to the children of friends. There does, however, appear to be a strong desire on the part of women to keep certain things within the mother's line.

Expectations about the future location of tools of trade and arguments over need tend to overlap. The daughter who is just setting up home may have a call on the furniture that older, more established siblings do not.

My family gave me their obsolete furniture which was on the basis of my setting up a home. I have a dining-room table which I grew up with as my table in Canberra. It's the table that my parents saved up for after marriage.

Another expectation has to do with levels of personal investment in particular objects. The dinner set that was a fortieth wedding anniversary present comes back in the distribution of the estate. The photographs taken in your first brownies' uniform are ultimately yours. Your claim on the sampler lovingly worked during a long, cold winter is undeniable. As the subject, the maker or giver, you have rights in that thing.

She likes to give things back to the people who gave them to her.

Shelley Schreiner came to Australia in 1974 from the U.S.A. She remains in contact with her mother and grandmother through visits and letters. In July 1987, Shelley's mother wrote to her daughter in Canberra of a visit to her eighty-one year-old mother.

If you have a chance, send Mom a card. She sent some dresses and things along for you. I'll get them to you. Also Mother wants you to have her Black Hills 'pinky' ring after she dies. (I hope she wrote that down.) She is still wearing it. She bought it with a cheque you gave her once. She likes to give things back to the people who gave them to her.

Returning what was given in a lifetime reflects the care with which the gift was originally made. From a daughter whose family is scattered across Australia:

I always spend a lot of time and so does the family on choosing birthday and Christmas gifts because it's a way of showing care even though the family member is a long way away. I've kept up that tradition and always take special care choosing things for my mother because it is my mother who feels the distance most keenly.

  We put energy and love into that gift in the beginning and really wanted it back. We take care in the choice of the gift. The things we give express our care and love. If we saw our relatives more often, then the gifts wouldn't be so important. But we use them as a way of communication, as a way of thinking of the person.

```
        URSULA
           |
        BARBARA
         1932-
           |
   JENNIFER RAINFORTH
         1954-
           |
         EMMA
         1984-
```

Decisions about who should have certain things enable us to talk about 'my' piano, string of pearls, library or painting, although we may not actually have it in our possession. It is when we come to assert these rights that we find ourselves balancing complex considerations.

She always said the moonstones were for me. I loved looking at them in their little velvet pouch, but I don't like to ask for them. I feel if I do it looks as if death is imminent but, if I don't ask, she thinks I don't care and will just as likely throw them out.

Getting possession of promised things is difficult. The person who stays in the family home has more chance of holding on to certain large items and collections of books and papers than family members who have moved out.

My sister stayed up in Swan Hill after Mum died, and she's still using the sewing machine. I hope she remembers Mum said it was for me. I use it if I'm up there, but bringing it down here would be a bit tricky.

Discussions about where property is to go after someone dies are often considered maudlin, and avoided. *There is some antique Ethiopian silver jewellery which my daughter's father bought in Africa and gave to me to hold in trust. The significance of that for me is in the wearing, not in the owning. His mother constantly says to my daughter, 'When I die, this will be yours, my dear,' and my daughter hates being told that. She doesn't like the idea of her grandmother dying, and I don't like the implied emotional manipulation with which it is said. It's a bit morbid.*

Sometimes the discussion is started by the person herself. Looking for reassurance that treasured items would not be lost, a mother said: 'Don't let the photographs finish up in an Op-shop as an item of curiosity for another generation, for people I don't know to buy and hang on their walls.'

Once an expression of interest and concern was forthcoming from her children, she stopped talking about destroying the photos.

By constant reference to her belongings and her will, one woman kept the family focused on her and their relationship to her.

My maternal grandmother was always 'shaking her will' at members of the family, and questions about her property were very important and caused continued strife, even after her death. The majority of her possessions and wealth went to Mum's younger brother, except those pieces specified for me.

Heirlooms and Hand-Me-Downs

Nothing was left to be fought over.

Where there has been a will, especially a 'tidy will', like that of Penny's Gran, conflict is minimized.

When she died, there was a very well-organized will. Grandma's father had left all the property to her in her lifetime. She could live on the proceeds of the house, and that was divided as he said. She left pieces of jewellery to each of us: a brooch with a blue stone to me and, to my sister, a diamante spray. To my mother there was a mourning brooch with a plait of my father's hair. She specified, and it was her decision, what went to whom. We didn't ask for them or admire them. All her clothes and effects went to the Salvation Army. The furniture is in my aunt's house because it is hers. Nothing was left to be fought over.

The memory of disputes over a will of an elderly relative is often enough to prompt later generations to devise a method of organizing matters better during the life of the owner.

Mum's got a list at the back of the sideboard, and we just write on it what she wants done with things. I saw this terrible fight over my grandmother's stuff between Mum's brothers and sisters, and I don't really want that to happen. I prefer to know where Mum wants it to go. She has that right.

The distribution may be organized in a variety of ways. It may be that the eldest has first choice, or that the family cuts the cards, throws the dice or works out a system on the basis of value or attachment to particular items. The strength of the claims is canvassed. The destination of fine things - embroidered cloths, napkin rings, the silver and the china - is susceptible to considerations of style: 'Will you appreciate and use it?' Should it come to me as the eldest?

At this point, there is often conflict between daughters-in-law and daughters. The wife of the eldest son lays claim to an embroidered cloth. She reasons it should come to her; it is part of the property that her husband now manages. The daughter argues that she would use and cherish it; it was, after all, with her that mother sat to embroider. The conflicts are not easily resolved and are easily revived.

Very often younger members of the family who had the time to talk to Grandma receive small items in her lifetime. Sometimes she leaves them something in her will to offset their junior status.

I was the baby of the family. My oldest sister can tell me all sorts of things about the family which I missed because I was the youngest. They were just discussions between the big girls and their mother. My grandmother lived in a caravan at the

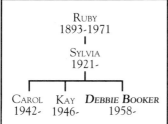

back of the house. I talked to her and played there. We were close and, when she died, I took her canasta set; it represented the time we had together. Taking the cards was a secret act of rebellion, which I can laugh about now, but I was surprised at the strength of the memory. My sisters say I could have had it if I'd asked.

Turning points in our lives are marked by the presentation of items of symbolic or economic importance. We receive special gifts on birthdays, when we put together a glory box, when a daughter comes home, a child is sick, in the face of of marital disputes, when setting up an independent home, on engagement and marriage and the birth of the first child. For those who do not marry or reproduce, leaving home and setting up alone may be the occasion to transfer some of these items. Some may never come into their inheritance.

For many reasons, the passage of objects from generation to generation is disrupted. One is attitudes to property. *My aunt was working class and gave everything away. She thought she had no right to keep things while others were in need.*

For another woman, property was a burden. She preferred to give things away rather than be shackled with the responsibility. Grandfather had been buying a house at Gladesville for fifteen years when my parents were married. He found that as a consequence of the way in which the loan was organized, he had only paid interest. It was a time of housing shortages, just after the war, and my parents had nowhere to go, so Dad took over the loan. By that time, the house was forty-odd years old. I lived there until I was eight, and there were no less than five adults and children and cousins in the house. Having to worry about owning things is not my idea of fun.

I hope someone will have the courage to dispose of my stuff in the way I should have done after my parents died.

Family traditions are the ties that bind and produce obligations for others.

My perception of generations is coloured by this feeling of obligation and duty and owing it to my parents. I live in comfortable circumstances and have considerable assets. But I feel encumbered and burdened by it, living in a mental and physical clutter, as much a victim of my family's wealth and pretensions as a beneficiary of it. Really, it is only my music and classical record collection that sustain me, and that is more connected to my friends in the orchestra and music society than to members of my family. As far as I'm concerned, there is too much junk in the world, and I hope someone will have the courage to dispose of my stuff in the way I should have done after both my parents died. The generations are creating too much, and there is no value in so much. It's better to have fewer objects and treasure them. I have no idea, and I don't think I really care about my things. The things I create are not so significant. I feel obliged to do something for my parents for things for which I am the custodian. I like things to go to people who admire them. They are the people who care about me.

In other families, the desire to protect reputations or to purge the house of all memories of the deceased, as part of the grieving process, meant that items stored there by other members of the family were lost. Some pieces considered to be in bad taste were simply sold.

There was a strong sense of the need to get rid of stuff and a haste to dispose of personal effects when mother died. Dad gave me a box of things that had been part of the house (a clock, a set of flying wall ducks), on the basis that if I didn't want them, they would be thrown away. I still have the clock, and the ducks went to a friend with a passion for kitsch.

Refugees and migrants came with little baggage and often a strong desire to leave the past behind. *We came to Australia as single migrants on a two-year contract. In the first few weeks in the hostel, people were allowed to get married, and many of us did. It was just, 'Who wants to get married? Here, sign the papers.' That was all about it. It was not long after that we heard our first news from Yugoslavia in years. We didn't know before who was dead or alive - maybe we wouldn't have got married if we'd known some things. But there you are - we had a new start in this country.*

Likewise, for those who lived through the anti-communist push of the fifties, there is a reluctance to recall the location of certain documents and books. Those Australians who lived through the Darwin cyclone lost many documents that provided links with their past. Bushfires, floods and cyclones could easily wipe out the accumulation of generations.

All the things we played with on holidays were there: everything, toys photographs, old bikes. After the fire at Aireys, there was just a lump of molten glass where the glass cabinet had been, hot and smokey. I picked up everything that was intact, including some teacups, and put them in a bag on the verandah at home. I didn't look at them for a couple of days and, when I did, the cups were reduced to fine powder.

Some things that were kept could not be identified. *Photographs were among the few things kept in my maternal grandmother's collection. There are ones where there is no one now alive who could identify most of the people in them. I suspect quite a few of them are of Grandmother's sisters and friends in Scotland before she emigrated in 1911. I went through them with my grandmother. They're important to me but not to Dad. It was Dad's sister who acted as the custodian of family history. Dad would give the things to me or to her, believing that girls were the ones to take care of family stuff.*

When elderly relatives are put in nursing homes, family properties are broken up. Personal items are taken along, but major pieces have to be distributed. In one story, the piano finds a home with the elderly woman but, in others, the members of the family take favourite and useful pieces and the remainder goes to the tip or a charity.

Where there are no relatives from whom to inherit, no one whose belongings you might hold in trust, the impulse seems to be to create an inheritance.

Well, I didn't have a grandmother. My mother came here as an orphan. But I adopted three spinster sisters, and they became my maiden aunts. They gave my mother a little worked padded box filled with doilies. I took it over as my inheritance. My mother fiercely kept all books, toys, report cards and photographs. They are being handed on to my sister's children.

Extending beyond blood relatives are those women we think of as sisters, as family, as our 'elective kin'. Items made in our lifetime may pass to these women. The bonds thus created mirror family ties.

I think of will-making as expensive and creepy, and the problem of pinning it all down was hugely complicated by wanting to make a bequest to feminist causes or friends. The impulse to pass on materials which are reminders of this generation's existence to the next is linked to the impulse to see that our values and ideas and discoveries live on after us also. It's so important to make sure that this time our ideas won't be swallowed again in silence. There is a real need to keep the stories going and keep the element of them as public as possible, and so it is less likely that the second wave of twentieth-century feminism will be lost as an account of women's experience of change.

So I listed the women to whom I felt close, and nominated the things that should go to them. The whole exercise was a legal dilemma because it is so much harder to leave things to non-blood related people and also because, as those elective relationships change over time, the will needs to be constantly updated.

I also wanted to leave some things to my nieces and nephews and to my godchildren who are the children of my former husband. My father cannot deal with the idea of my ex-husband's children, who are no blood relation, receiving things from me and therefore indirectly from my mother.

In some cases, it requires faith that future generations will care. *There are*

Sally White's gloves, worn by her grand-daughter Louise Palmer

Susan Andrews with her daughter Jane Simpson, O'Connor, Canberra

Alice Costello's family. Back: Great-grand daughters Regan Liddle and Felina Bruce, grand-daughter Valerie Bruce, daughters Elizabeth Rawson and Emily Liddle, great-grand-daughters Cheryl Edwards, great-great-grandchildren Marah Edwards and Leanne Liddle. Second Row: great-grand-daughters Derissa Rawson and Stephanie Rawson, Alice Costello. Front: great-grand-daughter Katrina Rawson, Alice Springs, Northern Territory

Floss Haig with her daughter, Diane Bell, and grand-daughter, Genevieve Bell, Highett, Victoria

treasures owned collectively which prove difficult to pass on when the collective owners disperse. What of the sculpture owned by the women's liberation house in Melbourne? What of the women's archive in Adelaide? In the end, it requires an act of faith to believe that there will always be another generation of women committed to protecting and preserving the collective history.

I left my papers to a woman colleague. It was the most precious thing on earth to me.

Protecting the future of our most precious belongings is anything but simple.

I have a loathing for the whole process of will-making because when I left my husband in the mid-seventies I had to make a will to ensure that my property would not immediately pass to him if I died. I realize now it was very naive. I left my papers to a woman colleague believing that she would turn them into a book. It was the most precious thing on earth to me.

Names, as we have seen, are important in linking women, and the practice of echoing given names from one generation to the next has a long history. In Joyce Caddie's family, the name and likeness were linked through a personal name. *My first grand-daughter is just as her mother was. They all carry the same name; Joy goes right through the line. There is Flora Joyce, Evelyn Joyce, Julia Joy and Bonnie Joy. Julia has followed her grandmother in the way she keeps her home, grows her own vegetables, makes her own bread. The older children follow this tradition more than the younger two. The hardship of the earlier years influenced the first two. They had to make do with second-hand clothes.*

Recently we find a renewed pleasure in retaining, or reclaiming names. Continuing to use a maiden name is one way of asserting continuity of identity. After divorce, it is a question many women ponder: to keep the name their children bear, to revert to that of their father, to choose a new name.

To honour her maternal grandmother on her one hundredth birthday and to mark her separation from her husband, whose name she had used for fifteen years, Leslie took the name of her grandmother. Cheryl looked to her maternal line and took her grandmother's first name 'Hannah' as her new surname.

A new name was a new beginning.

In the first four years of my marriage, in the mid-sixties, I had four children and was completely isolated. Then my husband went off with another woman. I knew we were not well suited, but we were married. I began to reconstruct my life. I went back to university, then got a job. I changed my name.

Cherished, coveted and cared for.

According to Meg Sekavs, 'Recording the stories of objects was part of getting to the beginning of things.' Here we have begun by mapping the daily routines and rituals of the generation born at the turn of the century and tracked through their daughters' and grand-daughters' memories of their mothers and grandmothers. The order they established and maintained structured households and bound all the family into a co-operative endeavour. Mother was revered as a good manager, the passing of the good old days of simple pleasures mourned. She worked hard, and it was visible labour. But she was bound within home and marriage; there was no career structure.

We teased out the links between the generations and found that certain objects were being used as markers. With the personal pieces came stories of who had the Jessie brooch, Mother's ring? The emotions engendered by such questions were not matters of nostalgia or greed. To dispose of such items ruptures the link between the object, the people who gave and received it and the work that went into making it. Its loss or sale was a violation of the trust in which the objects were held. In some direct way, the objects stand for people. They are cherished, coveted and cared for, and on them is inscribed the spirit and ideas of the maker or the previous holder.

The objects that are 'women's property' are often trivialized, and it is true that they are less valuable than 'the farm'. But we found in them ways of restructuring and reading our past that located women's experience and the links between women as central. The manner in which family histories are often written, archives established and public records ordered tends to deny this. What one generation bestows on the next gives significance to particular events and relationships. Bonds are created, ideas and values from which to construct a sense of self, of place, of belonging, spun.

CHAPTER FOURTEEN

IN SEARCH OF AUSTRALIAN WOMEN

In popular imagination anthropology is something that happens elsewhere, and anthropologists are people who trek to remote villages where they study primitive rites. On returning to civilization they tell of the vanishing world in which they have lived; of the differences and the similarities between their ways of thinking, doing and being and those of others. Although this is not a definition that most anthropologists would endorse wholeheartedly, it captures certain essentials of our practice.

Anthropological research involves fieldwork of a participant sort: by joining in the everyday lives of other people we come to appreciate their world view, to see and feel it as they do. In our attempts to explain these 'other worlds', we draw on models of human society and concepts of culture that allow us to compare across time and space. Our enterprise is broad and bold: we attempt to encapsulate whole societies, the logic of entire cultures. Anthropology is a study of the human condition; its methodology is participant observation; its approach holistic; its modelling comparative; its obsession otherness.

In researching *Daughters of the Dreaming* I did not travel to a foreign land but I did enter a world different from those in which I'd been socialized. The Aboriginal women with whom I worked had grown up in Australia and in certain respects we shared a history. But what it meant to be female and Aboriginal in Central Australia in the 1970s, those were matters about which I had much to learn. In *Generations* I have again focused the anthropological obsession with otherness - this time on woman as 'other' in the symbolic order, on the 'otherness' in self, on other Australias, some I know, others not.

It is not just because exotic field situations are scarce that anthropologists choose to study within their own society. A prerequisite of good anthropological practice is an understanding of self, and anthropological skills and modes of interpretation developed in the study of small-scale societies are appropriate to a study of our own society. It is not just members of 'primitive society' for whom kinship networks are important, for whom household organization or exchange relations are an integral part of the economy. My anthropological training led me to explore the operation of an alternate generation principle, to map the content of familial relations as lived experience. Finding ways of bringings these insights to bear on an understanding of Australian social structure and culture, however, entails crossing both disciplinary and psychological boundaries.

The anthropologist working in small-scale societies has at least some chance of knowing all members of her community, of writing a loving and faithful ethnography with real people talking about actual experiences; about the ebb and flow of their lives in relation to significant others. In *Generations* I wanted the immediacy of good ethnography, not generalized or abstracted portraits of what the 'average person in the street' believes or knows. A national stereotyping of Australian women as less feminine than the French, not obedient like mail-order brides, less precious than the British or more candid than our North American sisters was not going to be particularly helpful. Culturally, Australia is too diverse, and women do not comprise one homogeneous bloc. But a population of eight million is beyond even the most energetic ethnographer.

My research strategy evolved with the project. It was subject to endless revision, refinement and negotiation, but the essential features remained constant. I chose a nationwide team of ten assistant researchers. All had an interest in women's lives but each had access to different aspects of Australian society. Here considerations of age, residence, marital status, reproductive history, sexual preference, socio-economic status, ethnicity, religion, education and work experience were important. Each woman came to me highly recommended or, having worked with her before, I knew the quality of her work; most held qualifications in the fields of humanities and social sciences. I did trial interviews with friends and family. When I was satisfied that the format was sufficiently directive to elicit core data on biography, relations with female kith and kin and transmissions, but sufficiently open ended to pursue themes *in situ*, we began.

Each interviewer drew on different networks. My expectation was that if each interviewer sought out people in her own social field, we would produce intimate, direct and reflective material. In that we succeeded: matters of delicacy, humour, triumph and pain were all willing to be discussed. We learned more of our selves and families: it was informative, cathartic, indulgent, redemptive. For the most part there was no need to establish rapport. Shorthand references to events, places, relatives and jobs were intelligible. Mostly we could avoid gaffes and fill in details later.

The material generated during the research may be read as accounts of individual lives, but the interviews also fall into clusters that have their own dynamic. At this level they can be read as ethnographic sketches of a number of communities across Australia. We were able to explore the lives of a group of Christian wives, of second world war widows, of non-working wives of professional men, of career women, of lesbian women, and rural women in two different regions. Within each group we looked for variations in personal histories. The biographical data of one group of rural women included reference to being born in Yugoslavia; being a descendant of four generations in the region; being a member of the Brethren; and being an unmarried mother.

Wherever possible several generations were interviewed, though not always by the same person or in the same state. In all we conducted one hundred interviews: the assistant researchers completed fifty-five and I did the remaining forty-five, which included interviews with all the assistants. Most women agreed to be taped; sometimes we relied on notes. Wherever possible copies of tapes and transcripts were returned to those interviewed. This allowed checks for accuracy and elucidated women's priorities on the use of and access to the material. The transcriptions of the records of interview run to some 6,000 pages. From this and other sources I established a data base (on cards, not computer) and indexed as we went.

A number of features of the data base led me to believe that we tapped deep into the roots, growth and flowering of Australian culture. One is that most major events or themes of twentieth-century Australian history are mentioned. Another is the correlation between the data base and profiles of the Australian population in terms of features such as ethnicity, household units, marriage patterns, residential mobility. Also if an object seemed to have importance for a number of women, I would go back to my data base and, for the most part, I would find further examples.

I have relied heavily on the oral historical method, but the research design and methodology take us beyond mere recording and recounting. True, our ethnographic sketches were drawn on the basis of a few interviews but, at a number of levels, they have proved remarkably reliable and informative. There was that sense of closure after a certain number were completed. Once you've spoken to five non-working wives of professional men, four teachers who upgraded their qualifications as mature-age students, six residents of a mixed grazing and farming community, you know that further interviews will produce confirmation or elaborations but not new patterns. Whether these regularities will hold in another locale is another question. The closure may be a feature of the group itself. For the reasons outlined in chapter two (with reference to our group of over sixties in Melbourne) I do not think this was so. In allowing individual voices to carry the story line of *Generations*, I knew that they spoke from shared experiences: history and culture speaks through them.

In *Generations* I wanted to write of an Australia that would have resonance for women in all walks of life. It was for this reason I began within the domestic realm that area of activity that is at once central to survival and yet invisible in public discourse. Confinement within the home did not rule out political awareness or involvement. The kitchen was a site of political education, of listening to the radio, of analysing the latest strikes while salting pork, of learning to read while kneading bread, of imprinting hearth histories while sewing; of exchanges in a barter economy of home produce from vegie garden and orchard, simply sealed with a cup of tea. Careful ethnography threw up some helpful measures. A reliable indication of affluence may be the point at which a household acquired pillowcases with flaps or when the mincer was no longer the means of producing at least one weekly meal of leftovers.

Although their perspectives varied, most women were comfortable talking about their domestic routines. The order of things changes, and new skills are required, but within the domestic sphere women continue to manage space, time, financial resources and emotions. Their investment in relationships suggests the operation of another economy, one of the emotions, generated within the intimacy of households but played out with consequences for all in the larger society.

The division of things public from those private and things domestic from those political renders much of women's labour invisible and denies that constructions of self, forged in the little worlds of home, also give form to our cultural understandings of the socio-economic structures of the big world. For most women, the private flows into the public, the one is a construct of the other, but through various sleights of hand the division is presented as natural. The 1891 NSW Census, which introduced the division between 'breadwinner' and 'dependant', removed statistically a number of married women from the realm of productive labour. Women, however, still worked in the home and outside. This re-classification of domestic work provides a context for the texts on inside and outside work. Restricting herself to 'inside work' came to be considered 'proper' for a woman and demonstrated the prosperity of the nation. But only on established properties was it possible for women to withdraw from productive labour. Wives in poorer circumstances had to work outside. But 'outside work' was also a mark of self-sufficiency for a number of women who rejected the division as pre-ordained. Despite the legislative encoding of the expectations that all women could find security in marriage, women remained in the workforce. Their labour could be devalued, however, because they could be treated as 'temporary workers'.

The interest in social history over the last several decades has brought into focus the lives of the less articulate, of those who did not have the foresight or means to record their experiences for posterity, of those locked in the 'private' world of family. One way in which their lives have been retrieved is through oral history, another is by working with routinely generated records such as rate books and census returns, which expose the minutiae of daily life. In *Generations*, with specific reference to women, we have explored another point of access, the transmission of objects. The things given and bestowed by one generation on those that follow, the things inherited or bequeathed take us to the core of women's culture. Preoccupation with events in the public domain obscures the centrality of certain woman-to-woman relationships. In their secret hidden worlds, women make choices, albeit limited, which allow continuity of identity between generations and sustain a sense of worth and purpose. Transmissions of personal things are subversive of the patriarchial order but draw on principles of lineality and descent from the patriarchal order.

In recalling the stories of the transmission of objects a search for self was manifest. In looking at photographs of a female forebear there was a collapsing of images. It was, one woman explained, like a computer printout in which coloured dots showed which was from mother, grandma, and so on. That need to know ourselves as individuals with a unique past in part accounts for the personalization of objects. We see and hear ourselves reflected back in a number of forms but continually ask of the documentary record, Who am I? The objects are evidence of that link. The ones that are transmitted from generation to generation speak of a tradition of self-sufficiency, the constraints on women's independence, of hard selfless work, they recall a period when the task of management was visible and acknowleged as critical to survival.

These memories reach back to the closing decades of the nineteenth century, but the objects have a timelessness; their transmission transcends lifespan; they have a life force and logic of their own. The genealogies of particular categories of objects reveal that their transmission is a rule-governed activity that subverts the history of estates and allows continuity of identity from one generation of women to the next. It can be dismissed as of little consequence to those exercising power in the public domain because the pieces are not valuable. They are invested, however, with enormous sentimental and emotional value. They go to the heart of personal identity. Through them is articulated the economy of the emotions; from them we may read of the structural importance of certain generational ties.

In terms of property relations, the remnants of a dowry system whereby a woman takes her portion of her family property into marriage, were evident. The dimensions of a dowry were well worked out and discussed openly: the worth of a new wife was public knowledge. In a marriage based on romantic ideals of love, the role of the dowry diminishes and the woman herself becomes the object. The glory box, containing the essential for the establishment of a home, taken by a woman into marriage, was also a matter for public comment. The contents were inspected and assessed to determine the potential worth of the wife, but it was her labour, rather than family wealth, that was on show.

Married women have found it difficult to achieve and maintain financial independence. In the nineteenth century, restrictive practices on the holding and acquiring of property meant that women relied on husbands for financial support. For a father to will his property to a daughter would mean losing the identity of his estate: it would be known by the name of another lineage, that of her husband. After the passage of the Married Women's Property Act of 1882, a woman's legal identity was no longer treated as incorporated or merged with that of her husband. Although a married woman may now be in the same position in terms of the acquisition, holding and disposition of property as a single woman, and banks may no longer require a male guarantor for a housing loan, women both single and married do not hold the same sort of property as do men. A symmetry persists: the cryptic note, 'Daryl got the farm and Mum got the pearls,' has currency today.

Unmarried women in late nineteenth and early twentieth-century Australia often remained at home to help mother in the house or went into service in the home of another women. Their needs were thus taken care of, and there was no future generation dependent upon their bequests. Nonetheless, what property they had was theirs, and its final destination, whether intended, or by accident, provided a possible counter for the principle of primogeniture. In their lifetime, women have consistently bestowed objects of personal significance that were not covered by the formalities of property settlements. As women were able to own property in their own right, the category of objects that could be transmitted from one generation to the next expanded. Despite the increased possibilities, the principles underlying the transmission of objects appear to have remained remarkably constant. Bonds between and across generations of women can still be read from the traffic in personal things.

One of the dramatic changes in Australian society that is plain in the biographical material is the increasing intervention of the state in private aspects of family lives. Changes in the law and access to supporting mothers' benefits have meant that women no longer stay in unhappy and violent marriages because they have no other option; women are no longer regarded as property. There were some remarkable statements made about what they thought was expected of them as young married women in the 1920s, 1930s and even 1940s and the measures they were prepared to take to regain some control over their lives. On the other hand, the biography of Mimi Taylor can be read as a history of welfare and health policy failures. While her struggle to survive may have strengthened her, she did not need the indignity of being rejected by social security when benefits were available.

The texts as presented in *Generations* have a history, their own point of generation. The transcripts of the interviews make fascinating reading, but they require context and explication if they are to be available beyond a very small circle. In transforming the oral accounts to written texts I selected significant passages. I then edited and ordered the spoken words to form the texts that appear. The level of intrusion was minimal but necessary. A word-for-word transcription with 'ums' and 'ahs' may be of interest for some analysts but was irrelevant to my purpose. I did, however, want to retain the freshness, lightness and engaging quality of the spoken word. To catch nuances, tones, rhythms, styles of exposition, I saturated myself in the voices. I read the texts aloud to make sure they were utterable. The texts therefore are a rendition of the spoken word, which is recognizable as that person's speech but which I have edited to make readable. Many interviews weave back and forth and so I also provided an internal structure for some texts. I did not seek to put order into disorder but rather drew together observations on one topic to generate a text. These became evidence for the themes that had emerged in the interview process. Of course, one fed off the other, but I had set up the conditions under which the women might speak. Thus, although voices carry the narrative, they are mediated.

Generations is borne on the voices of Australian women of which mine is one. When I was a little girl Nanna, my mother's mother, spoke of home in England; my father's mother, we called her 'Ma', spoke of inner Melbourne. For each there was a wealth of emotional security in knowing and recalling those times. Nanna would retrace her steps through the labyrinth of London streets, and on my charm braclet hung little silver statues commemorating the British heroes who marked the way: proof of a pre-World War II England she knew I could never see. Ma loved music, and Dame Nellie Melba's farewell concerts were a favourite theme. She'd repeat her father's pronouncements on Burke and Wills, 'They'll never make it; they're not bushmen.' In this way the expedition became part of our experience.

These stories are part of the body of oral history I can tell about my family. In producing written versions they become *my* recollections, for these women are dead, and I don't have a record of their exact words. But I do have objects on which aspects of their lives are inscribed. To support her young family, Nanna took in sewing, and the walls of her workroom were bedecked with patterns, precious tools, fabric samples and photographs of the royal family. She sewed for my mother, myself and my daughter. I have her machine. My father's mother remained at home where she cared for her mother until she was married. In the 1920s she also found herself alone with two small children, but she didn't need to engage in paid labour. She fashioned exquisite taffeta pieces which adorned bonnets and lampshades. Her handiwork is evident in the sepia photograph in which she stands hat brim to hat brim with her six sisters. I knew them as wonderful eccentric women who fussed over my father and had an ever-ready supply of cucumber sandwiches and Herbert Adam lemon sponge, which they served from a trolley I still have. I suspect malnutrition contributed to their demise.

Their stories as family history, or biography, belong in a private world, and my search for Australian women has taken me into many such worlds. Once written, the accounts can be read by people with no direct knowledge of the individuals or the events. They may be seen as tales of intrinsic merit, be compared with the experience of others, but they may also be read as evidence of broader political, socio-economic and cultural forces. My grandmothers' stories as texts illuminate Anglo-Australian relations, the brevity of settler history, the celebration of female accomplishments, such as singing and sewing a fine seam, the exploitation of seamstresses, changes in family and household structures.

Working out which stories from which women and to what end has been my task. When I began, I didn't know where some paths would lead because there were no definitive maps. The process of exploration and discovery lies somewhere between the dense London my Nanna wanted me to know and the sparse land where Burke and Wills perished. The texts reveal the intimate details of the minutiae of many women's lives, but they are organized to be read as evidence of salient symbols, strategies, social structural arrangements, pervasive themes, an enduring dynamic culture. The format was one that accorded an individual woman the ability to reflect critically on her experience but permitted mapping of the forces that shape that consciousness of self. I draw on biography but in a way which is suggestive rather than exhaustive.

To know how to 'read' these stories, we need to know something of the conditions of their telling and recording. By whom? For what purpose? In response to what questions? To which audience? The questions I ask of the records and the construction I put on their lives is by no means fixed. Stories of raising children alone (as my grandmothers did) were discussed in hushed tones twenty years ago. No doubt different stories will be recorded in another twenty.

I have retained personal names because I did not want this to be a book of anonymous accounts: the voices belong to specific women. I also wanted to demonstrate that ordinary women have something to say. I hope that seeing the story of Mimi Taylor alongside that of Pat Giles will show that both have contributed to our society. A colleague pointed out to me that, save for the few who would recognize personal detail, pseudonyms would have sufficed. For me, it was part of the relationship that had been established during the interview. We had been entrusted with information about individual lives and, allowing them to read of themselves in a serious book, provided the historical legitimacy a number said they felt women had hitherto been denied.

Certainly we found women to be the bearers of oral histories of their families. Within this network they could choose who might and should be entrusted with family confidences. The extent of knowledge was restricted and privileged through their control of audience. In a sense this is a folk history, intended and of interest only to a limited audience. It is a resource into which we may dip for illustrative material of the private world of family and women. But it also offers a counterpoint to histories that focus on the public and noteworthy. The two, although intertwined, are not easily reconciled. The hearth history is essentially subversive in nature. It strikes at the public-private divide; it suggests that values attach to objects other than those of name and wealth; it exploits the ambiguity of the reliance on the existence of a women's only domain for its exposition.

Many of the women noted how pleasant it had been to speak of themselves in their own terms without constant correction or consideration of spouse or children, although achieving this often took considerable pre-planning. When other members of the family were present during the interview (as a matter of politeness, to clarify, because they insisted) the tone of the exchange changed. The mode of recounting of tales lost its laconic self-mocking edge and became more circumspect. The shift was subtle but suggestive of the existence of a domain of communication with a content of its own. Speech style also shifted and the readiness to use a vocabulary, metaphors and elliptical references to assumed shared experiences diminished. There was no need to elaborate: mere mention of the triumph on the occasion of the first successful pull start of the motor mower reverberated; the dynamic of the traffic in cuttings and recipes was immediately familiar. The interviews were conducted within women's domain and the language reflects this. For the male reader of *Generations* a certain leap of imagination may be necessary, for here women speak in a different register from that of public discourse.

I did interview a number of men and found that much of what their sisters, wives or mothers had related was on the fuzzy edge of their consciousness. Some dismissed the tales of objects as trivial women's stuff or as none of their business. Others wanted to be sure I had the stories 'right' and were anxious to hear what their wives and mothers had said. Still others exhibited an intellectual curiosity in the stories and provided insightful accounts of the genealogies of objects in all-male households. At least one old treadle now has an assured home.

Generations led me down some new paths, not all of which are traversed in the book. Here I am signposting those that bear on my observations about public and private spheres; women's investment in relations; the disjunction between spoken and written words, between stories for friends, known researchers, the general reading public and historical archives. The discriminations were fine, passsionate and revealing.

In researching and writing I was determined to include as wide a range of voices as possible. Some feared tokenism: 'Am I to be the ethnic of your study?' Another exclusion: 'When we came here we were migrants, then ethnics, when will we be Australians?' I relied on the research team having access to a broad cross-section of Australian women rather than a social survey approach. We did not, for instance, seek out particular ethnic groups. Here I note that one in five Australians is born overseas, and that statistic is duplicated in our groups. Throughout the project I thought hard about questions of representation, the 'typical' and the 'ordinary', privacy and self-censorship. I am still thinking about them.

When, in the research phase, women were invited to participate, and the nature of the project was outlined, some required confidentiality, others anonymity; some declined, still others sought me out. Women accustomed to handling interviews indicated confidently what was on and off the record. Several had spent time consulting their female kin before being interviewed; others consulted on receipt of transcript. Generally, career women, having allowed a story to be recorded, applied the test of truth to publication. By and large it was the non-working wives of men in established positions who did not wish to be named. The group most likely to ask to be consulted on text and context before being named in print were those whose lives were already part of the public record. They exercised care in re-working their transcriptions. Members of small communities were sensitive about being identifiable by name or residence: they did not want to be seen as 'putting themselves up'. From working-class women, the general sentiment was that their lives were already well documented in welfare records and, at least, this time, they'd seen what was written about them.

A worrying sign points to the path winding through 'the need to protect privacy' and 'avoiding the risk of events wearing a rosy glow'. Almost to a person, women did not want material published that might hurt others, especially mothers - often mothers with whom relationships were tense. In protecting others we protect ourselves, but there is also enormous energy invested in the maintenance of key relationships. Several asked that husbands (deceased, divorced and extant) not be identified. Respecting these demarcations of private and public territory did not limit my ability to draw upon the details to inform a generalized or structural account.

Of particular interest was that in the negotiations over their texts a number of women expanded their boundaries of the sayable and the 'private' moved into public discourse. Rather than damaging relationships, the move was redemptive. 'Did Nanna live with us during the war?' I asked. A factual question. Silence. Drawing on memory, I plotted the rooms of the house we had lived in during the war. Dad was away. I remembered his homecoming, the room where Nanna slept. Was this the memory of the two-year-old or a later recollection? Reference to the demobilization of troops in 1945-6 was one way of dating the memory. My mother dismissed the question: 'Things were tough then, I don't remember.' She did but it took some courage and some further research on her part to bring public record and private construction together. Yes, Nanna had lived there and, 'Things were tough.' She was not yet divorced. She was living with the man she was to marry years later. So powerful was the pain of this memory that her daughter had suppressed the information.

For my mother it was a topic to be avoided; to me it personalized the plight of deserted wives in the thirties and forties; for my daughter it was a residential pattern which would barely raise an eyebrow with her peers. We all learnt more of ourselves. In the telling of stories mothers spoke through daughters and achieved their historical moment. *Generations* provided the vehicle for some of the ambivalences in our relationship with our female kin to be brought to consciousness, to acknowledge that boundaries which ensnare us are not necessarily ones we wish to maintain.

An adjacent sign read 'self-censored'. In several interviews between close friends or family, certain areas were avoided. We all engage in a measure of self-censorship and tend to suppress different images in different contexts. It is possible to argue that silence, manipulation, adjustment or suppression of the past outweigh the benefits of using oral history as an important resource in any research. Demonstrating that memory was faulty or that someone had presented a more flattering self-image than was justified does not alter the fact that she told the story. What is necessary is to recognize that texts (both written and oral) are constructions and to note the silences. We did 'read' against other sources. We had access to letters, diaries, family trees and a range of scholarly research.

To tease out the myriad meanings of women's culture and weave patterns in the ethnographic record is a proper task for an anthropologist. In recent accounts of the lives of Australian women, we find reclamations of long forgotten texts and reinterpretations of old material. There is no doubt that we need to have 'documents' in which women's experience is recorded, and there are many reasons why these may be lost or organized in a fashion that creates a structure that fractures the continuity of women's experience.

Generations has been a search for 'documents', for ways of reading them, for modes of interpretation. I have allowed the women to speak for themselves wherever possible. Their accounts show women to be reflective and to know well the means by which their experience is rendered less important. They have a sense of the valour of their endeavours, even if only at a generation remove. What they lack is a way of imprinting these understandings and appreciations on the public consciousness. I hope *Generations* will stimulate debate and open new areas to research. I also hope that Australian women will find something of themselves in the pages.

NOTES

CHAPTERS 1, 2 AND 3:

Mapping the Domestic
Generations is not larded with references, but in researching and writing I drew on a rich tradition. In works like *Yesterday's Daughters: Stories of our past by women over seventy*, edited by Alma Bushell (Nelson, 1986), Edna Denmead, born in 1906, offers an account of the weekly routine that echoes that of Nar in chapter 1. The recollections of Dame Mary Gilmore in *Old Days: Old Ways* (Angus and Robertson, 1934, republished, 1986) of the second half of the last century merge with those of the rural women interviewed.

New Perspectives on Women and their Work
In the 1970s books such as *My Wife, My Daughter and Poor Mary Ann: Women and work in Australia* (Nelson, 1975) by Beverley Kingston; Miriam Dixson's, *The Real Matilda* (Penguin, 1976); and *Damned Whores and God's Police: The colonization of women in Australia* (Penguin, 1975), by Anne Summers, offered ways of 'reading' the documentary record that provided answers and generated new questions. Kay Daniels, in 'Feminism and social history', *Australian Feminist Studies*, no. 1, 1985, pp. 27-40, points to the paucity and bias of sources as one reason for the tendency to view women as victims in these accounts and issues a plea for renewed vigour by feminists in choosing and establishing the criteria by which history is written.

Kingston shows that in the second half of the nineteenth century most paid work for women was in domestic service, by 1901 accounting for almost half of such work. By 1920 the same work was being done by wives and daughters for no pay. Women, however, were still supporting themselves and others. By 1919 they did so on 54 per cent of the male wage. See Kaye Hargreaves, *Women at Work* (Penguin, 1982, p. 16). *Gentle Invaders: Australian women at work 1788-1974* (Nelson, 1974), by Edna Ryan and Anne Conlon, traces the emergence of the concept of male breadwinner and the nature of the campaigns for equal pay. They point to the inconsistences in the premises underlying the Harvester judgment of 1907, which provided for a basic wage designed to allow the working man to support himself and dependants on one wage while ignoring the high proportion of female breadwinners. Lynn Beaton's 'The importance of women's paid labour: women at work in World War II', in *Worth Her Salt* (Hale and Iremonger, 1982, pp. 84-98), edited by Margaret Bevege, Margaret Jones and Carmel Shute, carries the story to the war years when women were critical as paid workers.

The memories of women who were managing households early this century chart a period in which the transformation of the very shape of Australian households in terms of house design, family size, residental configuration, technological innovations, social structure, and family and personal relations occurred. In the1980s, attention has turned to these experiences. In 'Political arithmetic: the nineteenth century Australian census and the construction of the dependent woman', *Signs*, vol. 11, no.1, 1985, pp. 27-47, Desley Deacon analyses the manner in which 'market closure' was achieved by the reforms of the late nineteenth century. In her discussion of the New South Wales Public Service Act of 1895, Deacon shows that the justice of paying women less and creating distinctions on the basis of marital status was hotly debated. Kerreen Reiger's *The Disenchantment of the Home: Modernizing the Australian family 1880-1940* (O.U.P., 1985) and Jill Julius Matthews's *Good and Mad Women: The historical construction of femininity in twentieth century Australia* (Allen and Unwin, 1984) locate the inter-war period as critical to our understanding of the construction of femininity and housewifely domesticity, of the shift from woman as producer to woman as consumer. The economic crisis of the period from1880 to 1910 was the period when the state redefined production to mean remuneration so that paid work, originally part of a larger process, gained a new status. Women's wages were reduced; married women were discouraged from wage labour, and paid work became a male privilege; the technological rationality of 'experts' in mothering, sexuality, housework and childrearing invaded the home: 'good women' did not work. Lyndall Ryan reviewing Matthews and Reiger in 'Women and the home in Australia', in *Australian Feminist Studies*, no. 4, 1987, pp. 177-87, notes the need to cross theoretical and disciplinary boundaries in a search for ways of understanding women's experience.

Ann Curthoys addresses the structure of economic, social and cultural differences in 'The sexual division of labour: theoretical arguments' in *Australian Women: New feminist perspectives*, edited by Norma Grieve and Ailsa Burns (O.U.P.,1986, pp. 319-39). She concludes that the division arises from 'an interaction between bio-cultural tradition and practices on the one hand and the specific institutions of capitalist production on the other' (pp. 336-7).

Chapter three is based on the questions: Who did the work in your house? and Who paid the bills? Answers to the second question showed working-class women to be better informed about disposable income than wives and daughters of the middle class. Meredith Edwards reviews the literature on these issues in 'The distribution of income within households' in *Unfinished Business*, edited by Dorothy Broom (Allen and Unwin, 1984, pp. 120-36), and finds the assumption that incomes are pooled wanting. Patricia Tulloch, in 'Gender and dependency', *Unfinished Business* (pp. 19-37), explores the consequences of the high priority women give to caring for the relatively powerless. Ann Game and Rosemary Pringle offer a reconsideration of the production/consumption, public/private, work/non-work dichotomies in *Unfinished Business* (pp. 65-78). They argue that women's social reality does not mirror these distinctions, but that women frequently make them a strategy for survival at home and work.

Washing Day

The centrality of Monday was not just a woman's affair. Grazia Gunn in *Arthur Boyd: Seven persistent images* (A.N.G., 1985, p. 31) recounts that when Arthur Boyd's father operated his kiln on was- days, Arthur had to warn local residents around Murrumbeena of possible pollution. In some municipalities there were council regulations that prohibited burning off on a Monday. The importance of the Hill's Hoist to Australian wash-day technology is enshrined in the 'Ode to the Hoist' written on the death of Mr Lance Hill, aged eighty-three, by Ian Warden, *Canberra Times*, 11 March 1986. Citing a study undertaken in the U.S.A., Game and Pringle note that although the task of doing the laundry has lightened, the time spent has increased.

Cooking and Kitchens

In their documentation of changing work patterns, Game and Pringle point out that new tasks have been created by the extended possibilities with foods, including pre-prepared and processed foods. There is now the possibility of serving a different meal for each family member, and the invitation to create more elaborate dishes. Such are the 'liberating' effects of technology. The focus on the food and the places where it is handled illuminates cultural and social patterns. The naming of meals as dinner, tea or supper; whether eaten at midday, before or after dark; the cutlery and dishes used and the content of conversation reveal class distinctions and regional variations. High tea could reflect working-class origins (a meal of stodge to fill the workers) or be a matter of great elegance, with distinctions drawn between numerous delicacies. One example of the substantial changes in the material environment that were accompanied by conscious attempts to reform women's role in home management described by Reiger (and noted in the interviews) is the shrinking of the space allocated to kitchens. Books such as Anne Gollan's *The Tradition of Australian Cooking* (A.N.U. Press, 1978), Margaret Dunn's *Mother's Best Loved Recipes* (Rigby, 1974) and Wendy Walker-Birckhead's article, 'The best scones in town: old women in an Australian country town', in *Australian Ways: Studies in society*, edited by Lenore Manderson (Allen and Unwin, 1985, pp. 101-12) offer further ways of reading social histories from cooking and kitchens. In *Making a Life*, 'Salt pork to take away', Anne Gollan notes that the first closed fuel range arrived in Australia in the 1850s. It had two fires, one above and one below the oven. The one-fire stove is dated in Australia in the 1860s and gas in the 1880s. Aboriginal women's food preservation techniques are outlined in 'Gathered from Kaytej Women' by Diane Bell, in *Australians to 1788*, edited by D.J. Mulvaney and J. Peter White (Fairfax, Syme and Weldon Ass., 1987, pp. 238-51).

Aboriginal Australia

Under the *Aboriginal Land Rights (Northern Territory) Act*, 1976, claims may be brought to areas of vacant crown land but not to town land or pastoral leases held by non-Aborigines. In the land claim process, Aborigines give evidence before a judge who is appointed as Aboriginal land commissioner. Much history of Australia that is yet to be written is foreshadowed in evidence to these proceedings. For more of Jessie August and her family, consult exhibit 13 by Diane Bell to the *Cox River (Alawa-Ngandji) Land Claim* of 1982; for more of Topsy Nelson, the transcript of the *Warlmanpa, Warlpiri, Mudbara and Warumungu Land Claim*, 1982; a short biography by Diane Bell, 'Topsy Napurrula Nelson: teacher, philosopher and friend', in *Fighters and Singers: The lives of some Aboriginal women* (Allen and Unwin, 1985, pp. 1-18), edited by Diane Barwick, Isobel White and Betty Meehan. *Daughters of the Dreaming* (McPhee Gribble/ Allen and Unwin, 1983, pp. 50-89) provides more of the history of the central Australian area. Kenneth Maddock's, *Your Land is Our Land* (Penguin, 1983) gives a history of the passage and operation of the Land Rights Act.

'Village Australia'

The few empirical studies in which residential mobility is analysed pay little attention to gender. The household head is assumed to be the male, the breadwinner and the 'decision maker'. The factors that influence women's residential choices and the extent to which these are part of the decision to move remain unknown. Our interviews suggest that women are important in determining moves. The women interviewed in rural areas and in suburban neighbourhoods lived in stable communities, which were underpinned by the intimacy of face-to-face contact, kinship bonds, friendship and long association with the area. Leslie Kilmartin, David Thorns and Terry Burke, in *Social Theory and the Australian City* (Allen and Unwin, 1985, pp. 151-65), review the literature. Studies show intra-urban moves over relatively short distances and childhoods spent within the area. Residential mobility is not random but well structured. The move to the new suburbs is celebrated in Barry Humphries's *A Nice Night's Entertainment* (Currency Press, 1981), in which he pays tribute to Highett, 'the place of his dream' (pp. 30-1).

CHAPTERS 4 AND 5:

'Running up a Dress'

In her play 'Running up a Dress: a dialectic of sewing', Suzanne Spunner explores the feminine through what we learn from our mothers and how and what we teach our daughters. 'My mother made me in her own image on her machine, that reliable old Singer treadle...no fancy stitches, all plain sewing, well made, won't come apart at the seams, darts in the right place, hem even, pressed flat, not a pucker in sight, no loose threads... her daughter.'

A number of sources underline the importance of sewing as paid work. In Bernard Smith's *The Boy Adeodatus: The portrait of a lucky bastard* (Penguin, 1984, pp. 78-9), Tottie and her sister, Lily, buy a machine by monthly instalments at a cost of nine pounds, thirteen shillings. In 1885, Tottie in service and Lily by sewing save and are able to buy a home for their mother. All the women interviewed knew the price of their machines and the date they bought them. Societies such as the Queen's Jubilee Fund, described in *The Social Worker's Guide for Sydney and New South Wales*, compiled by J.C. Fox (Wright and Dawson, 1911, pp. 146-7), aimed to help by providing the tools of trade. The brief summary of the law of Landlord and Tenant included in John Herbert Plunkett's *The Australian Magistrate*, shows that in N.S.W. as of 1835 a man's tools of trade, horse or clothes 'in use' could not be taken for a rent debt. The legislation was extended to include other 'essentials', and under the 1898 *Distress for Rent Act* a woman's tools of trade (her mangle, typewriter, and sewing machine) could not be taken.

Embroidery

In *The Subversive Stitch: Embroidery and the making of the feminine* (The Women's Press, 1984), Rozsika Parker demonstrates that the notion that the ability to do fine work as a 'proper' feminine activity is recent. During the Victorian era medieval history was rewritten so that instead of acknowledging that both men and women embroidered, the activity became synonymous with femininity. Although sewing is no longer a wifely duty, it is not yet an acceptable activity in boardrooms. Christine Stoke describes the Daylesford embroidered banner project (*Lip*, vol. 6, 1981-2, pp. 6-13), which exploits these ambiguities. Madge

Cope's story of the apron protest is another example. See chapter 11.

Ann Stephen has brought to our attention the 'First Australian Exhibition of Women's Work' (*Lip*, nos. 2 & 3, 1977, pp. 73-80), which was held in 1907 at the Exhibition Building, Melbourne. Although neglected by art historians, it was considered significant at the time. It included work from women in all walks of life, including Aboriginal women. The skills of cookery, laundry and horticulture were displayed. Needlework was divided into three: plain, fancy and art, and there was a section for seamstresses whose weekly earnings did not exceed twenty-five shillings.

A cotton knitted bedspread, the work of five generations, seen outside the home for the first time in the display of women's work at the Diamond Valley Learning Centre in 1976, is described by Laurel Wilkinson (*Lip*, 1977, p. 83). The Great S.I.O. Exhibition at the Museum of Victoria, 23 August - 3 November 1985, brought forth a wealth of material, but it was all returned to people's homes. Certainly the Country Women's Association has provided a forum where tribute is paid to women's work, but much of women's fine work remains invisible because it as not seen outside the home. This argument is explored in detail by Jennifer Isaacs in *The Gentle arts: Two hundred years of Australian women's domestic and decorative arts* (Lansdowne Press, 1987).

CHAPTER 6 AND 7:
Holding Property
Halsbury Laws of England (fourth edition, Butterworths, 1979, pp. 628-9), has this to say of the situation that existed before the passage of The Married Women's Property Act, 1882 . A married woman was incapable of acquiring, enjoying or alienating independently of her husband any real or personal property. In equity, property might be given to a woman for her separate use, and such was protected during marriage. Any part remaining at her death was subject to her husband's rights at common law. Moreover, in equity, property could be so limited as to become a woman's separate property subject to a restraint preventing her alienating or anticipating the income of it during coverture.

The Piano
In the parliamentary debates of the 1898 session of the N.S.W. Legislative Council and Assembly (vol. XC111, pp. 325-32), the question of including a woman's piano as a 'tools of trade' was raised. Items given by charitable organizations such as the Queen's Fund were considered deserving of protection, but the purchase of a piano indicated comfortable circumstances. In *A New Britannia* (Pelican, 1970, pp. 117-19), Humphrey McQueen locates the piano at the 'pinnacle of working-class aspirations'. He likens it to the radiogram of today: it provided entertainment and the only opportunity that most people had of hearing classical music.

A Supply of Nails
In the *Australian Enquiry Book of Household and General Information* (Pater and Knapton, 1894, p. 205), Mrs Lance Rawson instructs women on the use of tools and the construction of basic furniture. There is no suggestion that this is an affront to her femininity.

The Swastika
Francis Budden and Marie McMahon (*Lip*, 1977, p. 65) discuss the use of this symbol in Australian fancywork.

Pearls
A customary royal practice is to present a girl child with one pearl on each birthday until, by the time she is twenty-one, she has a string of them.

Readings
In *Certain Chairs* (University of Queensland Press, 1968) Barbara Blackman writes evocatively of the pieces of furniture that have given continuity to her life in twenty homes in forty years. The manuscript 'The Rookes in Australia', 30 December 1979, pp. 1-17, and the appendix, pp. 1-25, is the possession of the author, Madge Cope, of Perth, W.A. The lives of the women of Melville Island, Northern Territory, are described in *Tiwi Wives* by Jane Goodale (University of Washington Press, 1971, pp. 47-8). Sue Bellamy writes of her work and her wish that her pieces not fall into the hands of men in 'Form - we are the thing itself' in the Women and Labour Publications Collective, *All Her Labours: Embroidering the framework*, vol. 2 (Hale and Iremonger, 1984, pp. 69-84).

CHAPTER 8, 9, 10 AND 11:

The Form of the Story

Nothing would please me more than to publish the extremely rich biographical material of the interviews. But even if the six thousand-odd pages were available, there would still be need for comment, explanation and context. A more promising task would be to work the existing materials into individual biographies. Recently there has been a flurry of publications of diaries and first-hand accounts of women's lives in the colonies such as *The Letters of Rachel Henning* (Angus and Robertson, 1986), which provide invaluable primary documents. A number of edited works link autobiographical sketches in thematic treatments. Jan Carter's *Nothing to Spare* (Penguin, 1981) records the stories of Western Australian grandmothers; in *Tall Poppies* (Penguin, 1984), Susan Mitchell talks to successful women; in *Different Lives* (Penguin, 1987), edited by Jocelynne Scutt, women reflect on the effect the women's movement had on their lives; in *Against the Odds* (Hale and Iremonger, 1984), edited by Madge Dawson and Heather Radi, professional women tell of their struggles; in Robyn Rowland's *Women Who Do and Women Who Don't* (Routledge and Kegan Paul, 1984), joining the women's movement is the topic. Individual autobiographies, such as that by Labumore: Elsie Roughsey, *An Aboriginal Mother Tells of the Old and the New* (McPhee Gribble/Penguin, 1984) and Amirah Inglis's *Amirah: An un-Australian childhood* (Heinemann, 1983), take us well beyond Anglo-Australia. The fifty biographical sketches in *Double Time: Women in Victoria - 150 years*, edited by Marilyn Lake and Farley Kelly (Penguin, 1985), highlight differences in class, race, religion, age and location as determinants of experience. In *Good Talk*, edited by Rhonda Wilson (McPhee Gribble/Penguin, 1985), ten ordinary Australian women speak of their extraordinary lives.

From all this activity one might conclude that women are well represented, but sources are limited. Barbara Jefferis, in *Three of a Kind* (Sisters, 1982, pp. 7-13), writes of her difficulty in tracing three generations of women. Not only name changes but the undervaluing by both men and women of the records women generate frustrated her.

Dale Spender has edited a special issue of *Women's Studies International Forum* (vol. 10, no.1) dedicated to 'Personal chronicles: women's autobiographical writings'. Ann Walters, in 'Self-image and style' (pp. 85-93), explores Estelle C.

Jelinek's *The Tradition of Women's Autobiography from Antiquity to the Present* (Twane, 1986) and the proposition that women's autobiographies have been excluded from the genre of 'proper' autobiography because their choice of subject matter, style and self-image do not fit male expectations and experience. It is also very difficult to move from individual lives to an understanding of the wider society and culture. Instead there is a faith in the unfolding of time as a framework for telling the story of a life. But the same experiences have an effect on people at different times and hold varying significance for them.

Family Histories
Careful reconstructions of the private worlds of family reveal their importance to the construction of the political domain. Patricia Grimshaw and others have done much to re-work and re-frame our understanding of our past. See 'Women and the family in Australian history', in *Women, Class and History*, edited by Elizabeth Windschuttle (Fontana, 1980, pp. 37-52); 'Women and the family in Australian history - A reply to the *Real Matilda*', in *Historical Studies*, vol. 18, no. 72, 1979, pp. 412-21 and *Families in Colonial Australia* (Allen and Unwin, 1985), edited by Pat Grimshaw, Chris McConville and Ellen McEwen.

We were directed to a number of sources on family history. Janet Shaw and Mary Smith, *A Douglas! A Douglas!* printed by K.L.A.N. Genealogical Supplies, 7 Wongaburra Street, Jindalee, Brisbane; Doreen Monro, 'Reminiscences of life in the Gulf Country in the 1930s by an ordinary housewife', Mitchell Library; Peter Verco's *Masons, Millers and Medicine* and *Thomas and Elizabeth Magarey*; *Social History of South Australia*, edited by Eric Richards (Wakefield Press, 1986), Dorothy Gilbert, 'Country life in the late nineteenth century', *South Australiana*, vol. 12, no. 2, September 1973, pp. 57-70; *The People of Perth: A social history of Western Australia's capital city*, (Perth City Council, 1979) by C.T. Stannage.

Argonauts Club
From 1941 onwards, the Argonauts (begun in the early 1930s), broadcast on A.B.C. radio, was a firm favourite with budding young writers and critics, who listened for their contributions and code names to be read.

Naturalization Act of 1903
This legislation needs to be read in the context of the anti-Chinese sentiments of the time, which no doubt distressed Ruby as Lew Din's wife, but there is no provision whereby she could be deported or her children denied citizenship.

Medieval Book Owners
Susan Groag Bell in 'Medieval women book owners: arbiters of lay piety and ambassadors of culture', in *Signs*, vol. 7, no. 4, 1982, (pp. 742-68), argues that book-owning women substantially influenced the development of lay piety and vernacular literature in the Middle Ages. Women frequently bought and inherited religious and secular books. As the owners and readers of books, 'as mothers in charge of children's education, as literary patrons who commissioned books and translations, as wives who married across cultural and geographic boundaries, women had a special and unique influence' (p. 743). In tracing the transmission of books from one generation to the next, she maps the development of a matrilineal literary tradition and postulates it may have influenced later generations (p. 767).

The 'Duchess'
Nancy Keesing in *Lily on the Dustbin: Slang of Australian women and families*

(Penguin, 1982, p. 38), explains the difference between 'duchess' as the embroidered runner and two flanking pieces and 'duchess' of which Mimi speaks as the dressing table; the latter is said to be a Queensland usage.

Epidemics
There was an outbreak of polio in N.S.W. and Queensland in 1904. In Victoria the first reports are from 1908. During 1919, in the influenza epidemic, 12,000 Australians died and some 58,528 passengers and crew were quarantined.

Kanaka Labour
Recruiting ceased in 1904. Since 1847, 57,000 Kanakas have worked in Australia.

Religion
This was a theme we pursued in most interviews, and the activities of one group associated with a church provided important links. Some pursued the topic obsessively, for others it arose incidentally. In a number of cases it was the horror attached to a 'mixed marriage' that lead women to re-think their position as Christians. Notably, tensions between different religions had lessened considerably in the past twenty years.

Sexuality
The ease with which this topic was discussed owes much to the interviews being conducted between friends. Most striking were the observations of older women that matters to do with sex were rarely discussed with peers. For several the interviews were the means through which they learnt of the youthful practices of contemporaries. This is also noted in *Dutiful Daughters* (Penguin, 1977), edited by Jean McCrindle and Shiela Rowbotham.

Within the group of lesbian women we interviewed, there was wide variation in class background and self-evaluations. Several expressed regret that their families could not accept their choice; not all were open about their sexual preference; not all were feminists. All, however, expressed concern about the future homes of their cherished belongings, and all had thought deeply about the consequences of bestowing 'family' objects on 'elective' kin. Nowhere was the recognition of the power of objects to confer kin-like status as marked; nowhere was the notion of what constituted 'women's property' so starkly drawn.

Politics
The interests of women interviewed included the C.W.A., W.E.L. and all political parties. Because Senator Pat Giles of Western Australia had agreed to participate, I decided to focus our treatment of politics in that state. After very few interviews, key people emerged and events were repeated. In each interview we found an interest in the life and work of Irene Greenwood and Katharine Susannah Prichard. The population of W.A. in the 1950s was around 600,000, of whom roughly half lived in Perth, and those who were female and politically active constitute a knowable group. This is a further dimension of the 'Village Australia' configuration discussed in chapter 2.

Chapter 12, 13 and 14:

Making Sense of It: Mothers and Daughters
This central relationship is the subject of Jane Flax's 'The conflict between nurturance and autonomy in mother-daughter relationships and within feminism', in *Feminist Studies*, vol..4, no. 2, 1978, pp. 171-89; Nancy Friday's *My Mother, My Self* (Dell, 1977); Judith Arcana's *Our Mothers' Daughters*,

(Women's Press, 1984); R. Wodak and M. Schulz, *Mother-daughter Relationships from a Cross-cultural Perspective* (John Benjamins, 1986). Albeit from different disciplinary backgrounds, these authors all deal with the tensions inherent in the relationship, the points of identification, the ambivalences. Nancy Chodorow in *The Reproduction of Mothering* (University of California Press, 1978) examines the pscho-dynamics of the construction of femininity and masculinity and emphasizes the different experience of boys and girls as they separate from their mothers and develop socially defined gender identities.

Language

Nancy Keesing's record of Australian domestic slang in current Australian draws on actual speech because she found that the usual sources (novels, Hansard, newspapers) suffered a heavy male bias. Who would record 'pinnie' for apron, pinafore? 'Tinnie' for tin of beer is always cited but not 'cardie' for cardigan or 'lippie' for lipstick. The texts of the interviews may be seen as constituting a register of women's speech. M.A.K. Halliday and Ruqaiya Hasan, in *Cohesion in English* (Longman, 1976, pp. 22-3), define a register as the set of meanings, the configuration, the specified conditions, along with words and structures that are used in the realization of the meanings. The controlling variables are field (the type of social action), tenor (role realization) and mode (symbolic organization).

Oral History

The merits of recording people in their own words are argued by Peter Spearritt in 'Growing up in the late 1930s: Rationale, methods and materials', in *Australia 1938*, Bulletin, no. 1, 1980, pp. 8-23, with particular reference to Wendy Lowenstein's *Weevils in the Flour* (Hyland House, 1979). Jacqueline Templeton, 'Exploiting our sources', no. 2, pp. 17-21, Wendy Lowenstein, 'They stamped on their heads', no. 3, pp. 33-5, and Bill Gammage, 'Some comments for oral history', no. 2, pp. 23-6, continue the debate.

Representation

Community profiles show that one in five Australians is born overseas. It is thus very difficult to speak of an enduring homogeneous Australian culture. Australia has always been a culturally diverse country. It is only recently, with policies of multiculturalism and recognition of land rights (albeit limited), that the merits of this diversity have come under scrutiny, been celebrated and disputed. Hitherto the dominance of the Anglo-Saxon tradition was so great that the influences such as Aboriginal, Islander, Chinese, Eastern European could be deemed non-existent: the bearers of other traditions were barely human, deported, interred, held in compounds, denied citizenship. Engaging a research assistant to deal specifically with 'Aboriginal women' or 'ethnic women' would have been cause for accusations of tokenism. There are, after all, many different ethnic and Aboriginal groups in Australia. Instead we interviewed women within local communities and networks.

Several Aboriginal groups have declared that participation in Bicentennial celebration is for them anathema: it is to celebrate their dispossession. For them, 1988 is a year of mourning. Several non-Aboriginal women chose not to be interviewed. Pip McManus did agree to be interviewed but wished to dissociate herself from what she called 'the official view of the Bicentennial' in 'celebrating two hundred years of colonization in this country'. Her wish was that we would deal with 'women in the Australian community in the widest context and be concerned, among other things, in promoting an alternative concept of community, that is co-operative, non-sexist and non-racist'. Some Aboriginal groups have been prepared to take advantage of money from the Australian Bicentennial Authority to mount various projects, many of which offer an alternative view to that of the pioneering legends of exploration of a hostile land by a bunch of brave Britishers.

Objects and Exchange
In *Antipodes* (Penguin, 1985, pp. 123-9), David Malouf writes of the things we hold 'in trust'. The nature of exchange is debated extensively by anthropologists. In *The Gift* (Cohen and West, 1970) Marcel Mauss examines the conditions under which a gift received must be repaid and the locus of the force which compels the return. Drawing on a wide range of case material he shows that the 'prestations', as he terms them, are obligatory and reciprocal and can not be understood in purely economic terms: affection, prestige, generosity, social and moral factors are also critical.

ACKNOWLEDGEMENTS

Diane Bell:
A series of mother and daughter photographs by Ponch Hawkes published in *Lip* in 1977 offered a starting point for this project. I had seen the photographs - one generation echoed the other in powerful ways - but I did not meet Ponch until late 1986. It was then that we began to work together on *Generations*, and the collaboration has been a joy. Our technical skills are very different, but we have rarely disagreed about what is significant.

Recognition of the range of possible applications of anthropology to the study of Australian society and culture may be clearer to an outsider than to one enmeshed in disciplinary debates, and this is certainly true of *Generations*. It was Hilary McPhee who invited me to think about writing a book on Australian women, and it was a feminist conviction that such a study would be productive that underscored the original questions and sustained the research and writing.

Through 1984 and 1985 I worked with McPhee Gribble on a proposal for the Australian Bicentennial Authority. By early 1986, McPhee Gribble were confirmed as the successful tenders for the volume. I had began informal research when the idea was first mooted, but the research phase did not begin in earnest until mid 1986. I had hoped to set aside twelve months to research and writing but, in July 1986, I took up the chair of Australian Studies at Deakin University. First semester of 1987, freed of teaching responsibilities, became my writing time.

Between June and December 1986, Genevieve Bell, Liz Cham, Floss Haig, Cheryl Hannah, Val Kear, Michele Kosky, Jane Lloyd, Patti Monro, Daphne Nash, Penny Peel, Michaela Richards and I recorded and indexed a hundred interviews. I am indebted to each of the assistant researchers. Their contributions go far beyond conducting interviews and indexing: they also located sources, negotiated, offered hospitality and sustained me through a torrid time.

More nimble fingers that I can count transcribed texts, typed drafts and manipulated the word processor. At the centre of the transcription process was Margaret Lanigan who, for some time, was the only person with an overview of the research. She typed most of the interviews, offered comments and eventfully became a 'subject' herself. Sylvia Baker, Judy Barber, Bev Bartlett, Genevieve Bell, Ella Day, Liz Jones and Jane Veale typed, photocopied, found things they thought might interest me, talked of their own experiences; everyone had something to add.

The help and enthusiasm of my fellow researchers, colleagues and staff at Deakin University has kept me going. Especially I thank Barry Alpher, Renate Klein, Shelley Schreiner, Gertrude Stotz and John von Sturmer who, with the assistant researchers, listened, looked after me and saved numerous elements of the electric jug.

Deakin University, especially the computing section, has been generous in terms of time and resources. The Australian Bicentennial Authority not only provided the grant to enable this book to be researched and written, but also offered opportunities to promote the work at various gatherings. I am grateful to the support team at McPhee Gribble: to Jane Arms for her thoughtful editing and good humour; to Pam Brewster for her design. Working with McPhee Gribble has taught me more about books than I learnt in any lecture theatre. Thank you for your patience, trust and wisdom. Most of all I thank all those who shared their lives with us and hope the book does justice to their generosity.

Ponch Hawkes:
I would like to thank Sandra Vitolins for help with printing, all the people around Australia who allowed me to take their photographs and those who took me into their homes - Michele Kosky, Bob Kosky, Andy Pearce, Lyn Keogh, Shaun Williams, Kate Legge, Greg Hywood, Marg Fletcher, Maureen Tehan, Jane Lloyd, Margot Hutchinson, Mike Mullins, Mary Christie, Andy Pierce and Michael Zerman - and my household and friends, who lived through the project with me - Jenny Saunders, Gail Davidson, Kaz Cooke, Paul Brant, Georgine Sparks and Laurel Frank.